D1612426

# Taiwan's Economic and Diplomatic Challenges and Opportunities

This book offers a diverse set of perspectives on the current state of Taiwan's economy and international relations, equally considering the challenges and opportunities that could forge Taiwan's future.

Featuring a range of interdisciplinary approaches, this edited volume has been written by some of the leading scholars on Taiwan's economy and international relations, as well as emerging scholars and writers with practical diplomatic, political, and civil society experience. Contributors cover themes from political economy and international relations to gender studies and civil society-led LGBT diplomacy. Readers will benefit from chapters outlining both the historical overview of Taiwan's development and more recent developments, with several chapters offering focused case studies into Taiwan's economy and international space. A balanced set of conclusions are reached, affording scope for both optimism and pessimism about Taiwan's prospects.

*Taiwan's Economic and Diplomatic Challenges and Opportunities* will appeal to students and scholars of international relations, economics, and Taiwan studies.

**Mariah Thornton** is an enthusiastic researcher of Chinese politics with an undergraduate degree in Chinese Studies from the University of Oxford and an MSc in the Politics of China from the School of Oriental and African Studies, University of London. From 2012 to 2013 she completed a year abroad at Peking University and later received the Huayu Scholarship from the Taiwan Ministry of Education to undergo intensive study of Mandarin at National Taiwan Normal University from 2015 to 2016. Mariah Thornton worked as a press and communications adviser at the Taipei Representative Office in the United Kingdom under Representative and former Foreign Minister David Y.L. Lin from 2018 to 2020.

**Robert Ash** (Bob Ash) is an Emeritus Professor at SOAS University of London, and Founder and Professorial Research Associate of the Centre of Taiwan Studies at SOAS. Before his retirement in 2020 he was Professor of Economics with reference to China and Taiwan, and Professorial Fellow of the SOAS China Institute. From 1986 to 1995 he was Head of the Contemporary China Institute at SOAS; during 1997–2001 he was Director of the EU-China Academic Network. From 1999 to 2013 Bob Ash was Director of the SOAS Taiwan Studies Programme and its Centre of

Taiwan Studies. In 2012 he received the Friendship Medal of Diplomacy from the Ministry of Foreign Affairs of the ROC Government in recognition of his efforts on behalf of Taiwan Studies in the UK and elsewhere in Europe. Bob Ash has held visiting research and teaching positions at universities in Australia, Hong Kong, France, and Italy. He has been researching China for more than 40 years and has written or edited 15 books, mainly on development issues relating to China, but also on issues relating to Taiwan and Hong Kong.

**Dafydd Fell** is the Reader in Comparative Politics with special reference to Taiwan at the Department of Politics and International Studies of the School of Oriental and African Studies (SOAS), University of London. He is also the Director of the SOAS Centre of Taiwan Studies. In 2004 he helped establish the European Association of Taiwan Studies. He has published numerous articles on political parties and electioneering in Taiwan. His first book was *Party Politics in Taiwan* (2005), which analysed party change in the first 15 years of multi-party competition. His second book was *Government and Politics in Taiwan* (2011) and the second edition was published in early 2018. He co-edited *Migration to and from Taiwan* (2013) and his next edited volume, *Social Movements in Taiwan*, under Ma Ying-jeou was published in 2017. His most recent co-edited book was *Taiwan Studies Revisited*, published in 2019. He is also the book series editor for the Routledge Research on Taiwan Series.

# Routledge Research on Taiwan Series

The *Routledge Research on Taiwan Series* seeks to publish quality research on all aspects of Taiwan studies. Taking an interdisciplinary approach, the books will cover topics such as politics, economic development, culture, society, anthropology and history.

This new book series will include the best possible scholarship from the social sciences and the humanities and welcomes submissions from established authors in the field as well as from younger authors. In addition to research monographs and edited volumes general works or textbooks with a broader appeal will be considered.

The Series is advised by an international Editorial Board and edited by *Dafydd Fell* of the Centre of Taiwan Studies at the School of Oriental and African Studies.
*Series Editor: Dafydd Fell, SOAS, UK*

For more information about this series, please visit: *https://www.routledge.com/Routledge-Research-on-Taiwan-Series/book-series/RRTAIWAN*

# Taiwan's Economic and Diplomatic Challenges and Opportunities

**Edited by
Mariah Thornton,
Robert Ash, and
Dafydd Fell**

LONDON AND NEW YORK

First published 2021
by Routledge
2 Park Square, Milton Park, Abingdon, Oxon OX14 4RN

and by Routledge
605 Third Avenue, New York, NY 10158

*Routledge is an imprint of the Taylor & Francis Group, an informa business*

*British Library Cataloguing-in-Publication Data*
A catalogue record for this book is available from the British Library

*Library of Congress Cataloging-in-Publication Data*
Names: Thornton, Mariah, editor. | Ash, Robert F., editor. |
Fell, Dafydd, 1970– editor.
Title: Taiwan's economic and diplomatic challenges and
opportunities / edited by Mariah Thornton, Robert Ash and
Dafydd Fell.
Description: Abingdon, Oxon ; New York, NY : Routledge, 2021. |
Series: Routledge research on Taiwan | Includes bibliographical
references and index.
Identifiers: LCCN 2020052392 | ISBN 9780367540739 (hardback) |
ISBN 9781000377330 (adobe pdf) | ISBN 9781000377347 (epub) |
ISBN 9781003091639 (ebook)
Subjects: LCSH: Taiwan—Economic conditions—1975– | Taiwan—
Economic policy—1975– | Taiwan—Foreign economic relations. |
Taiwan—Foreign relations—1945–
Classification: LCC HC430.5 .T38255 2021 | DDC 337.951249—dc23
LC record available at https://lccn.loc.gov/2020052392

ISBN: 978-0-367-54073-9 (hbk)
ISBN: 978-0-367-55029-5 (pbk)
ISBN: 978-1-003-09163-9 (ebk)

Typeset in Times New Roman
by codeMantra

# Contents

viii  *Contents*

# Figures

# Tables

# Appendix

# Contributors

**Robert Ash (Bob Ash)** is an Emeritus Professor at SOAS University of London, and Founder and Professorial Research Associate of the Centre of Taiwan Studies at SOAS. Before his retirement in 2020 he was Professor of Economics with reference to China and Taiwan, and Professorial Fellow of the SOAS China Institute. From 1986 to 1995 he was Head of the Contemporary China Institute at SOAS; during 1997–2001 he was Director of the EU-China Academic Network. From 1999 to 2013 Bob Ash was Director of the SOAS Taiwan Studies Programme and its Centre of Taiwan Studies. In 2012 he received the Friendship Medal of Diplomacy from the Ministry of Foreign Affairs of the ROC government in recognition of his efforts on behalf of Taiwan Studies in the UK and elsewhere in Europe. Bob Ash has held visiting research and teaching positions at universities in Australia, Hong Kong, France, and Italy. He has been researching China for more than 40 years and has written or edited 15 books, mainly on development issues relating to China, but also on issues relating to Taiwan and Hong Kong.

**Richard C. Bush** is a non-resident senior fellow of the Brookings Institution, where he worked for almost 18 years and focused first and foremost on Taiwan. Previously he worked 19 years in the Federal government: 12 years on Capitol Hill; two years as the National Intelligence Officer for East Asia; and five years as Chairman and Managing Director of the American Institute in Taiwan, the private entity through which the United States conducts substantive relations with Taiwan. He is now retired.

**Charles I-hsin Chen** is a Legislator in Taiwan's Legislative Yuan. He is also the Executive Director of the Institute for Taiwan-America Studies in Washington DC. He received his PhD in Economics from SOAS University of London and Postdoc in Cambridge University. He served as Spokesperson for Taiwan's Presidential Office and the Kuomintang Party. His articles have appeared in *Foreign Affairs, Foreign Policy, National Interest*, and numerous international newspapers.

**Chen Nai-chia** is a research fellow of the 'Taiwan Equality Campaign,' an organisation advocating for LGBTQ+ rights including full marriage rights for same-sex couples, workplace equality, and the political representation of LGBTQ+ people. She was part of the NGO lobby platform during the marriage equality campaign in 2019 in Taiwan. She has a Master of Science in International Politics from the School of Oriental and African Studies (SOAS), University of London, and her thesis was about LGBT Rights and Tongzhi Diplomacy in Taiwan. Before working in LGBTQ+ movements, Chen served as Press Officer of New Power Party and parliamentary aid in the Legislative Yuan in 2016 and 2017.

**Dafydd Fell** is the Reader in Comparative Politics with special reference to Taiwan at the Department of Politics and International Studies of the School of Oriental and African Studies (SOAS), University of London. He is also the Director of the SOAS Centre of Taiwan Studies. In 2004 he helped establish the European Association of Taiwan Studies. He has published numerous articles on political parties and electioneering in Taiwan. His first book was *Party Politics in Taiwan* (2005), which analysed party change in the first 15 years of multi-party competition. His second book was *Government and Politics in Taiwan* (Routledge, 2011) and the second edition was published in early 2018. He co-edited *Migration to and from Taiwan* (2013) and his next edited volume, *Social Movements in Taiwan under Ma Ying-jeou*, was published in 2017. His most recent co-edited book was *Taiwan Studies Revisited,* published in 2019. He is also the book series editor for the Routledge Research on Taiwan Series.

**Harry Harding** is University Professor of Public Policy and Senior Fellow in the Miller Center of Public Affairs at the University of Virginia, where he was the founding dean of the Frank Batten School of Leadership and Public Policy. He is also a Yushan Scholar at National Chengchi University in Taiwan. Harding has previously held appointments at Swarthmore College, Stanford University, and the Brookings Institution and part-time positions at Hong Kong University of Science and Technology and the University of Hong Kong. He served as Dean of the Elliott School of International Affairs at George Washington University and Director of Research and Analysis at Eurasia Group, a political risk advisory firm. A specialist on U.S.-China relations, his major publications on that topic include *Has U.S. China Policy Failed?* and *A Fragile Relationship: The United States and China since 1972.* He is now writing a sequel, *A Fraught Relationship: The U.S. and China from Partners to Competitors.*

**Jan Knoerich** is Senior Lecturer in the Economy of China at the Lau China Institute and Department of International Development, King's College London's School of Global Affairs. His research examines the business, political economy, and development dimensions of Chinese outward foreign direct investment (OFDI) and financial internationalisation. One strand of his research focuses on the political implications of mainland Chinese OFDI for host economies, including Taiwan. He has published in leading academic journals such as *New Political Economy* and the *Chinese Journal of International Politics* and co-edited a book with Paul Irwin Crookes on *Cross-Taiwan Strait Relations in an Era of Technological Change: Security, Economic and Cultural Dimensions* (Palgrave MacMillan, 2015). Before joining King's College London, he was a Departmental Lecturer at the University of Oxford's School of Interdisciplinary Area Studies and spent several years working for the United Nations Conference on Trade and Development (UNCTAD) in Geneva. He holds a PhD in Economics from the School of Oriental and African Studies (SOAS), University of London.

**Lee Chun-yi** is an Associate Professor and Director of Taiwan Studies Program at the School of Politics and International Relation (SPIR) at the University of Nottingham. Her current research project is geopolitical implication of China's Belt and Road Initiative. Chun-yi's past research includes 'Chinese Investment in Taiwan: Opportunities or Challenges to Taiwan's Industrial Development?' This project investigated bilateral cross-Strait economic activities and also its impact on both societies. It is a two-and-half year project, started in July 2014, finished in December 2016. Chun-yi's previous research project was 'Globalisation, national transformation and workers' rights: An analysis of Chinese labour within the global economy' with Prof. Andreas Bieler at SPIR. This project investigated the influence of different foreign investors on Chinese workers and labour rights. This is a three-year project, finished in September 2014.

**Lin Chu-chia** is a full professor at the Department of Economics, National Chengchi University (NCCU). Professor Lin served as the chairperson at the Department of Economics, NCCU, from 1992 to 1995 and he also served as the president of the Chinese Society of Housing Study from 1999 to 2002. Professor Lin was appointed as a Deputy Minister of the Mainland Affairs Council of Taiwan from October 2012 to January 2016, and he was appointed again as Minister, National Development Council, from February 2016 until May 2016. Professor Lin now teaches at the Department of Economics, NCCU. Professor Lin's major fields of research are cross-Strait economic relationship and housing economics, and he has published numerous books on economic relation across the Taiwan Strait and numerous papers in prestigious international journals.

**Lin Kun-chin** is a University Lecturer in Politics and Tun Suffian College Lecturer and Fellow at Gonville & Caius College, University of Cambridge. He is the Deputy Director of the Centre for Geopolitics and a senior fellow of the Centre for Industrial Sustainability at Cambridge. He is an editorial board member of *Business & Politics, Maritime Policy & Management,* and *Chinese Yearbook of International Law and Affairs,* and chair of the editorial board of the *Cambridge Review of International Affairs* (CRIA). Kun-chin was a Leverhulme postdoctoral fellow at the University of Oxford and taught at King's College London and the National University of Singapore. His research focuses on the politics of market reform in developing countries, federalism and regulatory issues in transport infrastructure and energy markets in China, industrial policy and privatisation of Chinese state-owned enterprises, and the economic and security nexus in maritime governance in the Indo-Pacific and the Arctic.

**Syaru Shirley Lin** is Compton Visiting Professor in World Politics at the Miller Center of Public Affairs at the University of Virginia and a member of the founding faculty of the master's program in global political economy at the Chinese University of Hong Kong. Previously, she was a partner at Goldman Sachs, responsible for private equity investments in Asia. She was appointed by the Hong Kong government as a member of the Hong Kong Committee for Pacific Economic Cooperation, and her board service includes Goldman Sachs Asia Bank, Langham Hospitality, and the Focused Ultrasound Foundation. Her current research project is focused on the challenges facing countries in East Asia in the high-income trap. She is the author of *Taiwan's China Dilemma: Contested Identities and Multiple Interests in Taiwan's Cross-Strait Economic Policy* (2016), which was also published in Chinese (2019). She earned an MA in international public affairs and a PhD in politics and public administration at the University of Hong Kong and graduated cum laude from Harvard College.

**Liu Da-nien** currently serves as the director of the Regional Development Study Center at the Chung Hua Institution for Economic Research (CIER), a leading economic think tank in Taiwan. His major research fields and publications cover topics of international trade and investment, industrial economics, multilateral trading systems, and regional economic integration. Dr Liu was involved in assisting Taiwan to join the World Trade Organization (WTO), participating in APEC activities, and forming Taiwan's bilateral Free Trade Agreements (FTAs), including the Economic Cooperation Framework Agreement (ECFA) signed in 2010 with China, Taiwan-New Zealand FTA and the Taiwan-Singapore FTA signed in 2013, which are important for Taiwan to expand its role in the international arena. Between 2014 and 2016, Dr Liu served as Deputy Secretary-General of the National Security Council, Office of the President in the Taiwanese government. He was an important advisor to the President and was mainly responsible for the international and cross-Strait economic and trade issues. Dr Liu also participated in the historic Ma-Xi meeting held in Singapore on 7 November 2015. The meeting was the first between the political leaders of the Taiwan Strait since 1945. In May 2016, he was awarded the First Class Medal by the Ministry of Economic Affairs for his contribution to Taiwan.

**Michael Reilly** is a Non-resident Senior Fellow in the Taiwan Studies Programme at Nottingham University. A former career diplomat, he spent over 30 years working for the UK Foreign & Commonwealth Office (FCO), principally handling UK policy towards East and South East Asia. His final FCO appointment was as Director of the British Trade and Cultural Office in Taipei from 2005 to 2009, the de facto British ambassador to Taiwan. He then joined BAE Systems, serving as the company's Chief Representative in China from 2011 to 2014. Since 2015 he has been pursing academic research, principally on the EU's relations with Taiwan and on Taiwan's railway history. In 2016 and 2019, he was a Visiting Fellow at Academia Sinica in Taipei under the auspices of the Taiwan Fellowship programme of the Ministry of Foreign Affairs of the Republic of China (Taiwan). He has a PhD in Economic History from the University of Liverpool and a diploma in Korean from Yonsei University in Seoul.

**Mariah Thornton** is an enthusiastic researcher of Chinese politics with an undergraduate degree in Chinese Studies from the University of Oxford and an MSc in the Politics of China from the School of Oriental and African Studies, University of London. From 2012 to 2013 she completed a year abroad at Peking University and later received the Huayu Scholarship from the Taiwan Ministry of Education to undergo intensive study of Mandarin at National Taiwan Normal University from 2015 to 2016. Mariah Thornton worked as a press and communications adviser at the Taipei Representative Office in the United Kingdom under Representative and former Foreign Minister David Y.L. Lin from 2018 to 2020.

# Acknowledgements

Completing an edited volume is always a complex and challenging process. This book was no exception and there were more than the usual share of storms in teacups along the way. There were moments when we wondered whether the project would fail, as is the case in so many publications based on workshop papers.

There are so many people we need to thank for making this project possible. The first place to start has to be the original workshop, entitled 'The Challenges and Opportunities of Asian Economic Integration Facing Taiwan under the Impact of Globalisation,' which was held at SOAS on 10–11 May 2018. We would especially like to thank our former PhD student and chapter author, Dr Charles Chen, for his work in designing the workshop, as well as identifying and liaising with speakers. Our SOAS colleagues, Laura Ritchie-Roberts and Chang Bi-yu, also played critical roles in helping to organise the event.

The Centre of Taiwan Studies would also like to thank Taiwan's Ministry of Foreign Affairs for its support over many years of our research on Taiwan. For this conference we worked closely with colleagues at the Taipei Representative Office to the UK in London. This cooperation was instrumental in the participation of Cabinet Minister John Deng, who spoke by video link about Taiwan's New Southbound Policy. We would especially like to thank then Deputy Ambassador Cheng for his opening remarks at the workshop, and we are also pleased to acknowledge the important liaison support of the Taipei Representative Office in the UK's Administration Division.

Bob Ash and Dafydd Fell owe a major debt of gratitude to Mariah Thornton, who valiantly stepped in and joined the editorial team when the project was experiencing one of its mini crises. Without your participation, Mariah, the project could not have been completed so smoothly. As is often the case in publication workshops, not all the conference papers made it into the book. This made it necessary to seek out some new chapters, and we would like to thank both Mariah and Chen Nai-chia for sharing their research in the book.

In 2020 we have been celebrating 20 years of Taiwan Studies at SOAS, and one of the most pleasing aspects of preparing this book for publication has been the opportunity to include the work of some of our former students. Jan Knoerich was a PhD student (2011) in Economics at SOAS; so was Charles Chen (2014), who also took a Development Studies in MSc (2003) at SOAS; Mariah Thornton (2017) and Chen Nai-chia (2018) are former Politics MSc students.

Lastly, we need – and it is a pleasure – to express very real thanks to all our contributors for having been so dependable in delivering their chapters and revised chapters on time. Bob and Dafydd have edited numerous edited volumes, and we thank you for having been the most reliable group of authors with whom we have worked!

Mariah Thornton
Robert Ash
Dafydd Fell
SEPTEMBER 2020

# 1 Taiwan's economic and diplomatic challenges and opportunities

*Mariah Thornton, Robert Ash, and Dafydd Fell*

Since the end of Japanese colonial rule in 1945, Taiwan has fluctuated between periods of optimism and pessimism over its position on the international stage (Fell 2018). Taiwan's ambitions in this respect have been tempered by a challenging global environment shaped by two competing superpowers: the United States and China. Hickey (2006) aptly described Taiwan's situation as 'a shrimp between whales.'

However, Taiwan has managed to navigate these turbulent circumstances over the past decades, emerging as an 'island of resilience.' In the spring of 1950, it looked only a matter of time before Taiwan would become incorporated as the latest province of the Communist People's Republic of China (PRC), but it was saved by the outbreak of the Korean War. Twenty years on, after the Republic of China (ROC) lost its seat in the United Nations and the United States switched diplomatic recognition to Beijing, there were serious doubts about the sustainability of Taiwan's de facto independence. Yet time and again Taiwan has found opportunities and solutions to survive and prosper against the odds. Facing the loss of formal diplomatic recognition, Taiwan successfully adopted more flexible strategies to expand its international space and enjoy unofficial but de facto diplomatic relations with most countries. In the 1980s Taiwan became known globally for having achieved an 'economic miracle'; in the 1990s its transition from authoritarianism to democratisation was hailed as a *political* miracle. Like the Korean peninsula, the Taiwan Strait is often seen as a potential source of international armed conflict. However, unlike the Koreas, Taiwan and China have been able to develop extensive economic ties and substantial cross-Strait trade despite their political differences. The purpose of this book is to shed light on the changing challenges facing Taiwan today and the ways in which it has sought to adapt to its changing environment.

As a state excluded from the international society by its authoritarian neighbour, Taiwan faces a unique set of circumstances in its efforts to maintain its position within the international economy and community. Nevertheless, Taiwan has made great strides to increase its international engagement both economically and diplomatically, and its efforts have yielded some impressive results. Its economy is highly ranked by several international organisations and think tanks around the world, and it remains an important trade hub in the Asian region. On the diplomatic front, Taiwan has 15 formal allies while maintaining substantial unofficial relations with most other nations across the world. It remains a full member of 33 international governmental organisations (IGOs) and an observer in 15 others (MOFA, 2020). Taiwan also contributes significantly to the international community in terms of striving towards UN Sustainable Development Goals (SDGs), such as alleviating poverty and hunger as well as achieving universal healthcare. The proportion of low-income households in Taiwan has been reduced to 1.6%, while its National Health Insurance programme covers 99.8% of the population as of 2019. Taiwan also provides development assistance and engages in several cooperation programmes with countries in the Pacific, Asia, Africa, and the Caribbean (Wu, 2019).

However, in recent years the PRC has intensified economic, military, and diplomatic pressures on the island as it pursues its ultimate goal of unifying Taiwan with China. In January 2019, Chinese leader Xi Jinping renewed the threat of force against the island in the event of unification under the 'one country, two systems' (Kuo, 2019). Since the landslide re-election of Democratic Progressive Party (DPP) presidential candidate Tsai Ing-wen in January 2020, China has continued flexing its military muscles by sending more warships to pass through the Taiwan Strait and fighter jets to invade Taiwanese airspace (The Telegraph, 2020a).

The global outbreak of the novel coronavirus 2019 (COVID-19) has also seen mounting evidence of disinformation campaigns from China, including hundreds of thousands of social media accounts aimed at influencing public perception of the pandemic as well as other events, including demonstrations over the death of George Floyd and the Hong Kong protests (The Telegraph, 2020b). According to evidence collected by the Taiwanese Investigation Bureau, Taiwan has been one of China's primary targets for fake news (MJIB, 2020). Furthermore, Beijing's passing of the Hong Kong National Security Law following months of protests in the Special Administrative Region throughout 2019 has widely been seen as the breakdown of 'one country, two systems' in Hong Kong and a sign of troubled times ahead for Taiwan.

Despite intense pressures from China as well as the severe impact of COVID-19 on the global economic system, Taiwan's economy has remained relatively strong and stable, albeit with some slowing of GDP growth in recent years. Prior to the outbreak of COVID-19, Taiwan's economy grew 3.3% during the fourth quarter of 2019, due in part to the effects of the US-China trade war which saw substantial benefits for Taiwan, Mexico, and the European Union (Nicita, 2019). Dubbed one of the four 'Asian Tigers' for high levels of economic growth from the 1960s to the 1990s, Taiwan has maintained an export-oriented and technology-focused strategy for economic development. Taiwan currently stands as the seventh largest economy in Asia according to the International Monetary Fund and is the 12th most competitive out of 141 economies in the world according to the World Economic Forum's 2019 Global Competitiveness Report (2019). Taiwan also ranks the 11th most competitive economy in the 2020 World Competitiveness Yearbook, compiled by the International Institute for Management Development, and enjoys a high degree of economic freedom (2020).

COVID-19 inevitably took a serious toll on Taiwan's economy. Nevertheless, its handling of the pandemic has won many plaudits. Not least, compared with many other countries, the economic impact of coronavirus in terms of its short-term hit on growth has been quite mild. According to data published by OECD and national statistical reporting agencies, the decline in Taiwan's GDP growth in the second quarter of 2020 was the lowest (−0.6%) of 38 countries included in the study (CNA, 2020).

However, despite these impressive economic credentials, Taiwan's contentious relations with China, the economically dominant power in the Asia, also present significant limitations to its economic integration in the region. As a result, Taiwan remains excluded from trade-facilitation integration in Asia as a member economy, despite becoming more integrated in terms of business (Bush, 2019). In addition, an increasingly authoritarian Beijing has stepped up its campaign to marginalise Taiwan by stealing its remaining diplomatic allies, blocking its participation in international summits, and pressuring companies overseas to downgrade Taiwan's status from a country to a province of China.

China's success in excluding Taiwan from the World Health Organization (WHO) and its annual World Health Assembly (WHA) has continued despite the urgent need for global cooperation to combat coronavirus and in the face of strong international support for Taiwan's inclusion. As of mid-September 2020, Taiwan has confirmed 495 cases of COVID-19 and seven deaths – relatively low numbers compared with those of other countries, and sufficiently low for Taiwan to be widely considered a success story (Taiwan Centers for Disease Control, 2020). Taiwan has also received praise from the international media for its effective and early response to the outbreak, as well as for its donations of personal protective equipment and medical supplies to countries hard hit by the virus. This has drawn increased international attention to the reasons for Taiwan's exclusion from the WHO and to China's behaviour in response to the pandemic (BBC, 2020).

Taiwan also remains shut out from several multi-lateral trade organisations, including negotiations over the Regional Comprehensive Economic Partnership (RCEP) trading bloc, comprising the Association of Southeast Asian Nations (ASEAN) member states, Australia, India, Japan, New Zealand, and South Korea. As the RCEP would account for 24% of global GDP and 46% of global population, Taiwan's exclusion threatens to cause significant economic losses (Wong, 2018). Taiwan has also been excluded from any involvement in China's grand vision for global economic integration: the Belt and Road Initiative (BRI). More broadly speaking, since the financial crash of 2008, Taiwan has remained on the fringes of these organisations, while ASEAN has ramped up economic integration. For example, in December of 2008, the ASEAN member states launched a charter to implement 'an EU-style community' by creating a single free-trade area for the region. Since Taiwan is not a member state, it cannot directly benefit from agreements made at a multi-lateral level. Taiwan's fate in the Comprehensive and Progressive Agreement for Trans-Pacific Partnership (CPTPP) also remains uncertain following the US's withdrawal from negotiations. In short, as other Asian countries become more economically interconnected, Taiwan has remained an outsider, squeezed out from this process by China.

On the diplomatic front, Taiwan has faced mounting pressure from China since the election of President Tsai Ing-wen in 2016. Since Tsai's ascension to power, Taiwan has been debarred from several key IGOs in which it had previously enjoyed observer status, including the WHA and the International Civil Aviation Organisations (ICAO). Beijing has also resumed its diplomatic war with Taiwan, offering substantial economic aid and trade deals to woo remaining diplomatic allies to switch recognition. As it stands, Taiwan currently maintains formal ties with 15 countries, but this number is likely to dwindle further as China increases pressure on Taiwan towards unification. Beijing has also launched a campaign to force private overseas enterprises and organisations to designate Taiwan as a province of China, further downgrading Taiwan's status and position in the international community. Following Tsai's re-election in January 2020, it is likely these trends in cross-strait relations will continue.

As Taiwan navigates these major shifts in global geopolitics, this volume seeks to analyse the challenges and opportunities faced by the country from economic and diplomatic standpoints.

## Origins and purpose

The origin of the book was a workshop on 'The Challenges and Opportunities of Asian Economic Integration Facing Taiwan under the Impact of Globalisation,' which took place at the School of Oriental and African Studies (SOAS), University of London in May 2018. After the conclusion of the workshop, participants were invited to expand their initial papers into chapters exploring different aspects on Taiwan's economic integration and diplomacy. In compiling this volume, our aim is to give an updated overview of Taiwan's economic and diplomatic situation during recent years. In so doing, we set out to explore not only the obstacles the island faces in building engagement with the international community, but also potential opportunities. We hope that this volume can provide valuable perspectives and insights into paths towards the country's greater economic integration and stronger diplomatic relations.

## Structure

The first half of the book focuses on Taiwan's economic policies at the domestic and international levels in order to provide a comprehensive understanding of the country's path to economic integration during the past decade or so. This section closely examines Taiwan's domestic economic transformation and its integration in the regional and global economy.

First, Lin Chu-chia analyses a wide range of economic data to show how and why Taiwan made a transition from an economy with a high economic growth rate and low unemployment to one with a low growth rate and moderate levels of unemployment. Lin cites a combination of both economic and political factors to explain this transformation, and views the year 2000 as the turning point between the two eras. Although his verdict on Taiwan's economic performance is quite pessimistic, he does offer several suggestions on how to tackle these challenges, such as adjusting energy policies and improving regional economic integration. This leads logically to Liu Da-nien's chapter, which focuses on how Taiwan can increase its Asia-Pacific regional economic integration. Liu also offers an analysis of Taiwan's economic development over the long term and reaches similar critical and pessimistic conclusions to those outlined in the previous chapter. In addition to external challenges such as changes in US policies on regional integration, Liu attributes blame to Taiwan's limited success in signing free trade agreements. He suggests a range of measures that Taiwan should pursue to enhance its economic integration, such as industrial upgrading and diversification. He is also at pains to emphasise that integration will only be possible in the context of stable cross-Strait relations.

While the analysis provided by Lin Chu-chia and Liu is set in the context of long-term patterns of economic change and challenges, Syaru Shirley Lin's chapter focuses more exclusively on current developments – in particular, the challenges which Taiwan now faces as a country caught in the high-income trap. She analyses the limited success of both the Ma and Tsai administrations in addressing the economic challenges underlying this phenomenon. She argues that Taiwan is in a double bind, which it can only escape by adopting policies that prioritise economic growth. But she also stresses the need for Taiwan to maintain its democracy and identity in the face of China's more assertive policies. For Shirley Lin, Taiwan faces a 'China dilemma.'

The next group of chapters looks in detail at four potential directions Taiwan could take to improve its economic links and integration: North, South, West, and East.

The important role of China in Taiwan's economic performance is recognised in earlier chapters. As Shirley Lin suggests, there has been much debate in Taiwan's election campaigns on how to handle economic integration with China. In 2008 and 2012, the KMT presidential contender, Ma Ying-jeou, depicted China as the solution to Taiwan's economic problems and warned of the dangers of DPP isolationism. Interestingly, the KMT appears to have returned to this rhetoric and policy platform in 2018 and 2019. Jan Knoerich and Lee Chun-yi address the China factor – or 'solution' – from the perspective of Chinese investment in Taiwan. Despite the liberalisation of Chinese foreign direct investment (FDI) under Ma after 2009, they find that Chinese investment in Taiwan has been surprisingly modest. They investigate the reasons why Taiwan has not attracted more investment from China despite its rapid expansion of multinational enterprises and FDI during the past decade. They conclude that the answer lies in a combination of business logic, unfavourable and discriminatory treatment of Mainland Chinese direct investment (MDI), as well as the unpredictable policy environment related to such investments. They are not optimistic that these trends will change significantly in the near future under the DPP. When Taiwan's leaders have warned of the security implications of excessive reliance on the Chinese market, they have tended to promote southward investment towards South East Asian countries, evidenced in Lee Teng-hui's Southbound policy of the 1990s. After the DPP returned to power, its most visible international initiative was the New Southbound Policy (NSP). In her sole-authored chapter, Lee Chun-yi looks at the impact of Taiwan's southbound policies from Lee Teng-hui to Tsai Ing-wen, and analyses the challenges and opportunities for Tsai's NSP vis-à-vis China's BRI. Using the key NSP partner Vietnam as a case study, Lee examines the advantages and disadvantages for the Taiwanese business community abroad under Tsai's NSP.

While most of the focus of Taiwan's economic integration has been on either China or South East Asia, the next two chapters discuss alternative opportunities East and Westbound. Lin Kun-chin and Charles I-hsin Chen's chapter questions the viability of the NSP. Instead, they suggest steering Taiwan's maritime trade eastward towards the Panama Canal, arguing that this would promise to boost US-Taiwan economic links and further reduce Taiwan's economic dependence on China. In contrast, to lessen economic dependence on China, Michael Reilly argues that Taiwan should look Westward to EU member states for opportunities. Reilly highlights the importance of reducing market access barriers in order to make Taiwan a more attractive destination for European exporters and investors, as well as advocating deregulation to make it easier for young entrepreneurs to develop new businesses. He argues that rebuilding a strong trading relationship with Europe can be the foundation of deeper and more wide-ranging ties.

The second half of the book explores challenges and opportunities for the country's diplomacy and status in the global community. Harry Harding provides a broad historical overview of the US government's policy towards Taiwan, looking specifically at three policy shifts: first, the US's initial placing of Taiwan outside the American defence perimeter in the Western Pacific; second, its extension of a formal security commitment to Taiwan following the outbreak of the Korean War in the 1950s; and finally, the US's de-recognition of the ROC and normalisation of relations with the PRC. In each case, Harding examines the impact of these policy shifts on Taiwan's diplomatic situation. In his chapter, Richard Bush examines how China has sought to benefit from Taiwan economically, while seeking to marginalise it politically, arguing that Taiwan's political marginalisation stems from the circumstances of its political history. Bush makes the case that since the Korean War, the PRC has striven to enhance its own legitimacy by shifting to political warfare and driving the ROC from the international system. He points out that the ROC survived on Taiwan longer than expected because it was able to maintain its economic and political freedom of action.

By contrast, the next two chapters look at the diplomatic challenges and opportunities with a focus on more recent developments. Mariah Thornton examines the different strategies Taiwan has pursued to increase its 'international space' under former President Ma Ying-jeou and current President Tsai Ing-wen. Thornton argues that Ma's strategy, which focused on economic integration and positive relations with China, did not translate into meaningful, long-term diplomatic gains for Taiwan. She argues that Tsai's more soft power-oriented and less China-focused strategy may in fact yield better results for Taiwan's international space over the long term. Chen Nai-chia and Dafydd Fell further examine a key aspect of Taiwan's soft power: its role as a leader for the advancement of LGBT rights in Asia. Chen and Fell note Taiwan's strong commitment to upholding human rights and highlight its reputation as one of the most democratic and liberal states in the region as a cornerstone of its international diplomacy. They use the 'Taiwan Tongzhi Hotline Association (Hotline)' as an example of how Taiwan is able to advance its image as a 'queer state' through Tongzhi diplomacy. Not only do they show how Taiwan's civil society-led LGBT diplomacy was distinct from the state-led model of many Western countries, they also reveal how the campaign to legalise same-sex marriage generated far greater international visibility than more traditional state-led public diplomacy efforts.

Taken together, all the chapters in this book offer diverse and important perspectives on the state of and prospects for Taiwan's economy and international relations. The approaches are also varied: some chapters offer broad historical overviews of Taiwan's development, while others are focused more narrowly on recent developments. The disciplinary mix is also very apparent, with chapters that embody economics, political economy, international relations, and gender studies, as well as a deliberately interdisciplinary orientation. Lastly, we reach a diverse set of conclusions which afford room for both optimism and pessimism about Taiwan's future.

## References

BBC. 2020. 'Coronavirus: Why Taiwan Won't Have a Seat at the Virus Talks', 17 May 2020, https://www.bbc.co.uk/news/world-asia-52661181

Bush, Richard C. 2019. 'From Persuasion to Intimidation: China's Approach to Taiwan and Taiwan's Response,' Brookings Institution, November 2019, www.brookings.edu/research/from-persuasion-to-coercion-beijings-approach-to-taiwan-and-taiwans-response/

CNA. 2020. 'CORONAVIRUS/Taiwan Disproves "Health or Economy" COVID-19 Argument: Study', China News Agency (CNA), 12 September 2020, https://focustaiwan.tw/society/202009120002

Fell, Dafydd. 2018. 'Cycles of Optimism and Pessimism in Taiwan.' Taiwan Sentinel, 22 January 2018, https://sentinel.tw/cycles-of-optimism-and-pessimism-in-taiwan/

Hickey, Dennis. 2006. *Foreign Policy Making in Taiwan: From Principle to Pragmatism*. London: Routledge.

International Institute for Management Development. 2020. '2020 World Competitiveness Yearbook', https://www.imd.org/wcc/world-competitiveness-center-rankings/world-competitiveness-ranking-2020/

Kuo, Lily. 2019. '"All Necessary Means": Xi Jinping Reserves Right to Use Force against Taiwan', *The Guardian*, 1 January 2019, https://www.theguardian.com/world/2019/jan/02/all-necessary-means-xi-jinping-reserves-right-to-use-force-against-taiwan

Ministry of Foreign Affairs (MOFA), Republic of China (Taiwan). 2020. 'IGOs in Which We Participate', https://www.mofa.gov.tw/enigo/Link3enigo.aspx?n=58BD38F4400A7167&sms=A72EC821FB103DD9

Ministry of Justice Investigation Bureau (MJIB). 2020. 'The Ministry of Justice Investigation Bureau's in-Depth Analysis of the Spread of the Mainland Produced False Misinformation,' '大陸製假訊息流竄　調查局深入解析,' 29 February 2020, https://www.mjib.gov.tw/news/Details?Module=1&id=570

Nicita, Alessandro. 2019. 'Trade and Trade Diversion Effects of United States Tariffs on China', *United Nations Conference on Trade and Development*, Research paper no. 37, https://unctad.org/en/PublicationsLibrary/ser-rp-2019d9_en.pdf

Taiwan Centers for Disease Control. 2020. 'CECC Confirms 1 More Imported COVID-19 Case; Woman Found to Have COVID-19 after Returning to Taiwan from France,' 8 September 2020, https://www.cdc.gov.tw/En/Bulletin/Detail/PBigenm-LzSk0rl1XCp0QA?typeid=158

The Telegraph. 2020a. 'Chinese Fighters Briefly Enter Taiwan Airspace: Taipei', 9 June 2020, https://www.telegraph.co.uk/news/2020/06/09/chinese-fighters-briefly-enter-taiwan-airspace-taipei/

The Telegraph. 2020b. 'Twitter Deletes 170,000 Pro-China Accounts', 12 June 2020, https://www.telegraph.co.uk/technology/2020/06/12/twitter-deletes-170000-pro-china-accounts/

Wong, Frank. 2018. 'What the CPTPP and RCEP Mean for China and Asia-Pacific Trade', *China Briefing*, 10 December 2018, https://www.china-briefing.com/news/cptpp-rcep-impact-china-asia-pacific-trade/

World Economic Forum. 2019. 'The Global Competitiveness Report 2019', http://www3.weforum.org/docs/WEF_TheGlobalCompetitivenessReport2019.pdf

Wu, Joseph. 2019. 'Building an Inclusive United Nations with Taiwan on Board', *The Diplomat*, 5 September 2019, https://thediplomat.com/2019/09/building-an-inclusive-united-nations-with-taiwan-on-board/

# 2 Economic development of Taiwan and structural change

## Retrospect and prospect

*Lin Chu-chia*

## I Introduction

For a long period of time Taiwan enjoyed an impressive economic performance, including a high economic growth rate, a low inflation rate, and a low unemployment rate.[1] However, after the new Democratic Progressive Party (DPP) regime came to power in 2000, the economic momentum of Taiwan quickly slowed down, generating higher unemployment, wage stagnation, and modest consumer price inflation.

During its period of buoyant economic growth, Taiwan also experienced dramatic structural change as its economic centre of gravity shifted from agriculture to manufacturing industry, and subsequently from manufacturing to the service industry. Meanwhile, as some manufacturing firms moved to mainland China in the 1990s, the focus of the manufacturing sector in Taiwan also sharply changed from labour-intensive industry to capital-intensive and technology-intensive activities.

Taiwan is a small-open economy which is highly dependent upon international trade. Now, as the economy has rapidly become integrated within the Asian-Pacific region, Taiwan has reached a point at which it should strengthen its involvement in the integration process, including signing Free Trade Agreements (FTA) with other countries and participating in multilateral FTAs, such as the Comprehensive and Progressive Agreement for Trans-Pacific Partnership (CPTPP) and the Regional Comprehensive Economic Partnership (RCEP) agreement.

In Section II, we examine the economic performance of Taiwan before and after the year 2000. In Section III, we will discuss the significant structural change that took place around 1990 and explain why Taiwan's economic momentum quickly slowed down under the new government regime, in terms of both GDP growth and the inflation rate. In Section IV, we will consider the process of Asian-Pacific economic integration and the importance of the China factor. We conclude this study by discussing the challenges for President Tsai Ing-wen and her administration (Section V).

## II  Economic development of Taiwan

### *No more Taiwan miracle*

Since the ruling party KMT (Kuomintang) moved to Taiwan in 1949, Taiwan has achieved rapid and sustained economic growth, with nominal per capita GDP having risen from US$164 in 1952 to US$24,337 in 2017. The annual growth rate during the past 65 years was 7.48%. However, it is clear that after 2000 the average growth rate declined sharply to 4.23% per year, and again fell to 2.45% between 2011 and 2017 (see Table 2.1).

There are several reasons to explain why the growth rate suddenly dropped after 2000: first, as a result of many manufacturing firms having moved from Taiwan to mainland China, the economic driving force in Taiwan shifted from the manufacturing sector to the service industry. Unfortunately, the growth rate of the service industry is usually lower than that of the manufacturing industry, thereby depressing the overall growth rate.

Second, although Taiwan had joined the WTO at the beginning of 2002, the significant slowing of the growth rate of global trade into the new century depressed Taiwan's GDP growth. With a trade dependence ratio as high as 140%, Taiwan's economy was hurt badly by the decline in international trade growth.

Third, the dispute surrounding the fourth nuclear power plant became critical for attracting investment in Taiwan. The construction of the fourth nuclear power plant had begun in March 1999 under the KMT regime. However, when DPP President Chen Shui-bian assumed office in May 2000, Prime Minister Chang Chun-hsiung suddenly announced (October 2000) that the

*Table 2.1* Taiwan's GDP (unit: US$, %)

| Year | Per capita GDP (US$)[a] | Average GDP growth rate (%) | Average inflation rate (%)[b] | Average unemployment rate (%) |
|---|---|---|---|---|
| 52–60 | 164 | 8.50 | – | 3.93 |
| 61–70 | 397 | 10.28 | 3.37 | 3.37 |
| 71–80 | 2,389 | 10.51 | 10.42 | 1.53 |
| 81–90 | 8,216 | 8.25 | 3.05 | 2.11 |
| 91–00 | 14,941 | 6.71 | 2.58 | 2.17 |
| 01–10 | 19,278 | 4.23 | 0.94 | 4.63 |
| 11–17 | 24,337 | 2.45 | 1.00 | 4.03 |
| 1952–2017 | – | 7.48 | 3.58 | 3.06 |
| 1952–2000 | – | 8.86 | 3.83 | 2.60 |
| 2001–17 | – | 3.50 | 0.97 | 4.38 |

Source: *Taiwan Statistical Data Book 2018*, Table 1-1, pp. 19–24, National Development Council, ROC (Taiwan).

Note:
a  The figure is the per capita GDP at the last year of that period.
b  The figure is the consumer price index, CPI.

government intended to cease construction of the plant. This policy decision not only caused huge political turmoil, but also had a major impact on both domestic and foreign investment since businessmen feared that Taiwan would suffer electricity supply shortages. Although the construction of the fourth nuclear power plant re-commenced in February 2001 after the Legislative Yuan passed a law forcing the government to do so, by the end of President Chen's regime in 2008 the plant remained uncompleted. Only in 2014 under KMT President Ma Ying-jeou's administration the construction of the nuclear power plant was finally completed. However, in response to huge political pressure from the opposition party, in April of that year Prime Minister Jiang Yi-hua announced that operational implementation of the fourth power plant, which had never been activated, would be suspended indefinitely.[2]

The dispute surrounding construction of the fourth nuclear power plant had two significant effects on investment in Taiwan. First, potential investors were concerned about the possibility of future shortages of power supplies. Second, when the DPP won the presidential election for the first time in 2000 and immediately decided to cease construction of the fourth nuclear power plant, many businessmen in Taiwan worried that the likelihood of future changes of central government administrations would undermine the consistency of important economic policies. Indeed, in 2001 the growth rate of investment was −17.9%, which remains to this day a historical low point for Taiwan. Table 2.2 shows that the annual growth rate of gross fixed capital formation in Taiwan from 1991 to 2000 was 7.31%, and fell to a mere 2.61% from 2001 to 2010.[3] In fact, the investment rate (total investment divided by national income) was only 20.60% in 2002, and it has remained at a very low level thereafter (in 2017 it was 20.46%). However, during the same period the savings rate in Taiwan was increasing (it rose from 27.99% in 2002 to 35.61% in 2017). In short, the excess savings rate also rose sharply from 7.39% to 15.15%. The deterioration in the investment environment is one of the crucial reasons for the high excess savings rate.[4] Finally, thanks to the low investment rate, GDP growth was −1.3% in 2001, the first year since 1952 in which Taiwan had recorded a negative GDP rate of growth.

*Table 2.2* Average annual growth rate of GDP, by expenditure (unit: %)

| Year | GDP | Consumption | Investment | Government expenditure | Export | Import |
|------|-----|-------------|------------|-----------------------|--------|--------|
| 1952–60 | 8.50 | 19.45 | 21.56 | 25.40 | 23.12 | 23.97 |
| 1961–70 | 10.28 | 11.73 | 13.01 | 17.08 | 25.92 | 19.62 |
| 1971–80 | 10.51 | 20.02 | 19.62 | 26.02 | 28.35 | 29.32 |
| 1981–90 | 8.25 | 11.74 | 12.92 | 8.97 | 10.22 | 9.01 |
| 1991–2000 | 6.71 | 9.35 | 7.31 | 9.62 | 10.40 | 11.07 |
| 2001–10 | 4.23 | 2.79 | 2.61 | 3.62 | 7.11 | 6.95 |
| 2011–17 | 2.45 | 3.04 | 2.29 | 0.08 | 1.90 | 0.37 |

Source: *Taiwan Statistical Data Book 2018*, Table 2-a, p. 4, National Development Council, ROC (Taiwan).

When the economy slowed down after 2000, consumer price inflation also fell to a low level. The annual inflation rate averaged 3.58% during the past 65 years, but from 2001 to 2017 the corresponding figure was as low as 0.97% per year. Several factors explain Taiwan's low inflation rate after 2000. First, the sudden economic slowdown significantly restrained effective demand, resulting in a reduction in the inflation rate. Second, Taiwan had also experienced very low growth in wages, and stable labour costs are commonly translated into supply price and inflation rate stability. Finally, from 1998 until his retirement in 2018, Perng Fai-nan – a conservative economist who was very effective in controlling inflation – held the key position of President of Taiwan's Central Bank.[5]

As for the unemployment rate, it moved in exactly the opposite direction to that of the inflation rate. The average unemployment rate from 1952 to 2000 was 2.60% per annum, but it increased to 4.38% from 2001 to 2017. In the 1960s, the Taiwanese government successfully implemented an export-oriented policy and emphasised labour-intensive industries, such as clothes, toys, and electric and electronic products. With high labour demand, these industries generated a great many job opportunities, which in turn held the unemployment rate in Taiwan at a very low level of around 2% per year from the 1960s.

However, this situation began to change when Taiwanese firms started to invest in mainland China after the 1990s. When these firms moved their production activities to the mainland, they also shifted their labour demand to China. A further knock-on effect was that they released large numbers of workers in Taiwan. While some of these shifted their jobs to services, more elderly workers with lower skills were unable to do so, as a result of which they became unemployed. This became known as the 'hollowing out' effect. Thus, the unemployment rate gradually increased, and by 2000 it had reached 3%.

When the economy of Taiwan quickly slowed down after 2000, the demand for labour also declined, causing the unemployment once more to rise. In the year of the dot-com bubble the unemployment rate in Taiwan had risen to 5.2%, and by the time of the international financial tsunami it had reached 5.9%. Thereafter it fell back to around 3.8% in 2018. But it is safe to predict that it will never again fall below 3%.

While economic growth slowed after 2000, the inflation rate was also low, enabling per capita GDP in terms of PPP to remain quite buoyant. For instance, in 2000 Taiwan's per capita GDP in both nominal and purchasing power parity (PPP) terms (US$14,877 and US$21,590) was higher than that of South Korea (US$11,947 and US$16,452) (see Table 2.3). However, in 2017 per capita GDP in Taiwan (US$24,398) was lower than that of Korea (US$29,749) in nominal terms, although in real terms (US$50,592) it was much higher (US$38,548). The reason was, quite simply, that over a long period of time Taiwan's inflation rate was much lower than that of Korea.[6] Although many in Taiwan complained about the low growth rate and low wage

*Table 2.3* Per capita GDP and by PPP (unit: US$)

| Country/area | 2000 | | 2017 | |
|---|---|---|---|---|
| | *Per capita GDP* | *Per capita GDP by PPP* | *Per capita GDP* | *Per capita GDP by PPP* |
| Japan | 38,534 | 26,850 | 38,344 | 42,818 |
| USA | 36,433 | 36,433 | 59,894 | 59,894 |
| UK | 27,828 | 26,425 | 39,975 | 44,364 |
| Hong Kong | 25,578 | 26,776 | 46,091 | 61,528 |
| Singapore | 23,793 | 40,978 | 59,990 | 95,507 |
| Taiwan | 14,877 | 21,590 | 24,389 | 50,592 |
| Korea | 11,947 | 16,452 | 29,749 | 38,548 |
| China | 959 | 2,918 | 8,677 | 16,682 |

Source: IMF, World Economic Outlook Database, October 2018. https://www.imf.org/external/pubs/ft/weo/2018/02/weodata/index.aspx.

rate, in fact (as these estimates suggest) the purchasing power in Taiwan was relatively favourable, compared with most countries. For example, in 2017 Taiwan's per capita income (US$50,592 in PPP terms) was even higher than that of the UK (US$44,364).

## The importance of trade

Another important feature of Taiwan has been its high trade dependency ratio. Taiwan is a small-open economy which is highly dependent on international trade. In Taiwan reference is commonly made to international trade being the engine of its economic growth. Through international trade, Taiwan has been able to expand its production sufficiently to realise scale benefits, to lower production costs, and to increase its international competitiveness. Against the background of relatively high GDP growth before 2000, as Table 2.4 shows, the trade dependency ratio (i.e., total trade divided by GDP) also rose dramatically – from a mere 16.9% in 1952 to 134.8% in 2010 – subsequently falling to 117.7% in 2017. The slowing of export growth is likely to be one of the reasons for slowing economic growth in Taiwan after 2000.

Taiwan's government chose a so-called export-oriented policy in the 1960s. A critically important initiative was the establishment of Taiwan's first export-processing zone (EPZ) in Kaohsiung in 1965 – the first EPZ to be set up in Asia. In terms of promoting exports from Taiwan, it was very successful. Table 2.4 shows that between 1960 and 1970 the trade dependency ratio increased from 16.6% to 60.1%.

After 1990, when Taiwan businessmen started to invest in mainland China, exports to China also rapidly increased. Today the China market accounts for about 40% of Taiwan's total exports. Another important factor which facilitated an increase in Taiwan's trade dependency ratio

*Table 2.4* The changing structure of GDP, by expenditure (unit: %)

| Year | Consumption | Investment | Government spending | Export | Import |
|------|-------------|------------|---------------------|--------|--------|
| 1952 | 64.7 | 8.4 | 34.0 | 4.9 | 12.0 |
| 1960 | 59.0 | 10.7 | 35.6 | 5.7 | 10.9 |
| 1970 | 56.4 | 17.7 | 18.5 | 30.0 | 30.1 |
| 1980 | 55.1 | 23.3 | 20.8 | 32.3 | 31.4 |
| 1990 | 53.4 | 21.2 | 17.2 | 44.6 | 39.9 |
| 2000 | 59.9 | 24.1 | 13.7 | 53.0 | 50.9 |
| 2010 | 53.1 | 23.6 | 14.9 | 70.9 | 63.9 |
| 2017 | 53.0 | 20.5 | 14.1 | 65.2 | 52.5 |

Source: *Taiwan Statistical Data Book 2018*, Table 2-a, p. 4, National Development Council, ROC (Taiwan).

after 2000 was Taiwan's membership, from January 2002, of the World Trade Organisation (WTO) – an event which significantly facilitated Taiwan's export expansion. Thus, between 1990 and 2010 the trade dependency ratio rose from 84.5% to 134.8%. However, after the international financial tsunami of 2009, the growth rates of both exports and imports fell sharply, as a result of which trade dependence declined from 134.8% (2010) to 117.7% (2017).

## III  Structural change in Taiwan

As economic development proceeded, Taiwan also experienced significant economic structural change. This manifested itself in various ways:

• First, agriculture's share of GDP fell steadily. In 1952 the agricultural contribution was almost one-third; by 2017 the corresponding figure had fallen to a mere 1.70% (see Figure 2.1).
• Second, alongside buoyant economic growth, between 1960 and 1988 the industrial share of GDP increased from 26.90% to 42.28%. But it subsequently declined sharply to 31.28% in 2000, since when its share has remained stable at around 35%. One of the reasons why industry's share of GDP fell so quickly is that after 1990 significant flows of investment moved from Taiwan to China, causing the manufacturing share in Taiwan to contract.[7] Taiwanese businessmen had begun to invest in mainland China in the late 1980s, when the Taiwanese government ended martial law and allowed its citizens for the first time to visit their relatives in mainland China. During 1990–2000 large amounts of Taiwanese investment flowed into mainland China, most of which was undertaken by manufacturing firms. When these firms shifted their production operations from Taiwan to mainland China, the GDP share of the island's manufacturing sector fell sharply until the end of 2000.

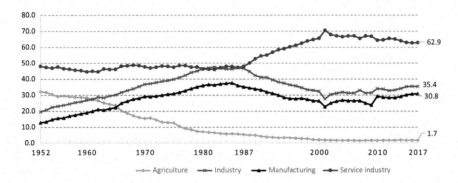

*Figure 2.1* Percentage shares of GDP, by industry.

- Finally, between 1988 and 2000 the service sector's contribution to GDP rose significantly (from 52.83% to 66.74%), thereafter remaining stable. There are several reasons why the service sector expanded so quickly after 1990. First, throughout the 1980s the Taiwanese government enforced strong financial liberalisation: around 1984, for example, the Central Bank of Taiwan liberalised the interest rate and allowed all state-owned banks to decide their own interest rate structure. Moreover, the Central bank also liberalised the foreign exchange market, including freeing the foreign exchange rate and allowing the unfettered purchase and sale of foreign exchange. Finally, in 1991 the government sanctioned the entry of 13 privately owned banks into the market.

The rapid contraction of the manufacturing sector, following the removal of many firms to mainland China, was another important reason why the service sector grew so rapidly after 1990. As manufacturing production declined, large numbers of workers were laid off. At the same time, as the service sector was liberalised, it started to hire more labour, thereby strengthening the momentum of service sector growth. Only in about 2000, when large-scale investment flows from Taiwan to mainland China ceased, did this process of structural change halt.

Alongside the rapid contraction of the manufacturing sector in and after 1988, the structure of exports also underwent a significant change. In Figure 2.2, we see that Taiwan's exports increasingly changed from the production of goods with a high labour intensity to those with a low labour intensity. Simultaneously, there was a shift (see Figure 2.3) from goods with a low *capital* intensity to those with a high *capital* intensity, as well as one (Figure 2.4) from a low to a high *technology* intensity. The main factor shaping these changes was the fact that so many labour-intensive firms moved from Taiwan to mainland China after 1990, thereby affecting exports. The nature of these changes suggests that when Taiwanese businessmen started to invest in mainland China, the manufacturing sector in Taiwan was upgrading, rather than hollowing out.[8]

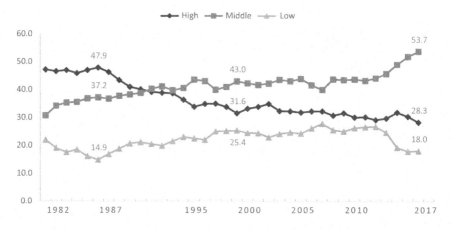

*Figure 2.2* The changing structure of exports, by labour intensity.

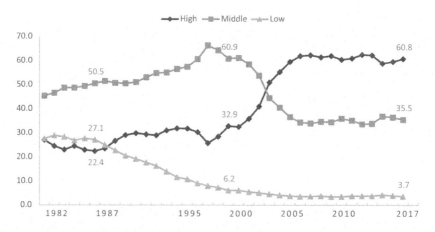

*Figure 2.3* The changing structure of exports, by capital intensity.

### *Changes in employment structure and wages*

As production in Taiwan shifted towards the manufacturing and service sectors, the sectoral distribution of employment followed a parallel pattern. Table 2.5 shows that the employment share of agriculture dropped from 19.50% in 1980 to 4.90% in 2017, while that of manufacturing also contracted from 42.52% to 35.79%. In contrast, the employment share of service increased sharply from 37.98% to 59.31%.[9]

Another important feature of the labour market in Taiwan is the stagnation of wage rate that occurred after 2000. From Table 2.6, we see that the monthly wage for manufacturing increased from US$196.7 per month in 1980

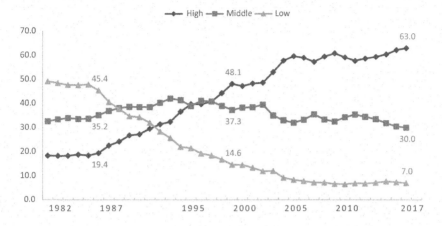

*Figure 2.4* The changing structure of exports, by technology intensity.

*Table 2.5* Sectoral shares of employment (unit: %)

| Year | Agriculture | Industry | Service |
|------|-------------|----------|---------|
| 1980 | 19.50 | 42.52 | 37.98 |
| 1985 | 17.45 | 41.57 | 40.98 |
| 1990 | 12.85 | 40.83 | 46.32 |
| 1995 | 10.55 | 38.74 | 50.71 |
| 2000 | 7.79 | 37.23 | 54.99 |
| 2005 | 5.94 | 36.40 | 57.67 |
| 2010 | 5.24 | 35.92 | 58.84 |
| 2015 | 4.95 | 36.03 | 59.02 |
| 2017 | 4.90 | 35.79 | 59.31 |

Source: *Taiwan Statistical Data Book 2018*, Table 2-9b, p. 38, National Development Council, ROC (Taiwan).

to US$696.8 per month in 1990 (implying an average annual growth rate of 13.5%), while the monthly wage in the service sector also rose from US$254.6 in 1980 to US$788.4 in 1990 (growing by 12.0% per year). When Taiwan's GDP growth fell sharply after 2000, the growth rate of monthly wages also fell sharply. Table 2.6 shows that the annual growth rate of the monthly wage in both manufacturing and service sectors was only 1.5% between 2001 and 2017.

There are several reasons to explain why wages stagnated in Taiwan after 2000: first, as Huang (2015) has pointed out, the shift of so much production activity to mainland China in the 1990s released many workers in Taiwan and thereby depressed the overall wage rate. Second, Haepp and Hsin (2016) found that many vocational schools and colleges were restructured and became universities at the end of the 1990s, which greatly increased the supply of college graduates, thus generating a drag on wage rates for college graduates. Third, Lin and Yang (2018) argued that the deterioration in terms of trade of Taiwan's exported products

# 18 *Lin Chu-chia*

*Table 2.6* Monthly wage of employees by industry

| Year | Industry | | Service | |
|---|---|---|---|---|
| | Monthly wage (US$)[a] | Average annual growth rate (%)[b] | Monthly wage (US$) | Average annual growth rate (%) |
| 1980 | 196.7 | – | 254.6 | – |
| 1990 | 696.8 | 13.5 | 788.4 | 12.0 |
| 2000 | 967.2 | 3.3 | 1,090.8 | 3.3 |
| 2010 | 1,127.2 | 1.5 | 1,245.1 | 1.3 |
| 2017 | 1,249.9 | 1.5 | 1,406.5 | 1.8 |

Source: *Taiwan Statistical Data Book 2018*, Table 2-12, pp. 43–44, National Development Council, ROC (Taiwan).

Note:
a  Monthly wage does not include bonus or other benefits usually paid at the end of every year. Here, monthly wage is converted from NT$ by average exchange rate of that year.
b  Average annual growth rate is the average rate during the ten-year period.

was another factor which caused the growth rate of wages to be lower than that of productivity.

## IV Regional economic integration and the China factor

### *Regional economic integration*

As the role of the WTO in reducing tariffs worldwide weakened, regional economic integration began to strengthen after 2000. According to the WTO, up to March 2018 more than 500 FTAs had been signed, of which 305 were actually operational. Economic integration within the Asia-Pacific region also accelerated sharply after 2000. In Table 2.7, we see that as of 2017 Singapore had signed 22 FTAs with 60 countries, giving it the highest FTA coverage ratio (86.89%) in East Asia. South Korea had signed 15 FTAs with 52 countries, with an FTA coverage ratio of 64.44%, while mainland China had signed 14 FTAs with 22 countries, with a coverage ratio of 33.73%. The corresponding figures for Taiwan are the lowest among all the countries shown, with seven FTAs and a coverage ratio of only 9.74%. In the absence of more involvement in FTAs, the competitiveness of exported goods will be increasingly eroded, thereby damaging Taiwan's export prospects in the years to come.

In June 2010 Taiwan signed the Economic Cooperation Framework Agreement (ECFA) with mainland China (its largest trading partner, accounting for about 28% of Taiwan's global merchandise trade). Taiwan and mainland China published 'early harvest lists' – i.e., a list of items and services eligible for tariff reductions and early market access. Taiwan listed 267 items, on which tariffs would be reduced to zero within a three-year period (2011–13). These items accounted for about 10.5% of all imports from China

Table 2.7 FTA coverage ratio, by countries, 2017

| | Singapore | | Korea | | Japan | | China | | Taiwan | |
|---|---|---|---|---|---|---|---|---|---|---|
| | Country | Trade percent of the world (%) | Country | Trade percent of the world (%) | Country | Trade percent of the world (%) | Country | Trade percent of the world (%) | Country | Trade percent of the world (%) |
| Signed | 60 (22 FTAs) | 86.89 | 52 (15 FTAs) | 64.44 | 20 (16 FTAs) | 39.52 | 22 (14 FTAs) | 33.73 | 8 (7 FTAs) | 9.74 |
| In force | 32 (21 FTAs) | 76.65 | 51 (14 FTAs) | 64.29 | 16 (14 FTAs) | 22.71 | 21 (13 FTAs) | 33.70 | 8 (7 FTAs) | 9.74 |
| Contact | Canada | 0.29 | Mexico | 0.79 | Korea | 5.57 | RCEP | 30.94 | China | 18.13 |
| | Pakistan | 0.21 | Japan | 10.5 | GCC | 7.55 | GCC | 3.46 | | |
| | Ukraine | 0.01 | CJK | 31.18 | Colombia | 0.15 | CJK | 14.02 | | |
| | Mexico | 0.52 | Indonesia | 2.03 | Turkey | 0.22 | Sri Lanka | 0.12 | | |
| | Turkey | 0.17 | GCC | 13.06 | EU | 10.77 | Maldives | 0.00 | | |
| | RCEP | 55.38 | RCEP | 46.52 | CJK | 26.75 | Israel | 0.29 | | |
| | TPP | 30.89 | SIECA | 0.18 | RCEP | 47.05 | Norway | 0.18 | | |
| | Total | 88.08 | Total | 84.31 | Total | 84.97 | Total | 53.61 | Total | 27.86 |

Source: Bureau of Foreign Trade (BOFT), Taiwan, ROC. https://www.trade.gov.tw/, 2018.03.20.

as of 2010. Meanwhile, Beijing listed 539 early harvest items, on which tariffs would be reduced – these accounting for 16.1% of mainland China's imports from Taiwan.

Table 2.8 shows that during 2011–17 the annual growth rates of exports from Taiwan to mainland China for goods under the 'Early Harvest Programme' (EHP) were higher than those of *total* exports from Taiwan to mainland China. The average annual rate of growth of EHP goods exported from Taiwan to mainland China was 4.25%, compared with a negative −0.66% for all goods exported from the island to mainland China. In other words, the EHP succeeded in raising the growth rate of goods exported from Taiwan to mainland China by about 5% per year.

However, we should also consider the effect of the EHP on goods imported from mainland China to Taiwan. In Table 2.9, we find that the average annual growth rate of imported goods from mainland China under the EHP (3.45%) was about the same as the annual growth rate of *all* imports (3.52%). This implies that the impact of the EHP on imports was insignificant. Furthermore, the total tariff exemption for goods exported from Taiwan to mainland China was US$5.13 billion – a much larger figure than that from mainland China to Taiwan (US$0.45 billion).[10]

There are two important regional multilateral FTAs which are crucial for Taiwan, since Taiwan's trade involvement with both of them is very large. One is the Comprehensive and Progressive Agreement for Trans-Pacific Partnership (CPTPP); the other is the Regional Comprehensive Economic Partnership (RCEP) agreement.[11]

CPTPP was signed in late 2015 under the name of TPP, and expected to take effect in late 2017. However, when the then newly elected president of the USA, Donald Trump, retreated from TPP in January 2017, the agreement

*Table 2.8* The result of the Early Harvest Plan, export to mainland China (unit: US$ billion)

| Year | Total exports to mainland China | | Goods exported to mainland China under the Early Harvest Plan | | |
|------|-------------|------------------|-------------|------------------|--------------------------------|
|      | Total value | Growth rate (%) | Total value | Growth rate (%) | Estimated tariff exemption |
| 2011 | 85.24 | 9.36 | 17.99 | 18.18 | 0.13 |
| 2012 | 82.67 | −3.02 | 18.58 | 3.26 | 0.57 |
| 2013 | 84.12 | 1.76 | 20.55 | 10.60 | 0.72 |
| 2014 | 84.74 | 0.73 | 21.07 | 2.50 | 0.83 |
| 2015 | 73.41 | −13.37 | 19.01 | −9.67 | 0.84 |
| 2016 | 73.90 | 0.67 | 19.12 | 0.60 | 0.92 |
| 2017 | 88.98 | 20.41 | 22.74 | 18.73 | 1.12 |
| Estimated total tariff exemption | | | | | 5.13 |

Source: Customs Administration, MOF, Taiwan. https://eweb.customs.gov.tw/, 2018.02.14.

*Table 2.9* The result of the Early Harvest Plan, import from mainland China
(unit: US$ billion)

| Year | Total imports from mainland China | | Goods imported from mainland China under the Early Harvest Plan | | |
|------|---------|--------------|--------|--------------|-----------|
| | Total value | Growth rate (%) | Total value | Growth rate (%) | Tariff exemption |
| 2011 | 44.09 | 21.28 | 5.05 | 27.95 | 0.02 |
| 2012 | 41.43 | −6.17 | 4.89 | −3.21 | 0.05 |
| 2013 | 43.34 | 4.11 | 4.97 | 1.74 | 0.06 |
| 2014 | 49.25 | 12.80 | 5.45 | 7.41 | 0.08 |
| 2015 | 45.26 | −8.10 | 5.29 | −2.90 | 0.08 |
| 2016 | 43.99 | −2.80 | 4.75 | −10.27 | 0.08 |
| 2017 | 50.04 | 13.74 | 5.39 | 12.98 | 0.08 |
| Estimated total tariff exemption | | | | | 0.45 |

Source: Customs Administration, MOF, Taiwan. https://eweb.customs.gov.tw/, 2018.02.14.

was nullified. However, the remaining 11 signatories decided to rename the
agreement as CPTPP and in March 2018 they formally endorsed it, with
the intention that it should officially take effect on 30 December 2018.
Moreover, South Korea, Thailand, and even the UK showed an interest in
participating in CPTPP. Since two-way trade between Taiwan and CPTPP
constitutes about one-quarter of its total trade, the importance of Taiwan's
membership is self-evident. However, if Taiwan were unable to join in the
near future, its exclusion would necessitate tariff charges with detrimental
effects on its economy.

RCEP is notionally constituted by ASEAN 10 and six other countries
(mainland China, Japan, Korea, New Zealand, Australia and India). It has
been under negotiation since 2011, and (as of June 2020) 29 rounds of talks
have already taken place.[12] Though the degree of openness of RCEP is much
less than that of CPTPP, the importance of RCEP is suggested in the finding
that in 2017 the value of bilateral trade vis-à-vis RCEP members constituted
about 57% of its global trade.[13]

As a small and open economy, it is desirable that Taiwan should participate in as many FTAs possible, including CPTPP, RCEP and FTAs with
mainland China and other countries.[14]

## The 'China factor'

After the KMT retreated from mainland China to Taiwan in 1949, people
on both sides of the Taiwan Strait were not allowed to visit each other until
1987. In November of that year, the Taiwanese government ended martial
law, and for the first time, on humanitarian grounds, permitted Taiwanese
citizens to visit their relatives in mainland China. Subsequently, Taiwanese
businessmen took advantage of the more relaxed circumstances and began

to invest in mainland China. In addition to the two sides sharing the same language and other cultural characteristics, a major factor which encouraged so many Taiwanese firms – many of them engaged in labour-intensive industrial activities – to invest in mainland China was the existence of an abundant labour supply available at a very low cost. (In 1990, labour costs in China were about 10% of those facing producers in Taiwan.) Another important factor was the appreciation between 1986 and 1988 of the New Taiwan Dollar from NT$38:US$1 to NT$26:US$1 – a development which hindered the continued expansion of Taiwanese firms' exports to the rest of the world.

As industrial production increasingly shifted from Taiwan to mainland China, shipments of parts and semi-finished goods across the Taiwan Strait also accelerated. The outcome was a rapid rise in bilateral trade from 1990. Table 2.10 shows that between 1990 and 2017 exports from Taiwan to mainland China increased from US$8.6 billion to US$130.2 billion, while trade in the reverse direction rose from US$1.8 billion to US$51.6 billion. Meanwhile, Taiwan has enjoyed a huge trade surplus vis-à-vis mainland China. In 2017, for instance, Taiwan's bilateral surplus was US$78.7 billion, or more than one-third greater than its global trade surplus, including China (US$58.0 billion). Taiwan's trade dependency ratio with China has also steadily increased. For example, the mainland market's share of Taiwan exports increased from 6.5% in 1990 to 41.0% in 2017, while the import share also rose from 1.4% to 19.9% during the same period (see Table 2.11).

While more than 70% of exports from Taiwan to mainland China comprise parts and semi-finished products, Taiwanese subsidiaries in mainland China have incorporated these goods into final products which are then sold to other countries. As a result, some Taiwanese firms – the most important of which are Hongfujin, Foxconn, Tech-Front, and Pagatron (based on data

*Table 2.10* Bilateral trade across the Taiwan Strait (unit: US$ billion)

| Year | Taiwan to China | China to Taiwan | Total trade | Taiwan's surplus with mainland China | Taiwan's surplus with the world |
|------|------|------|------|------|------|
| 1980 | 2.3 | 0.8 | 3.1 | 1.6 | 7.8 |
| 1985 | 9.9 | 1.2 | 4.4 | 8.7 | 10.6 |
| 1990 | 8.6 | 1.8 | 10.3 | 6.8 | 12.5 |
| 1995 | 26.5 | 4.9 | 31.4 | 21.5 | 8.1 |
| 2000 | 35.6 | 8.4 | 44.0 | 27.1 | 8.3 |
| 2005 | 77.7 | 22.2 | 99.9 | 55.5 | 15.8 |
| 2010 | 114.7 | 37.6 | 152.3 | 77.2 | 23.4 |
| 2015 | 109.3 | 45.6 | 154.9 | 63.6 | 51.8 |
| 2017 | 130.2 | 51.6 | 181.8 | 78.7 | 58.0 |

Source: *Cross Strait Economic Statistics Monthly, No.298 (2017-02)*, Table 1, p. 2-1, Mainland Affairs Council, ROC (Taiwan).

*Table 2.11* Dependency ratio of bilateral trade across the Taiwan Strait (unit: %)

| Year | Taiwan | | | Mainland China | | |
|------|--------|--------|-------------|--------|--------|-------------|
| | Export share | Import share | Total trade share | Export share | Import share | Total trade share |
| 1980 | 1.2 | 0.4 | 0.8 | 0.4 | 1.2 | 0.8 |
| 1985 | 3.2 | 0.6 | 2.2 | 0.4 | 2.3 | 1.6 |
| 1990 | 6.5 | 1.4 | 4.2 | 1.2 | 8.2 | 4.5 |
| 1995 | 23.7 | 4.8 | 14.6 | 3.3 | 14.7 | 8.0 |
| 2000 | 24.0 | 6.0 | 15.2 | 3.4 | 11.1 | 6.6 |
| 2005 | 39.1 | 12.2 | 26.2 | 2.9 | 8.5 | 5.4 |
| 2010 | 41.8 | 14.9 | 29.0 | 2.2 | 6.1 | 4.0 |
| 2015 | 39.0 | 21.4 | 30.5 | 2.0 | 8.5 | 4.8 |
| 2017 | 41.0 | 19.9 | 31.5 | 1.9 | 8.4 | 4.9 |

Source: *Cross Strait Economic Statistics Monthly No.298 (2017-02)*, Table 2, p. 2-2, Mainland Affairs Council, ROC (Taiwan).

for 2005 and 2017 – see Table 2.12) – have become leading exporting companies in mainland China.

The total value of exports generated by the top 20 Taiwanese exporting firms was, as of 2017, about US$127.3 billion. Since there are nearly 100,000 Taiwanese firms operating in mainland China, the total value of exports by *all* Taiwanese firms is likely to be at least US$200–300 billion annually, which would account for between 10% and 15% of China's total exports.[15]

The rapid increase in bilateral trade across the Strait has had two important effects on Taiwan's economy: first, the removal of increasing numbers of manufacturing firms from Taiwan to mainland China after 1990 prompted significant structural change in Taiwan, as manufacturing industry gave ground to service industry, and labour-intensive industry retreated in favour of more capital-intensive and technology-intensive activities. Second, the accelerated growth of 'intra-industry trade' across the Strait[16] has resulted in Taiwanese firms becoming major participants in the supply chain of *mainland* producers – a development that underlines the inescapable fact that Taiwan's economic future has become dependent on that of mainland China.

## V The challenges facing President Tsai Ing-wen's administration

In the first two years of President Tsai's regime, GDP growth fell sharply to 1.51% (2016) and 3.08% (2017) (see Table 2.13). In 2017 the performance of the foreign sector remained quite buoyant, with exports and imports rising by 7.43% and 5.28%, respectively. Conditions were more challenging in the domestic sector, where private consumption increased by only 2.54% in 2017, while private investment actually declined (−0.12%). DGBAS shows GDP growth to have been 2.63% in 2018, a little lower than that of 2017; and according to the same source the corresponding figure for 2019 was marginally

*Table 2.12* Top 20 exporting companies in mainland China

| Rank | 2005 | 2017 | Export (US$ billion) |
|---|---|---|---|
| 1 | Hon Hai/Foxconn Technology Group (Zhengzhou)[a] | Hongfujin Precision Electronics (Zhengzhou) Co., Ltd | 28.7 |
| 2 | Tech-Front (Shanghai) Computer Co., Ltd | Tech-Front (Shanghai) Computer Co., Ltd | 20.6 |
| 3 | Motorola (China) Electronics Ltd | Shenzhen Foxconn Technology Group | 16.9 |
| 4 | Maintek Computer (Suzhou) Co., Ltd | Pegatron (Shanghai) Corporation | 14.5 |
| 5 | China Putian Corporation | Shenzhen Huawei Technologies Co., Ltd | 13.0 |
| 6 | Inventec Corporation | Pegatron (Suzhou) Corporation | 11.6 |
| 7 | Nokia (China) Investment Co., Ltd | Micron Technology (Xi An), Inc. | 10.7 |
| 8 | Samsung Semiconductors (Suzhou) | Huizhou Samsung Electronics Co., Ltd | 9.7 |
| 9 | China International Marine Containers (Group) Ltd (CIMC) | Huawei Terminal (Dongguan) Co., Ltd | 9.5 |
| 10 | China Great Wall Computer Shenzhen Company Limited | Tech-Front (Chongqing) Computer Co., Ltd | 9.4 |
| 11 | Renbao Electronic Technology (kunshan) Co., Ltd | China Petroleum & Chemical Corporation | 7.8 |
| 12 | TPV Electronics (Fujian) Co., Ltd | Hongfujin Precision Electronics (Chengdu) Co., Ltd | 7.8 |
| 13 | China National Petroleum Corporation (CNPC) | Win Smart Co., Ltd | 6.3 |
| 14 | Inventec Appliances (Shanghai) Co. Ltd | Intel Products (Chengdu) Co., Ltd | 6.3 |
| 15 | China National Offshore Oil Corporation (CNOOC) | China National Petroleum Corporation (CNPC) | 5.8 |
| 16 | Orient International (Holding) Co., Ltd | Foxconn Precision Electronics (Taiyuan) Co., Ltd | 5.8 |
| 17 | Sinochem Group | Midea Group | 5.7 |
| 18 | Intel Products (Shanghai) Co., Ltd | Inventec (Chongqing) Co., Ltd | 5.7 |
| 19 | China Petroleum & Chemical Corporation (Sinopec) | Intel Trading (*Shanghai*) Co., Ltd | 5.5 |
| 20 | Dell (China) Company Limited. | Orient International (holdings) Co., Ltd | 5.5 |

Source: Ministry of Commerce, PRC. http://tjxh.mofcom.gov.cn/article/n/201812/201812 02812624.shtml, 2018.12.03.

Note:
a   The ones in boldface are Taiwanese firms.

*Table 2.13* Current GDP growth rates, by sectors (unit: %)

| Year | Total GDP | By sectors | | | | |
|---|---|---|---|---|---|---|
| | | Consumption | Government spending | Investment | Export | Import |
| 2016 | 1.51 | 2.37 | 3.60 | 2.36 | 1.92 | 3.08 |
| 2016Q1 | −0.14 | 2.79 | 6.52 | 0.10 | −4.22 | −1.51 |
| 2016Q2 | 1.22 | 1.74 | 2.30 | 0.22 | −0.01 | −0.54 |
| 2016Q3 | 2.08 | 2.81 | 3.43 | 3.49 | 3.44 | 4.65 |
| 2016Q4 | 2.79 | 2.11 | 2.49 | 5.34 | 8.00 | 9.41 |
| 2017 | 3.08 | 2.54 | −0.63 | −0.12 | 7.43 | 5.28 |
| 2017Q1 | 2.94 | 1.97 | −4.46 | 4.88 | 7.29 | 7.22 |
| 2017Q2 | 2.50 | 2.32 | 1.43 | 1.07 | 4.89 | 4.95 |
| 2017Q3 | 3.36 | 2.64 | 1.61 | −2.41 | 11.39 | 7.00 |
| 2017Q4 | 3.48 | 3.23 | −1.23 | −3.26 | 6.10 | 2.31 |
| 2018(f) | 2.66 | 2.17 | 2.95 | 3.59 | 3.37 | 4.68 |
| 2018Q1 | 3.15 | 2.55 | 6.63 | 0.36 | 6.42 | 6.19 |
| 2018Q2 | 3.29 | 2.29 | 5.87 | 0.02 | 6.33 | 4.53 |
| 2018Q3(p) | 2.27 | 1.80 | −1.50 | 5.40 | 1.21 | 4.64 |
| 2018Q4(f) | 2.02 | 2.05 | 1.54 | 8.25 | 0.39 | 3.53 |
| 2019(f) | 2.41 | 2.23 | 0.26 | 5.40 | 3.06 | 2.94 |
| 2019Q1(f) | 2.28 | 2.02 | −2.87 | 4.86 | 1.54 | 1.30 |
| 2019Q2(f) | 2.18 | 2.17 | −3.47 | 7.93 | 2.84 | 3.11 |
| 2019Q3(f) | 2.53 | 2.39 | 3.23 | 3.67 | 3.68 | 3.33 |
| 2019Q4(f) | 2.64 | 2.33 | 3.72 | 5.33 | 4.02 | 3.92 |

Source: *Statistical Abstract of National Accounts*, Directorate General of Budget, Accounting and Statistics (DGBAS), ROC (Taiwan). https://www.dgbas.gov.tw/ct.asp?xItem=43553&ctNode=5624&mp=1, 2018.11.30.

higher at 2.71%. In short, the situation has become one described as 'foreign sector hot, domestic sector cold.' A new challenge that has arisen more recently is that because of the trade dispute between the USA and China, global trade in 2019 suffered a significant contraction. These forces will constrain Taiwan's foreign sector performance. Meanwhile, reversing the slow economic momentum of the domestic sector in Taiwan will not be easy to achieve within a short period of time, given the nature of the DPP administration's long-term goals, such as establishing a 'nuclear-free homeland' by 2025.

From the perspective of 2019, there were several major challenges facing President Tsai in the future: the first of these derived from the DPP government's decision to cut about one-third of pension payment for all retired governmental agents, effective as of 1 July 2018.[17] The likely impact of this policy initiative will be not only to reduce government officers' willingness to work hard, but also to reduce daily consumption for those affected by the decision and thereby slow down the economic momentum of Taiwan in future years.

A second challenge relates to the low incentive to undertake investment, which seems likely to persist for the foreseeable future. Taiwan businessmen have long complained about Taiwan's shortages of important production factors, such as electricity, water, land, technology, and skilled workers.[18]

Such shortages help explain why both domestic and foreign investment have been so sluggish in recent years.

The third challenge is that Taiwan must seek to expand its participation in regional economic integration, such as joining CPTPP and RCEP, and signing FTAs with the USA, Japan, etc. Achieving FTAs with these two countries requires Taiwan to solve the pork issue (with the USA) and the issue of nuclear-contaminated food (with Japan). Both these issues carry strong political overtones for the DPP. Thus, for example, in the '9-in-1' election in November 2018, Taiwan voted in a referendum that the Taiwanese government should maintain its ban of imports of food products from areas near Fukushima in Japan. A few days later, the Japanese Foreign Minister, Taro Kono, stated that the continuation of this ban would make it difficult for Taiwan to achieve membership of the CPTPP.

Furthermore, the China factor has always been a crucial issue for Taiwan in its efforts to participate in international forums. It is clear that in the absence of ECFA and the 1992 Consensus, mainland China's political stance would make it difficult for Taiwan to join RECP or to sign bilateral FTAs.

Finally, the most serious domestic challenge facing the DPP is the energy issue – in particular, the policy of seeking to establish a nuclear-free homeland by 2025. In pursuit of its goals, the DPP has given three major guarantees, including establishing a nuclear-free homeland, ensuring no electricity shortages, and holding electricity prices unchanged up to 2025. In order to attract more domestic and foreign investment in renewable energy sources (especially solar energy and wind energy), Tai Power, an SOE and monopoly firm in Taiwan, has guaranteed to purchase all the electricity produced by such sources of renewable energy at a constant price of NT$6 per kWh for the next 20 years.[19] According to this plan, 800 wind generator fan sets will be built before 2030 at a cost of around NT$720 billion. Moreover, Tai Power has pledged to spend NT$1.3 trillion in total for the next 20 years, or NT$65 billion per year – the equivalent of about 3% of total government spending each year.

Notwithstanding the Taiwanese government's commitment to inject huge sums of money in order to attract investment for the development of clean energy, projections of future energy production suggest that it will still be difficult to fulfil planned changes in the structure of energy production. In Table 2.14 we find that currently 46.6% of electricity production derives from coal, 34.6% from LNG, 8.3% from nuclear, 4.7% from gasoline, and 4.8% from renewable energy. The corresponding targeted figures for 2025 are 30% (coal), 50% (LNG), and 20% (renewable energy). The implied increase in the contribution of renewable energy from 4.8% to 20% in just seven years seems virtually impossible to fulfil. No less challenging are the looked-for reduction in the contribution of coal and increase in that of LNG. In particular, a major problem in expanding the use of LNG is the difficulty of finding environmentally suitable locations in which to construct several large LNG containers that will be needed if Taiwan is to increase LNG sufficiently to

*Table 2.14* The share of electricity production,
by type of energy input (unit: %)

| Type of energy | 2017 | 2025 |
|---|---|---|
| Coal | 46.6 | 30.0 |
| LNG | 34.6 | 50.0 |
| Nuclear | 8.3 | 0.0 |
| Gasoline | 4.7 | 0.0 |
| Renewable energy | 4.6 | 20.0 |

Source: *Energy Statistics Handbook 2018*, Table 16, p. 86, Bureau of Energy, Ministry of Economic Affairs.

enable it to supply half of total electricity production. Indeed, the DPP's efforts to bring about such major changes in the energy structure[20] have already made power supplies so fragile in Taiwan that a mass power shortage could happen at any time.[21]

A further problem is that before LNG supplies reach a level sufficient to provide 50% of primary energy by 2025, the Taiwanese government will have to increase the usage of coal in order to replace the gap that will open up as nuclear power sources are closed down. In fact, Tai Power had originally planned to build a new large coal-fired power plant in the north-east of Taiwan. However, most people living in northern Taiwan oppose this construction project for fear that it will cause excessive air pollution, and in the face of political pressure, since prior to the '9-in-1' election the DPP government decided to abandon the Shen-Au project.

In November 2018, in two referendums held during the election, Taiwanese voted in favour of the proposition that Taiwan should 'establish an energy policy that undertakes not to construct any new coal-fired power plants or generators or expand existing facilities (including the expansion of the Shen Au Power Plant).' In a second referendum voters also voted in favour of abolishing the first paragraph of Article 95 of the Electricity Act, whereby 'all nuclear-energy-based power-generating facilities shall cease to operate by 2025.'[22]

In the '9-in-1' local election – Taiwan's mid-term election – held at the end of November 2018 the ruling DPP fared badly, losing seven of the 14 county seats which they had previously held. By contrast, the opposition KMT gained seven seats so that they controlled 15 counties instead of the previous eight. A major factor accounting for the DPP's collapse in votes was Taiwan's poor economic performance. The most popular slogan in the election for the then newly elected city mayor of Kaohsiung, Han Kuo-yu, was 'Goods could sell out, people could get in, and Kaohsiung could make a fortune!'[23]

In conclusion, the moral of this analysis seems clear: against the background of weak domestic consumption, a low investment rate and increasing international competition, the Taiwanese government must redouble its efforts to create a stronger domestic investment environment (for example, by putting in place an effective sustainable energy policy) in order to attract more domestic and foreign investment. At the same time, it must also work harder to sign FTAs with other countries, as well as seeking to participate in the CPTPP and RECP.

### *Postscript*

In January 2020 President Tsai Ing-wen won the most recent presidential election by a large margin. There were many reasons for her victory over the challenger, Han Kuo-yu. One of these was the success with which throughout the election President Tsai simultaneously maintained a very strong stance vis-à-vis China, while keeping a close relationship with the USA. Nevertheless, the fact – and a major challenge – remains that in the wake of the trade war between the USA and China, political relations between the two countries worsened, as has the political relationship between Taiwan and China. At the same time, following the trade war bilateral trade between Taiwan and China has contracted.

COVID-19 has had a similar impact as the trade war between the two giants. As of the time of writing, President Trump insists that he will demand huge payments from China to compensate for having allegedly delayed informing relevant parties of the contagious reality of COVID-19 – an accusation which both China and the WHO deny. Whatever the precise outcome, there is no doubt that the relationship between the USA and China will further deteriorate in the wake of the COVID-19 pandemic. So will the relationship between Taiwan and China.

Another consequence of the trade war is the reshuffling of production chains among East Asian countries, especially for foreign firms (and Taiwanese firms) in China. In 2019 more than 150 Taiwanese firms announced their intention to shift investment worth US$23 billion from China back to Taiwan in order to relocate some of their production activities from the Mainland to Taiwan and thereby avoid the high tariff which they would otherwise face if they wished to export from China to the USA. Meanwhile, for the same reason many Taiwanese firms are looking for investment opportunities elsewhere in East Asia.

Since COVID-19 may well have a similar consequence as that of the trade war between the USA and China, there is a real possibility that the reshuffling of production chain will intensify. This should present the Taiwan government with a major opportunity to enhance and strengthen incentives in order to attract Taiwanese firms operating in China to shift more investment back to Taiwan.

From the perspective of mid-2020, however, a difficult challenge for the government in Taipei is that of maintaining a stable relationship with China, while relations between the USA and China continue to deteriorate

– not least in a context in which the DPP administration has chosen to stand alongside the USA. The uncertainty and unpredictability of these changing circumstances raise profound questions for the Taiwanese government. To what extent will tensions with China damage the economic relationship across the Strait? And how will it be possible for Taiwan to maintain a sufficiently durable relationship with China to enable it to continue to enjoy its trade surplus vis-à-vis China? Finding answers to these questions will be a huge challenge during President Tsai Ing-wen's second term of office.

## Notes

1  On Taiwan's economic performance before the 1990s, see Kao and Lee (1991, 1995).
2  To reduce pressure from the opposition party, President Ma promised that the Fourth Nuclear Power Plant would not be activated until put to a popular vote through a future referendum.
3  Though there may be other reasons – for instance the dot-com bubble in 2000 – to explain the sluggish rate of investment, the dispute surrounding the fourth nuclear power plant was certainly a critical contributing factor.
4  The figures are from Table 16 in National Income Statistical Abstract, February 2020, p. 41 (Directorate General of Budget, Accounting and Statistics, Executive Yuan, Taiwan).
5  Mr Perng was awarded Grade A as the president of Central Bank for 15 consecutive years until his retirement in 2018.
6  During 2001–17, the average annual inflation rate of Taiwan and Korea was 0.97% and 2.56%, respectively.
7  Some described this as the 'hollowing-out' of Taiwan's manufacturing sector.
8  For a detailed discussion on Taiwanese investment in mainland China, see Kao et al. (1992, 1995, 2006).
9  On the impact of Taiwanese investment in mainland China on the structural change in Taiwanese economy, see Lin (2005, 2008).
10  For a detailed discussion of the potential impact of ECFA on Taiwan, see Chu (2009) and Lin (2013).
11  For a detailed discussion of the road map for Taiwan to participate TPP, see Chen and Liu (2014).
12  Because of the COVID-19 pandemic, the 29th round (April 2020) took the form of a video conference.
13  According to Hsu (2015), if Taiwan were to join RCEP, Taiwan's GDP could fall by 0.10%, compared with a potential decline of 0.90% if it remained outside RCEP.
14  For a detailed discussion of the potential interaction between ECFA and East Asia economic integration for Taiwan, see Lin (2011).
15  In fact, for a long period of time the total export share contributed by foreign firms in mainland China has always been high. For instance, the total value of exports of foreign firms was US$977.6 billion in 2017, or 43.19% of China's total exports (US$2,263.5 billion).
16  According to the theory of comparative advantage, the goods traded between two countries usually belong to two different industries, which is called 'inter-industry trade.' For example, the USA sold airplanes to Taiwan, while Taiwan sold computers to the USA. However, the major goods sold from Taiwan to

mainland China are parts and semi-products in the electric and electronic industry, while the major goods sold from mainland China to Taiwan are final products also in electric and electronic industry. Since both of them are in the same industry, it is called 'intra-industry trade.' Moreover, the major trading partners across the Taiwan Strait are Taiwanese firms in both sides of the Strait.

17 About 333,000 retired government employees are thought to have been affected by this policy.

18 For more details about production factor shortages, see The 2017 White Paper from the Chinese National Federation of Industries, Chapter 2, pp. 9–19.

19 At the same time, the average price that Tai Power charges to the public in Taiwan is set at only around NT$2.7 per kWh.

20 For instance, two years after coming to power the DPP government shut down two nuclear power generator sets, one in the First Power Plant and the other one in the Second Power Plant. The result was rapidly to reduce the reserve capacity of electricity production to less than 5%. On one occasion (15 August 2017) this caused a total blackout in Taiwan for about two hours.

21 To reduce the probability of mass power shortages, in March 2018 the DPP government decided to reactivate the second nuclear power generator set in the Second Nuclear Power. However, the shadow of mass power shortage continues to hang over the public and most businessmen in Taiwan.

22 After the passing of the referendum, the DPP government promised to remove the relevant clause in the Electricity Act, although the government spokesperson Kolas Yataka said that the goal of 2025 nuclear-free homeland policy would not be changed by the government.

23 During the election, Han emphasised the importance of economic freedom for the city of Kaohsiung and he claimed that if he won the election, he would help the firms in Kaohsiung to export more to the world and attract more international tourists to come to the city, so that its citizens could make more money.

## References

Chen, T.C., and D.N. Liu, eds. 2014. *From ECFA to TPP: The Road Map of Regional Economic Integration of Taiwan*, Prospective Foundation, Taipei (in Chinese).

Chinese National Federation of Industries. 2017. *The 2017 White Paper*, Taipei (in Chinese).

Chu, C. eds. 2009. *ECFA: To Create a New Episode of a Mutual Benefit Relation across the Taiwan Strait*, Prospective Foundation, Taipei (in Chinese).

Haepp, T., and P.L. Hsin. 2016. 'Is Taiwan's Workforce Underpaid? Evidence from Marginal Product of Labor Estimates at the Company Level.' *Journal of Social Sciences and Philosophy*, 28(2), 299–331.

Huang, D.S. 2015. 'On the Wage Stagnation of Taiwan: Trade and FDI Partners under Globalization.' *Review of Social Sciences*, 9(1), 33–58.

Kao, C., and J. Lee. 1991. *The Taiwan Experience: 1949–1989*, Commonwealth Publishing Co. Ltd., Taipei (in Chinese).

Kao, C., and J. Lee. 1995. *The Taiwan Experience: Past and Future*, Commonwealth Publishing Co. Ltd., Taipei (in Chinese).

Kao, C., J. Lee, and C.C. Lin. 1992. *An Empirical Study of Taiwan Investment in Mainland China*, Commonwealth Publishing Co. Ltd., Taipei (in Chinese).

Kao, C., J. Lee, and C.C. Lin, eds. 2006. *The Twenty-Year Experience of Economic Relationship across the Taiwan Strait*, Commonwealth Publishing Co., Taipei (in Chinese).

Kao, C., C.C. Lin, C. Hsu, and W. Lin. 1995. *The Taiwan Investment Experience in Mainland China: A First-hand Report*, Commonwealth Publishing Co., Ltd., Taipei (in Chinese).

Lin, C.C. 2005. *The Economic Relation across the Taiwan Strait and the Economic Development of China*, Commonwealth Publishing Co., Taipei (in Chinese).

Lin, C.C. 2008. *Back to the Economic Plateau: Cross-Strait Economic Relation and the Future of Taiwan*, Kao-Pao Publishing Co., Taipei (in Chinese).

Lin, C.C. eds. 2011. *ECFA and East Asia Economic Integration*, National Policy Foundation, Taipei.

Lin, C.C. 2013. *Going East Asia and Trading the World: ECFA and the Prospect of Industrial Development of Taiwan*, Commonwealth Publishing Co., Taipei (in Chinese).

Lin, Y.L., and T.T. Yang. 2018. 'Decoupling of Wage Growth and Productivity in Taiwan: An Empirical Investigation.' *Academia Economic Papers*, 46(2), 263–322.

# 3 How can Taiwan enlarge its role in the process of Asia-Pacific economic integration?

*Liu Da-nien*

## I Introduction

The World Trade Organization (WTO) Doha Round trade talks have sought to bring about a level of trade liberalisation (in terms of both depth and breadth) that promised to be the greatest ever achieved since the WTO's predecessor, the General Agreement on Tariff and Trade (GATT), was first initiated. Unfortunately, the sheer scale of the Doha Round's ambitions has prevented any significant progress from being made. With trade liberalisation at the global level having stalled, there has been a continuing worldwide upsurge in efforts to achieve regional economic integration (Lee et al., 2008; Whalley, 2008; Albertoni, 2018). Regionalism has become a trend that has not only affected functions of the WTO, but also severely impacted global trade, investment, and even the industrial division of labour.

From Taiwan's point of view, a significant finding is that countries around the world have accelerated the signing of FTAs to eliminate both tariff and non-tariff barriers over the past decade or so. This has seriously impacted Taiwan's foreign trade performance. In particular, the vogue for large-scale FTAs in the recent years has had a major impact on Taiwan, which is heavily dependent on foreign trade, is closely integrated with global supply chains, but itself has been able to sign only a handful of FTAs.

The USA announced its withdrawal from the Trans-Pacific Partnership (TPP) after US President Trump assumed office, despite his emphasis on fair trade and the benefits of bilateral pacts. However, the Comprehensive and Progressive Agreement for Trans-Pacific Partnership (CPTPP), formed by the remaining 11 countries of the TPP, will still have a great influence on Taiwan's future. The creation of large-scale FTAs in the future will also impact Taiwan. How Taiwan responds to this new trend and associated challenges will significantly shape Taiwan's future development.

This chapter mainly analyses how Taiwan can assume a greater role and make breakthroughs in the trend of regional economic integration. It is structured as follows: the first section is an introduction. The second section summarises global trends and the most recent developments in regional economic integration. The third section describes Taiwan's participation in regional economic integration and the difficulties that have been encountered. The fourth section explains the nature of the adjustments which Taiwan should make in its industry and economic system in order to increase its chances of making a breakthrough in regional integration, as well as enhancing its role in the Asia-Pacific's regional economy. The fifth section is the conclusion of this chapter.

## II Developments and trends in regional economic integration throughout the world

### A Overview of developments in regional economic integration

The WTO began the Doha Round of negotiations in 2001. It was the most in-depth and extensive round of negotiations ever to have been carried out, although because of negotiation difficulties significant progress has yet to be made towards trade liberalisation. The only progress to date has been the Trade Facilitation Agreement (TFA) and Information Technology Agreement (ITA II), completed in 2013 and 2015, respectively.

Since multilateral negotiations of the WTO have stagnated, countries are turning from multilateral to bilateral endeavours. According to WTO statistics (WTO, 2020), a total of 479 regional FTAs have taken effect between 1950 and 2020 (Table 3.1). Of these FTAs, 428 took effect after the WTO was established in 1995, accounting for nearly 90% of all regional FTAs. Some 318 FTAs (more than 60%) took effect after 2005, showing that FTAs have become the main focus of trade policies in most countries.

### B The new trend of regional economic integration throughout the world

Regional economic integration promotes trade and cooperation between countries, but opening the market to other countries has generated a number of issues, such as its impact on weaker industries, more severe unemployment,

*Table 3.1* Number of regional FTAs throughout the world

| Year | Number of regional FTAs |
| --- | --- |
| 1950–9 | 2 |
| 1960–9 | 2 |
| 1970–9 | 11 |
| 1980–9 | 10 |
| 1990–4 | 26 |
| 1995–9 | 38 |
| 2000–4 | 72 |
| 2005–9 | 128 |
| 2010–14 | 104 |
| 2015–20 June | 86 |
| **Total** | **479** |

Source: www.wto.org.

and widening income and wealth gaps. As a result, increasing opposition to globalisation has led to the UK's decision (June 2016) to exit the EU, the rise of political parties advocating populism in various countries, and Donald Trump's victory in the US Presidential Election (November 2016). These can all be viewed as important representative examples of anti-globalisation, and they have greatly impacted global economic and trade development. They have also brought changes to regional economic integration. Key aspects of recent developments can be summarised as follows.

### (A)   The US bilateral promotion of fair trade

Donald Trump's trade policy revolves around fair trade and reducing the trade deficit. The USA has evaluated the 14 FTAs that are already in effect. It is also using a variety of trade measures to prevent unfair trade practices by its trade partners, and it has resorted to tax reform and infrastructure expansion to safeguard its interests.

The adoption of these measures shows that the USA is using its domestic laws rather than WTO rules to quickly respond to other countries' unfair trade policies, and is forcing countries to the negotiation table in order to meet its conditions. Such policies have not only precipitated a trade war between the USA and China that has changed the global economic situation, but has also demonstrated that bilateral FTAs are no longer part of US trade policy.

### (B)   Regional economic integration carried out through bilateral FTAs and large-scale FTAs

Recent and current development trends indicate that opposition to globalisation has not affected regional economic integration, and suggest that countries other than the USA will continue to participate in integration through bilateral FTAs and large-scale FTAs (Ciuriak, Xiao, & Dadkhah, 2017; Rachel, 2018).

## III   Taiwan's participation in regional economic integration

In contrast to the rapid actions of other countries in signing FTAs, Taiwan's path has been extremely difficult. The following section describes Taiwan's participation in regional economic integration.

Prior to Taiwan's accession to the WTO in 2002, all of Taiwan's efforts were focused on securing WTO membership. By contrast, it was felt that pursuing FTAs would only result in the delaying of Taiwan's accession to the WTO. But after becoming a member of the WTO, Taiwan began to actively explore possibilities for signing FTAs with other countries as a major focus of its economic diplomacy. Taiwan held preliminary talks with a large number of countries, including Japan, ASEAN member states, the USA, and the small group of countries with which Taiwan has maintained formal diplomatic relations.

From Taiwan's point of view, in addition to the economic benefits that FTAs would bring, securing the signing of FTAs would also represent a major diplomatic breakthrough. In short, FTAs promised to have dual significance. However, precisely because of the significant diplomatic benefits that securing FTAs would bring Taiwan, the island's efforts to negotiate FTAs with other countries have encountered major obstacles. Eleven years on from Taiwan's accession to the WTO, Taiwan's concrete achievements in terms of securing FTAs have been limited to the signing of FTAs with five countries in Central America with which Taiwan has formal diplomatic relations: Panama, Guatemala, Nicaragua, Honduras, and El Salvador (Ministry of Economic Affairs, 2020).

The reason why Taiwan's progress in securing FTAs with other countries has been so slow is of course the China factor. As a result of China's rapid economic growth, as well as China's active efforts to secure participation in regional economic integration following its accession to the WTO in 2001, countries throughout the world have focused on developing the opportunities that have emerged as a result of the opening up of the China market, while also coming under pressure from China to reject overtures from Taiwan. When forced to choose between Taiwan and China, foreign countries have pragmatically chosen China, making the securing of FTAs with China their main objective. The process of negotiating an FTA is inevitably related to the issue of national sovereignty. Wary of how China might respond, other countries have been reluctant to proactively seek trade negotiations with Taiwan, and this has had a major impact on Taiwan's efforts to negotiate FTAs.

Given the difficulty that China's interference caused to Taiwan's efforts to negotiate FTAs, in order to achieve a breakthrough in this regard Taiwan naturally reoriented the focus of its efforts towards those countries with which it had formal diplomatic relations, where China's ability to interfere would be reduced. These countries are mostly located in Central and South America, Africa, and the island countries of the Pacific Ocean. In terms of the size of their economies and the maturity of the relevant systems and structures, countries located in Central or South America have offered the best potential for negotiating FTAs, and it is in this region that Taiwan has had most success in signing FTAs.

It was only after the thawing in cross-Strait relations between Taiwan and China in 2008, and the commencement of negotiations for the signing of the *Economic Cooperation Framework Agreement* (ECFA) with China in 2009, that the obstacles to Taiwan's negotiating of FTAs with other countries grew less pronounced.

In 2013 Taiwan secured a number of major breakthroughs in its efforts to secure greater participation in regional economic integration. On 10 July 2013 the *Agreement between New Zealand and the Separate Customs Territory of Taiwan, Penghu, Kinmen, and Matsu on Economic Cooperation* (ANZTEC) was signed, followed on 7 November the same year by the signing of the *Agreement between Singapore and the Separate Customs Territory of Taiwan, Penghu, Kinmen, and Matsu on Economic Partnership* (ASTEP). The signing of these FTAs with New Zealand and Singapore represented a major step forward in terms of Taiwan's ability to successfully negotiate FTAs with countries other than those with which it has formal diplomatic relations. However, given the rapid pace of regional economic integration, Taiwan still has a long way to go to catch up.

Proactive participation in regional economic integration has been a key element in the foreign trade policy of almost all countries. An examination of the FTAs that have been negotiated in the past few years shows that there has been a trend towards large-scale FTAs that to some extent compete with one another; at the same time, the range of issues addressed by FTAs has grown broader, and their economic impact has grown more pronounced. In addition, it has become more common for existing regional groupings to establish their own regional FTAs. Overall, FTAs have become an extension of countries' economic and diplomatic clout. From Taiwan's perspective, as a country heavily dependent on international markets, the negative impact of these trends has been enormous.

Of course, Taiwan's government is aware of this situation and has been actively seeking to expand its FTA network. The Cross-Strait Service Trade Agreement with China in 2014, however, raised concerns about being too dependent on China, and led to the Sunflower Movement, which forced all subsequent negotiations of the ECFA to be terminated. The establishment of the DPP administration in 2016 led to tense cross-Strait relations and put Taiwan in an even more difficult position with respect to FTAs.

## IV  Taiwan's role and response strategy

### A  Trends in Taiwan's exports

Turning now to how Taiwan can play an important role in regional economic integration in the context of a changing global situation, we begin by considering changes in Taiwan's position in the Asia-Pacific.

Manufacturing industry has always been the core of Taiwan's economic development due to its long-standing export-oriented trade policy. In the face of rising labour costs in Taiwan, labour-intensive companies whose continued competitiveness required them to lower prices were forced to move their production bases overseas. As labour-intensive industries moved to China and Southeast Asian countries, capital-intensive industries continued to develop in Taiwan, and manufacturing industry has remained the core of Taiwan's development. As a result of downstream manufacturing industries relocating overseas and remaining industrial activities moving towards mid- and up-stream, Taiwan's external trade connections and supply chain in Asia have changed (Liu & Shin, 2012).

Table 3.2 shows that between 1996 and 2017 intermediate and capital goods accounted for an increasing share of Taiwan's exports. During 2011–17 almost 80% of exports were intermediate and capital goods.

Table 3.3 shows that Taiwan's exports to developed countries, such as the EU, the USA, and Japan, have been decreasing, while those to emerging

*Table 3.2* The change in the structure of Taiwan's export products

|  | Raw materials (%) | Intermediates and capital goods (%) | Consumer goods (%) |
|---|---|---|---|
| **Average share of exports in 1996–2000** | 1.71 | 74.51 | 23.78 |
| **Average share of exports in 2001–5** | 1.28 | 78.07 | 20.64 |
| **Average share of exports in 2006–10** | 1.10 | 78.95 | 19.95 |
| **Average share of exports in 2011–17** | 1.25 | 79.13 | 19.62 |

Source: Collated from Taiwan Customs data.

*Table 3.3* The change in Taiwan's export markets

| Country | Average share of total exports | | | |
|---|---|---|---|---|
|  | 1996–2000 (%) | 2001–5 (%) | 2006–10 (%) | 2011–17 (%) |
| 1  China (including Hong Kong) | 23.90 | 35.03 | 40.48 | 40.02 |
| 2  ASEAN | 12.43 | 12.78 | 14.86 | 18.35 |
| 3  USA | 24.51 | 17.64 | 12.47 | 11.43 |
| 4  EU | 15.31 | 12.94 | 10.69 | 8.64 |
| 5  Japan | 10.17 | 8.42 | 6.83 | 6.44 |
| 6  South Korea | 2.10 | 2.97 | 3.46 | 4.24 |
| 7  Australia | 1.44 | 1.20 | 1.24 | 1.15 |
| 8  India | 0.46 | 0.60 | 1.08 | 1.13 |
| 9  Canada | 1.31 | 1.00 | 0.74 | 0.78 |
| 10 Mexico | 0.64 | 0.60 | 0.58 | 0.65 |
| Total | 100 | 100 | 100 | 100 |

Source: Collated from Taiwan Customs data.

countries, such as China, ASEAN, and India, have been significantly increasing. Between 2011 and 2017 almost 60% of Taiwan's exports were to China and ASEAN countries, highlighting the increasingly close direct trade relationships that have been established between Taiwan and Asian countries.

Figure 3.1 shows the increasing share of intermediate and capital goods exported by Taiwan to ASEAN and, especially, China. Meanwhile, exports of intermediate and capital goods to the EU, Japan, and the USA continued to decline. Taiwan mainly exported consumer products to the USA, ASEAN, and the EU, followed by China and Japan.

All this shows that Taiwan has adjusted its industry structure to accommodate changes in the production environment, and is now even more focused on the production of mid- to upstream products. Taiwanese companies view Asian countries as a base for processing and exports, and their investments have driven trade and brought industries in Taiwan and Asian economies to work closer together. In particular, the division of labour between industries in China and ASEAN countries has shown an upward trend.

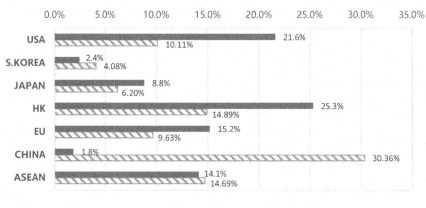

*Figure 3.1* Changes in product categories exported by Taiwan: intermediate goods.
Source: Taiwan customs statistics.

Taiwan's consumer products are still mainly exported to the USA and the EU, but exports of intermediate goods and capital goods to these destinations have declined, and direct trade relations have weakened as well. *Indirect* exports to Europe and America have increased through processing and production chains in China and ASEAN countries.

In summary, a symbiotic relationship between Taiwan's pattern of foreign trade and its overseas investment has evolved. Taiwan's overseas investments are mainly in China and Southeast Asia, which Taiwan basically views as its overseas processing bases. Taiwan exports intermediate goods and capital goods to China and ASEAN for processing into consumer goods, and finally exports the consumer goods to countries in Europe and America, thereby forming a triangular pattern of trade. Even though it has worked hard to expand the global market for consumer goods, the triangular trade described above remains at the heart of Taiwan's foreign trade relations.

When the end consumer product market is in recession – e.g., cf. the US subprime mortgage crisis and the European debt crisis – exports from processing bases in China and Southeast Asia to Europe and America will decline, and Taiwan's exports to China and ASEAN will also significantly decline because of this trade pattern. Effects of this chain reaction are growing stronger further upstream, and countries upstream of the production chain are impacted more – described as the 'bullwhip effect' – with a major impact on Taiwan (Figure 3.2).

The IT and electronics industry represents a large part of Taiwan's industry structure and is more susceptible to international fluctuations. Table 3.4 presents estimates of the nominal value of production of Taiwan's four main

## Consumer Goods

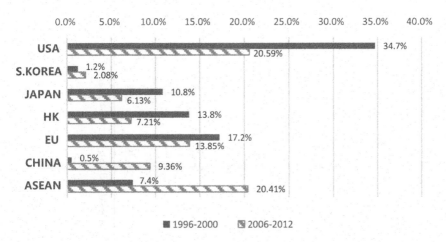

*Figure 3.2* Changes in product categories exported by Taiwan: consumer goods.
Source: Taiwan customs statistics.

industries in 2000–16, and shows the IT and electronics industry to have been the fastest growing, with its share of total production value rising to reach 31.3% in 2016. Under the impact of Taiwan's industrial policy, its industry structure has clearly shifted towards the IT and electronics industry. The outcome has been to bring about an excessive concentration of Taiwan's exports in IT and electronics products. Electronics and ICT products have consistently accounted for at least 30% of Taiwan's total exports. Due to the higher income elasticity of ICT and electronics products, consumers can easily defer consumption. Hence, any fluctuations in the global economy will considerably impact Taiwan's economy, while also limiting its ability to make adjustments.

Changes in the added value of Taiwan's exports, which reflect on vertical division of labour, are further analysed based on the export pattern described above. Table 3.5 shows a downward trend in the value added of Taiwan's exports, decreasing from 68.54% in 1995 to 54.55% in 2011. This shows the problem Taiwanese domestic industries have faced in moving up the value chain.

### B  Taiwan's challenges

#### (A)  Economic aspect

Taiwan has been impacted even more by the large-scale FTAs that continue to grow evenlarger around the world due to this trade pattern throughout the world. The division of labour and industrial supply chains in each region covered by FTAs will affect Taiwan's position in the industrial chain in Asia. By way of illustration, the case of the CPTPP is further described below.

Table 3.4 Changes in nominal industrial production in Taiwan, 2000–16 (units: NT$ billions, %)

| Industry | Nominal industrial production in 2000 | Share of total (2000) (%) | Nominal industrial production in 2011 | Share of total (2011) (%) | Nominal industrial production in 2016 | Share of total (2016) (%) | Growth rate (2000–2016) (% per annum) |
|---|---|---|---|---|---|---|---|
| **Overall Industrial Production** | 11,087.38 | 100.00 | 18,147.08 | 100.00 | 19,624.50 | 100.00 | 3.63 |
| B Mining and quarrying | 36.65 | 0.33 | 146.14 | 0.81 | 25.61 | 0.13 | -2.22 |
| C Manufacturing | 9,556.88 | 86.20 | 17,173.15 | 94.63 | 17,335.38 | 88.34 | 3.79 |
| Metallurgy and machinery manufacturing industry | 2,695.92 | 24.32 | 4,410.73 | 24.31 | 4,766.85 | 24.29 | 3.63 |
| IT and electronics industry | 2,910.29 | 26.25 | 5,948.85 | 32.78 | 6,143.71 | 31.31 | 4.78 |
| Chemical industry | 2,267.49 | 20.45 | 4,865.41 | 26.81 | 4,180.48 | 21.30 | 3.90 |
| Food and textile industry | 1,683.18 | 15.18 | 1,948.16 | 10.74 | 2,244.34 | 11.44 | 1.81 |
| D Electric power and gas supply | 376.26 | 3.39 | 629.80 | 3.47 | 684.69 | 3.49 | 3.81 |
| E Water supply and pollution prevention | 89.47 | 0.81 | | | 229.24 | 1.17 | 6.06 |
| F Construction | 1,028.12 | 9.27 | | | 1,349.58 | 6.88 | 1.71 |

Source: Collated from data compiled by the Directorate General of Budget, Accounting and Statistics (DGBAS), Executive Yuan.

*Table 3.5* Value added of Taiwan exports

| Year | Taiwan (%) | USA (%) | China (%) | Korea (%) | Japan (%) | EU (%) | Other (%) |
|---|---|---|---|---|---|---|---|
| 1995 | 68.54 | 4.27 | 0.75 | 1.26 | 8.38 | 3.96 | 5.22 |
| 2000 | 66.43 | 4.33 | 1.02 | 1.57 | 7.55 | 3.35 | 5.23 |
| 2005 | 60.90 | 2.86 | 2.34 | 1.57 | 5.99 | 3.10 | 8.45 |
| 2008 | 53.96 | 2.68 | 3.46 | 1.16 | 4.88 | 2.93 | 12.68 |
| 2009 | 60.52 | 2.43 | 3.28 | 1.19 | 4.82 | 2.67 | 9.76 |
| 2010 | 56.34 | 2.68 | 3.46 | 1.38 | 5.34 | 2.78 | 10.45 |
| 2011 | 54.55 | 2.60 | 3.91 | 1.31 | 4.94 | 2.87 | 11.61 |
| 1995–2005 difference | −7.64 | −1.41 | 1.59 | 0.31 | −2.39 | −0.86 | 3.23 |
| 2005–11 difference | −6.35 | −0.26 | 1.57 | −0.26 | −1.05 | −0.23 | 3.16 |

Source: Calculated from 'OECD Inter-Country Input-Output (ICIO) Tables, edition 2015,' (http://www.oecd.org/sti/ind/input-outputtablesedition2015accesstodata.htm).

First, Table 3.6 shows that members of the CPTPP already have a complete FTA network, and after it takes effect the CPTPP will bring about the further integration of the 11 member countries. Of these 11 countries, Taiwan has an FTA only with New Zealand and Singapore. Besides the impact on tariffs, the CPTPP continues to apply the strict country of origin regulations of the TPP to strengthen the division of labour between industries and supply chain connections within the region. Since Taiwan mainly exports intermediate goods, this may weaken Taiwan's previous role in the CPTPP's supply chain, or even cause the production chain to break. This is a challenge Taiwan must face.

Looking in greater detail at the challenges that regional economic integration can be expected to pose for Taiwan in the future, the key factor is the CPTPP, which is currently the most significant regional trade arrangement in the Asia Pacific region. The CPTPP already has 11 member nations and has been advocating a strengthening of the intra-regional supply chain. This means that in the future the CPTPP will implement strict rules of origin (RoO) provisions, which will consolidate the linkage of supply chain in the region and promote the development of the intra-regional division of labour, but which may have a negative impact on Taiwan (Platzer, 2012; Doan & Xing, 2017).

Taking Taiwan's textile industry as an example, Taiwan currently exports large quantities of yarn and fabric to Vietnam, where it is processed into garments for export to the CPTPP region. Under the current 'yarn forward' approach adopted for the CPTPP's rules of origin in relation to garment manufacturing, Vietnam will be required to use yarn produced in another/other CPTPP member country/-tries in order to benefit from preferential tariff treatment when exporting garments to the CPTPP. This promises to disrupt the existing Taiwan-Vietnam-CPTPP supply chain, with the most serious adverse effect being felt by Taiwan. Given the strictness of the CPTPP's rules of origin requirements, a similar situation is likely to emerge in other industries.

*Table 3.6* FTAs between members of the CPTPP

| | Japan | Canada | Australia | Mexico | Malaysia | Singapore | Vietnam | Chile | Peru | New Zealand | Brunei |
|---|---|---|---|---|---|---|---|---|---|---|---|
| Japan | | ■ | △ | △ | △ | △ | △ | △ | △ | ■ | △ |
| Canada | | | ■ | △ | ■ | ■ | ■ | △ | △ | ■ | ■ |
| Australia | | | | ■ | △ | △ | △ | △ | △ | △ | △ |
| Mexico | | | | | ■ | ■ | ■ | △ | △ | ■ | ■ |
| Malaysia | | | | | | △ | △ | △ | ■ | △ | △ |
| Singapore | | | | | | | △ | △ | △ | △ | △ |
| Vietnam | | | | | | | | △ | ■ | △ | △ |
| Chile | | | | | | | | | △ | △ | △ |
| Peru | | | | | | | | | | ■ | ■ |
| New Zealand | | | | | | | | | | | △ |
| Brunei | | | | | | | | | | | |

Source: Prepared by this study.

Note: △ indicates a bilateral FTA was signed.

■ indicates new connection from joining the CPTPP.

*(B)  Political aspect*

For Taiwan, securing membership of the CPTPP means not only complying with the requirements of the CPTPP in regard to economic issues; because of Taiwan's unique diplomatic status, it will also require Taiwan to take account of the 'China factor.'

Membership of the TPP is open to all APEC member economies. In principle, however, the process of applying for membership of the TPP cannot be completed until the applicant economy has completed negotiations with all existing CPTPP members in regard to the terms and conditions of accession.

Taiwan currently does not have formal diplomatic relations with any of the 11 existing CPTPP member states. By contrast, not only do the 11 CPTPP member states all have formal diplomatic relations with China, they also have important investment and trading links with China. If relations between Taiwan and China remain tense, attempts by Taiwan to secure membership of the TPP will likely be subject to interference by China. Although China is not currently a member of the CPTPP itself, the dramatic growth of the Chinese economy means that the amount of influence it is able to exert within the international community is growing steadily larger, and will affect Taiwan's ability to secure accession to the CPTPP. It may well be that while refraining from making a formal, public statement of opposition to Taiwan's membership of the CPTPP, China will privately ask existing CPTPP members to adopt a cautious attitude towards the negotiation of CPTPP membership for Taiwan in order to drag out the process of bilateral negotiation as long as possible, or even to issue a direct refusal to accept Taiwan's membership of the CPTPP.

Even if Taiwan does succeed in securing participation in the second round of CPTPP accession talks, Taiwan's past experience when attempting to secure membership of international organisations suggests that China will insist on the adoption of the same model used in regard to Taiwan's and China's accession to the WTO, whereby China requested that Taiwan not be allowed to join the WTO before China[1]. In other words, China would ask the CPTPP to agree that Taiwan should not be given membership of the CPTPP before China. Although China's stance towards the CPTPP has become less oppositional, with Beijing expressing a more positive attitude towards the CPTPP, at the same time it has promoted other FTAs (such as the RCEP) as a counterweight to the CPTPP. Nevertheless, China's economic and trading systems are still very far from being in conformity with the CPTPP's requirements. Overall, it is highly unlikely that China will join the CPTPP. If China were to adopt the WTO model, Taiwan's accession to the CPTPP will be delayed considerably.

The cross-Strait relationship will be even more problematic in the wake of Tsai Ing-wen's landslide victory of presidential election in 2020. As a result it is more difficult for Taiwan to make progress in regional economic integration in the future.

## C  Taiwan's response

### (A)  Industry

#### 1 BRAND PROMOTION

Taiwan is bound to face an increasingly challenging export environment as the CPTPP and more FTAs begin to take effect. Since Taiwan mainly exports intermediate goods, strict place of origin requirements in future FTAs to strengthen the bond between industries in the FTA region will cause Taiwan's exports to be even more squeezed.

The added value of Taiwan's exports is not high due to Taiwan's focus on manufacturing. OEM products account for a significant proportion of exports, resulting in intermediate goods accounting for a high share of exports. Taiwan lacks global brands and has relatively weak capacity to integrate downstream of the value chain. This has resulted in the relatively low share of end consumer products in Taiwan's total exports. This is why Taiwan is more easily directly affected by the global economy. In future, Taiwan must find ways of accelerating brand building through marketing.

Branding is a difficult road. The 2016 Interbrand Survey showed that the total value of the world's top 100 brands reached US$18 trillion in 2015. None of these brands was Taiwanese. Even though the majority of the top 100 brands belong to Western countries, Japan already has six brands, South Korea has three, and China has two. The value of Taiwan's largest brand (ASUS) is only about 40% of the value of the world's 100th brand. Taiwan must catch up.

#### 2 INDUSTRY DIVERSITY

Besides changing the model for connecting to the world, Taiwan must also expand the ways in which it makes connections. An important reason why in recent years Taiwan's economy has been severely impacted by the global financial crisis is the concentration on ICT products and lack of diversity. Taiwan should actively develop new products and new industries in line with development trends in the global market. In short, Taiwan must redefine its role in global industries. In recent years countries in Europe and America have been reviving their industries through the implementation of re-industrialisation and 'Industry 4.0' strategies. The 'red supply chain' China is actively building has placed great pressure on Taiwan's production. The rise of a new digital economy has changed the structure of industries, and mobile communications have created new business models. Taiwan has not been able to effectively engage in such changes and seize the market opportunities of a new generation of products. The inference is that it should actively engage in innovation to develop new generation industries.

*(B) System*

1 OVERALL REGULATORY REFORM

In addition to adjusting to effects of market opening, Taiwan must also carry out system reform. Taiwan will need to implement an inventory-taking of domestic laws and systems, and to identify where they are in conflict with the requirements of major FTAs. It will need to formulate clear plans with regard to adjustment procedures and timetables, to ensure that all necessary revisions of relevant laws and regulations are completed. In so doing, it will show itself to be a mature economy able to meet the most rigorous requirements of any FTA.

Taiwan must also have a thorough understanding of the issues that are of concern to major countries. Areas on which it will need to focus include promoting reform of the agricultural sector and state-owned enterprises, enhancing the transparency of administrative procedures, and formulating relevant guidance measures as early as possible in order to be able to respond to the negative impact of market opening on Taiwan's less competitive industries. This proactive approach will demonstrate Taiwan's commitment to securing membership and help Taiwan secure the support of other countries.

In the case of the CPTPP, besides the emphasis on traditional market opening in the agricultural, industrial, and service sectors, the CPTPP also stresses the need to reduce non-tariff barriers. The non-tariff barriers with which the CPTPP is concerned are not limited to 'on the border' measures; they also include member states' 'behind the border' systems and regulatory frameworks (Polanco Lazo & Sauve, 2018). Areas such as e-commerce, competition law, environmental protection, finance, telecommunications, intellectual property rights, government purchasing, investment, legal harmonisation, transparency, natural person status, labour rights, etc., all fall within the scope covered by the CPTPP. These are areas where Taiwan will need to make adjustments in the future.

*(C) Communication*

1 INTERNAL COMMUNICATION

The main emphasis in internal communication should be on improving communications with industry, the Legislative Yuan (Taiwan's legislature), the labour force, and ordinary citizens. It might be advisable for the government to form multi-disciplinary expert advisory teams and to canvass the views of ordinary members of the public, workers, students, industry organisations, etc. This would help the government get a clearer picture of citizens' attitudes and related trends in industry, which would serve as a useful reference point when negotiating with other countries, as well as for the government's own decision-making; at the same time, this process of canvassing citizens' views should also help to build consensus within Taiwan regarding efforts to secure future FTA membership, thereby reducing the level of domestic uncertainty in this regard.

2 EXTERNAL COMMUNICATION

Cross-Strait relations are currently at an impasse. If Taiwan is to reduce China's influence and gain greater opportunity to participate in economic integration, Taiwan must offer greater economic incentives to other countries. From the perspective of industrial and trade developments, Taiwan must emphasise its ability to strengthen the division of labour and create a 'win-win' situation in the Asia-Pacific when participating in regional economic integration. In the case of the CPTPP, Taiwan should not be too heavily focused on its own interests, emphasising the risk of Taiwan becoming marginalised or stressing the benefits that CPTPP membership would provide for Taiwan. Instead, Taiwan should focus on the perspective of its counterpart, and make clear to it the positive effects that Taiwan's membership promises to deliver.

The areas in which in the future Taiwan is well placed to make a contribution include the following:

1   Taiwan's position in the global industrial supply chain can help maintain the integrity of the supply chain in the Asia-Pacific.

Taiwan is an important part of the international supply chain. According to the Global Competitiveness Report 2018 issued by the WEF, Taiwan's global ranking was 13th among the 140 countries that were rated. Taiwan ranked fifth in the industrial cluster development. Taiwan's globalisation experience and foundation for supply chain integration will help countries integrate resources, create economic and trade opportunities, increase the production efficiency of supply chains, and optimise resource allocation. This will benefit the completeness and stability of international supply chains, and help drive economic and trade development in the Asia-Pacific.

Taiwan is an important supplier of ICT products for the world, and plays a key role in the global supply chain for numerous products, such as notebooks, tablet PCs, motherboards, CDs, DSL terminals, LCD monitor, foundry, and wireless network products. By participating in regional economic integration, Taiwan can enhance cooperation and development opportunities for member states in the field of electronics and ICT.

2   Taiwan's strength in investments and trade can drive industrial development and economic growth in the Asia-Pacific.

Taiwan has a tight network of investments in the Asia-Pacific, and plays a key role in industrial technology transfer within the region. On the one hand, Taiwan is independently developing or obtaining technologies from advanced countries. On the other hand, Taiwan is transferring technologies to emerging countries through its investments. Taiwan can enlarge its role in providing capital and technology transfer by participating in regional economic integration. The partnership between Taiwan and member states in investment and trade can create even more opportunities for industrial and economic development to the benefit of all parties.

Apart from the macro-perspectives described above, Taiwan also promises to make significant contributions to major countries in the Asia-Pacific.

For Japan, Taiwan serves as a hub in the production network of developing countries in East Asia for many industries, such as steel, machinery, electronics, and ICT. Japanese, Taiwanese, and Southeast Asian countries' industries are engaged in the vertical division of labour and trade. Taiwan's exclusion from regional economic integration will negatively impact Japan's overall economic interests.

Small and medium enterprises (SMEs) in Taiwan and Japan complement each other very well. If Taiwan is able to participate in regional economic integration, this will benefit investments between SMEs in Taiwan and Japan. The complementary advantages both sides enjoy in technology and market development abilities will give SMEs in Taiwan and Japan the opportunity to jointly develop markets.

For East Asia, Taiwan plays an important role in the production network in Southeast Asia for steel, plastics, electronics, and electrical equipment. If Taiwan is excluded from economic integration, this will negatively impact the industrial development of Southeast Asian countries. Participating in integration will help Taiwan increase its investment in Southeast Asia, and will create even more technology spill-overs and employment opportunities.

## V Conclusion

In the past Taiwan maintained a high rate of GDP growth. Indeed, its record and performance as one of the fastest growing economies in the world have been described as an 'economic miracle.' In recent years, however, Taiwan's economic growth has clearly hit a bottleneck and has even started to go downhill. In the eight years from 2000 to 2018, Taiwan's economic growth rate was lower than the global growth rate, and was even negative for the first time in two of those years. Stagnant economic growth also resulted in slow per capita GDP growth in Taiwan. Taiwan's GDP per capita almost doubled in the ten years from 1990 to 2000; in the 17 years from 2000 to 2017, however, it increased by only about 55%.

Many reasons can be put forward to explain Taiwan's stagnant economy, but the slow progress of its participation in regional economic integration is indisputably one of the more important factors affecting Taiwan's trade and industrial development. The significant growth in the number of FTAs throughout the world in recent years has significantly impacted Taiwan. The development of bilateral and multilateral – and increasingly all-embracing – FTAs has taken an even greater toll.

In the future, Taiwan must accelerate its industrial transformation, promote diverse industries, and build brands. Internally, Taiwan must strengthen communication for consensus building. Externally, Taiwan must utilise its economic strength to persuade others that Taiwan's participation in regional economic integration is beneficial to the region and will generate a 'win-win' outcome.

Of course, Taiwan must understand that stable cross-Strait relations are an essential precondition of any breakthrough in FTAs. This is part of the reality of today's international realpolitik. However undesirable it may seem, Taiwan must face this undeniable fact. If harmonious cross-Strait relations cannot be maintained in the future, the road ahead for Taiwan's involvement in FTAs will only become harder.

Finally as the COVID-19 pandemic wreaks havoc on the world, countries are even more keenly aware of the importance of maintaining supply chain stability and guaranteeing industrial security. Given the inefficiencies of the multilateral WTO, the best option is to use FTAs to facilitate trade and consolidate supply chains by initiating industrial cooperation.

If these conditions were fulfilled, regional integration would accelerate throughout the world, encouraging the establishment of new FTAs and the expansion of the membership and scope of existing FTAs. This, in turn, would stimulate further competition. In such a process Taiwan cannot afford to be left behind.

## Note

1   GATT (document C/M/259): 'Many contracting parties, therefore, had agreed with the view of the People's Republic of China (PRC) that Chinese Taipei, as a separate customs territory, should not accede to the GATT before the PRC itself.'

## References

Albertoni, Nicolás. 2018. 'The New Dynamics of the International Trading System.' *Global Policy* 9 (1), pp. 156–8.

Ciuriak, Dan, Jingliang Xiao, and Ali Dadkhah. 2017. 'Quantifying the Comprehensive and Progressive Agreement for Trans-Pacific Partnership.' *East Asian Economic Review* 21 (4), pp. 343–84.

Doan, Thang N., and Yuqing Xing. 2017. 'Trade Efficiency, Free Trade Agreements and Rules of Origin.' *Journal of Asian Economics* 55, pp. 33–41.

Fefer, Rachel F. 2018. 'USA Trade in Services: Trends and Policy Issues.' *Congressional Research Service*, R43291.

Lee, Jong-Wha, Innwon Park, and Kwanho Shin. 2008. 'Proliferating Regional Trade Arrangements: Why and Whither?' *The World Economy* 31 (12), pp. 1525–57.

Liu, Da-nien and Hui-tzu Shih. 2012. 'New Economic Development Opportunities for Taiwan in the Post-ECFA Era.' *Asie.Visions* 51, Ifri Center for Asian Studies.

Ministry of Economic Affairs, Bureau of Foreign Trade. 2020. 'Our Country's FTAs.' https://www.trade.gov.tw/Pages/List.aspx?nodeID=764

Platzer, Michaela D. 2012. 'USA Textile Manufacturing and the Trans-Pacific Partnership Negotiation.' *Congress Research Service (CRS)*, R42772.

Polanco Lazo, Rodrigo and Pierre Sauve. 2018. 'The Treatment of Regulatory Convergence in Preferential Trade Agreements.' *World Trade Review* 17 (4), pp. 1–33.

Whalley, John. 2008. 'Recent Regional Agreements: Why So Many, Why So Much Variance in Form, Why Coming So Fast, and Where Are They Headed?' *The World Economy* 31 (4), pp. 517–32.

World Trade Organization. 2020. 'Regional Trade Agreements Database.' http://rtais.wto.org/UI/PublicMaintainRTAHome.aspx

# 4 Taiwan in the high-income trap and its implications for cross-Strait relations

*Syaru Shirley Lin*

## Background to Taiwan's double bind

After decades of impressive growth, Taiwan achieved the status of 'high-income economies,' according to the World Bank's definition of approximately $12,000 gross national income per capita, more than three decades ago.[1] In so doing, Taiwan experienced an economic miracle. It not only built a high-income society with a solid middle class, avoiding the middle-income trap that has plagued so many other emerging economies. But even more miraculously, the majority of Taiwanese, ordinary workers and elites alike, benefited from increasing prosperity creating an unusually high degree of equality compared with other economies making the same transition. During its evolution from middle-income to high-income status, Taiwan relied primarily on the export of more highly valued products. But today Taiwan can no longer compete with countries that are catching up technologically, but still enjoy lower labour costs. Taiwan also finds it difficult to promote innovation or upgrade to still higher value-added services in order to provide the economic benefits that a wide spectrum of society has come to expect. Overall, established economic patterns fail to satisfy expectations of the voters, whether in aggregate or per capita terms. Furthermore, Taiwan also became a new democracy, and the top-down industrial policy-led economic planning of the past gave way to a more consensus-driven way of policy-making.[2] Such participatory politics in a highly democratic society has made it difficult to make the necessary economic trade-offs among policy alternatives, often leading to political gridlock or oscillating policies. The latest trade-off, for example, is the classic one of 'guns vs. butter,' because the pressure to invest more in the military to keep up with the Chinese threat complicates Taiwan's ability to meet these other socio-economic priorities (Newsham 2020).

Like its other East Asian neighbours, Taiwan's growth dropped from double digit in the 1960–80 to single digit from 1988 to now, except for 2010 in the aftermath of the global financial crisis. More importantly, wages have stagnated for two decades except for some high-skilled workers. Ever since Taiwan reached the high-income status, it has struggled to remain competitive.

This coincided with cross-Strait two-way trade (excluding Hong Kong) growing to become over a fifth of Taiwan's total trade from 2008 onwards, with exports to China reaching an all-time high in 2018 to constitute 29% of Taiwan's total exports. Furthermore, the majority of Taiwan's cumulative foreign direct investments are still in China. In other words, Taiwan escaped the middle-income trap only to enter a high-income trap with structural problems that include an ageing population, wage stagnation, rising welfare entitlements, inflated housing costs, over-regulated markets, and what many regard as excessive dependence on China. Furthermore, inequality has widened, and social tensions and political unrest are increasing. As in other countries caught in the high-income trap, there is a perception that the 'other' – especially emerging markets and immigrants – are to be blamed for job loss, slower growth, and social problems. For Taiwan, however, the 'other' is primarily mainland China, whose insistence on eventual unification is seen as an existential threat to many Taiwanese, even though the large Chinese economy appears to others to be the most obvious solution for Taiwan's sluggish economic growth. This 'double bind' between fearing China yet being compelled to integrate with it economically has had important political implications in Taiwan's highly democratic environment. Voters have been dissatisfied with all the political parties, in terms of both the solutions they have proposed to stimulate growth and fairly distribute the gains, and their policies towards mainland China.

After former President Ma Ying-jeou of the Kuomintang (KMT) initiated a period of extensive liberalisation of cross-Strait economic relations under the flagship Economic Cooperation Framework Agreement (ECFA), signed in 2010, Taiwanese voters rejected such a strategy by voting overwhelmingly for the Democratic Progressive Party (DPP) to control both the executive and legislative yuans in 2016 and 2020. Because of the DPP's historical commitment to independence, and its refusal to reassert a commitment to unification with China, this has led to a cross-Strait stalemate, with Beijing making increasingly assertive efforts to penalise Taiwan economically, marginalise it internationally, and pressurise it militarily. Briefly in 2018, Taiwanese voters changed their minds and returned 15 KMT mayors out of 22 cities. However, the newly elected Kaohsiung mayor and 2020 KMT presidential candidate Han Kuo-yu's surprising emergence and sudden fall by a popular recall within two years, together with DPP president Tsai Ing-wen's landslide re-election in 2020, again signalled how quickly Taiwanese voters can change their minds. Nonetheless, Han's appeal – especially his advocacy of closer economic relations with China – highlights the importance of such an alternative in the debate on Taiwan's economic future.

These dramatic political developments have occurred in the context of the combination of Taiwan's deepening high-income trap, the rising power of China, and the consolidation of Taiwanese identity, especially among the youngest generations. The resulting double bind simultaneously pulls Taiwan both towards China and away from it. As Taiwan's political leaders face increasing popular demands to escape from the high-income trap, expanding economic ties with China is an option that is economically compelling but politically untenable. This is because the island's citizens want to safeguard their Taiwanese identity against growing pressure from Beijing for unification. Thus, Taiwan's economic policy continues its historic pattern of oscillating between cross-Strait economic liberalisation and restriction (Lin 2016). While Taiwan has long experienced a version of this China dilemma, it is more acute for Tsai's administration than for any previous government because of the difficulty in diversifying Taiwan's economy to avoid deeper dependence on China and the prospect that a challenging global recovery from the 2020 pandemic will further dampen Taiwan's economic growth.

## The first half of the double bind: Taiwan's high-income trap in the context of East Asia

Like many other high-income economies, Taiwan's attainment of high-income status paradoxically coincided with the start of an economic slowdown. The decline in growth is the basis of many of the related issues facing high-income societies. Reaching high-income status may have been difficult, but maintaining consistent rates of economic growth in order to retain that status and deliver welfare benefits to a broad spectrum of society – particularly health care, education, and retirement benefits – has proven even more challenging (Figure 4.1).

For nearly five decades after 1960, only 13 out of 101 economies graduated from the middle-income category to high-income status, and the five East

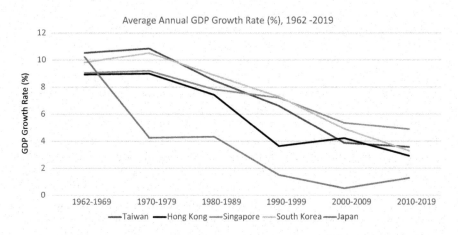

*Figure 4.1* Average annual GDP growth rate by decade (– percent), 1962–2019.
Sources: All data from World Bank, *World Development Indicators*, except Taiwan's data from Directorate-General of Budget, Accounting and Statistics, Executive Yuan, Republic of China (DGBAS).

Asian economies were the poster children, especially if viewed from a real GDP per capita measured by purchasing power parity.[3] More countries in recent years have joined the high-income ranks and have remained there, including Chile, the Czech Republic, Estonia, Poland, and Uruguay. However, several other countries that attained high-income status have been unable to stay there, moving in and out of the category. Croatia, Hungary, and Latvia fell out but rejoined, while Russia, Argentina, and Venezuela came in, but have subsequently been downgraded to upper-middle-income status, where they are now competing with other countries in that status such as Malaysia, Kazakhstan, and Turkey which are quickly moving up the ladder.[4] Having finally reached high-income status, countries like Taiwan must find a sustainable path forward. Unless they can continue to grow at a consistent rate, they may stall economically or even fall back. Continued growth may be necessary to meet rising demand for more benefits, maintain national status and military capability. Economically, studies have shown that inequality inhibits further growth (Ostry 2014). Furthermore, the social and political implications of the high-income trap for the middle class in these wealthy societies are far reaching, since uneven distribution in favour of the elites leads to political alienation, and growing support for extreme political platforms. Faced with rising inequality and high youth unemployment, these societies are becoming more polarised as they search for potential solutions.

More fundamentally, the structural factors which have led these economies into the high-income trap are not easily addressable in the short term (Manyika et al. 2015). Although troubled more by deflation than asset inflation, Japan, the first East Asian country to enter the trap, remains deeply enmeshed in slow growth, demographic decline, and debt. Other advanced economies in Asia, like Taiwan, South Korea, Hong Kong, and Singapore, as well as their counterparts in the West, have also suffered from their own versions of the high-income trap. Since 2015, all five Asian economies grew between only 2% and 4% (Figure 4.2). With estimated 2.7% GDP growth in 2019, Taiwan was actually the best performing economy in this group. But with the COVID-19 crisis, all of them are projected to contract, including Taiwan whose growth may decline by as much as 4%, according to the IMF.[5]

During its eight years in office, Ma Ying-jeou's government did make a serious effort to address the deep structural problems confronting Taiwan's economy. But Ma's solution relied on doubling down on economic integration with mainland China both to ensure cross-Strait stability and to stimulate Taiwan's economy. During his administration, Ma tried to mollify Beijing in order to maintain a stable economic environment, encouraging more two-way trade with China as well as permitting Chinese investments in Taiwan. Ma reaffirmed the '1992 Consensus,' which acknowledged that Taiwan was part of China and committed Taiwan to eventual unification with the mainland. He also met China's President Xi Jinping in Singapore just a few months before Taiwan's January 2016

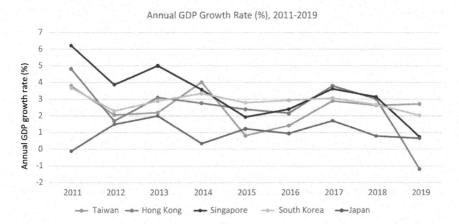

*Figure 4.2* Annual GDP growth rate for East Asia (– percent), 2011–19.
Sources: All data from World Development Indicators, World Bank except Taiwan's data from DGBAS.

presidential election, the first Taiwanese president to meet with his mainland counterpart (Lin and Chung 2018). But the economic results of this strategy were unspectacular: GDP growth rate dropped to under 2% in Ma's last two years in office and Taiwan's trade surplus with China also fell to a ten-year low in 2015. Disappointing economically, Ma's approach was nothing short of disastrous politically: a proposed service trade agreement with China, one of the most important elements in his policy of promoting deeper integration with the mainland, could not be ratified because of mass protest, and then the KMT lost the presidency and control of the Parliament to the DPP in 2016.

To make matters worse, China's own economic growth has begun to slow as it enters its own middle-income trap, reducing the prospect that China can serve as an engine of growth for Taiwan. This situation has been exacerbated by U.S.-China rivalry: the trade war threatens the profitability of Taiwanese manufacturers in China who export goods to the United States, and the technology war and export controls on sensitive technology have compelled Taiwanese businesses, particularly in the semiconductor industry, to stop taking Chinese orders. After the global financial crisis, Taiwan's economy recovered gradually and under the DPP since 2016, growth has been higher than in other East Asian high-income economies, yet it has been under 3%. Expectations need to be adjusted to anticipate around the same level of growth for the long term, if not lower when there are crises like the pandemic (Liu 2020). And reliance on China has been slow to drop. Due to rising costs and the trade war, Taiwanese investments in China have declined, but trade has kept growing and in 2018 under President Tsai Taiwan's trade surplus with China reached nearly $97 billion – an all-time high.

Economically, Taiwan has been seeking to enhance value-added manufacturing, focusing on the digital economy and software in order to move
beyond the lower-end information communications technology industry
that has dominated its export economy thus far. However, higher costs,
lack of innovation, and increasing competition from emerging markets, including lower-income and middle-income countries, are producing obstacles that seem insurmountable (Liu and Shih 2013). Moreover, in a fully
democratic Taiwan, public pressure has mounted for a fairer distribution of
economic gains to wider segments of society. While the whole country has
become more affluent, inequality has grown as Taiwan has become more
integrated into the global value chain because the benefits have gone dispro-
portionately to large corporations and elites (Chi and Kwon 2012; Lee and
Lin 2017). More and more people find it a struggle to maintain their standards of living even as a small segment of the population becomes extremely
wealthy.

The combination of slower growth, wage stagnation, and growing inequality has a serious political impact on high-income economies.[6] Several
interrelated trends occur when the overall economy becomes less competitive: terms of trade become less favourable, technological change becomes
accelerated, enriching a small group of elites rather than the middle class,
and economic returns become increasingly skewed towards business owners rather than workers. While other East Asian economies have also seen
real wage growth slow since 2000, the gap between economic growth and
wage growth has been much greater in Taiwan, as reflected in the declining
share of labour compensation as a percentage of GDP (Figure 4.3). After the
global financial crisis, Taiwanese workers suffered even more; even though
productivity was increasing, real wages did not keep pace and unemployment rose (Huang and Huang 2020). Average real wage levels for Taiwanese
in eight out of 19 sectors have been negative since 2000, especially in export-
oriented manufacturing. The only sectors where wages grew significantly
were related to services, including finance, hospitality, and leisure.

In an effort to sustain growth, governments of high-income Asian economies have resorted to quantitative easing with interest rates kept low for
a prolonged period of time – more than two decades in Japan. Elsewhere
around the world, low interest rates have also been made possible partly because of low inflation, due largely to cheap imports from China (*The Economist* 2004). After each financial crisis and the 2020 pandemic, it became
compelling to keep interest rates low to stimulate the economy, and quantitative easing became the norm. Under competitive pressure, more and more
markets adopted such loose monetary policies and no country wanted to be
the first to tighten (Shirakawa 2019). But monetary stimulus policies are less
effective in high-income societies like those in East Asia with shrinking labour forces, ageing populations, and declining household consumption. Yet
as such a policy became prevalent around the world, it produced a vicious
cycle where economies do not recover and rates can never be raised. Few

*Figure 4.3* Compensation of employees as percentage of GDP, Taiwan, 1981–2017.
Source: DGBAS.

have confidence that change will actually happen because of the entrenched nature of these global financial patterns (Palley 2013).

The unhappy result of low interest rates has been asset inflation and rising levels of household debt. The cost of living in Asian cities has risen markedly, with housing becoming completely unaffordable for young adults, more than a third of whom live with their parents (Chow 2016). Government statistics of 2018 show that in order to purchase a median price apartment in Taipei, one would have to save more than 15 years of income in order to do so without leverage (Figure 4.4). Therefore, families have had to resort to heavy debt in order to purchase a home and household indebtedness as a percentage of GDP has risen to be one of the highest in Asia, exceeding 80% since 2004 (Central Bank of the Republic of China 2019) (Figure 4.5).

The problems produced by low interest rates and accommodative monetary policy are intertwined with the consequences of increasing financialisation, whereby the financial sector has become a more important part of the economy (Davis and Kim 2015). Capital gains through asset appreciation and other forms of unearned income have become more important than earned income, which also benefits large companies and older generations who are asset-rich (Palley 2013). And financial institutions have more influence over the economy compared with the manufacturing industry, thereby creating the 'Wall Street vs. Main Street' divide. Global capital flows continue to increase, new financial instruments keep emerging, and regulation tightens in order to rein in the speculators. Paradoxically, market risks and contagion still spread, while global over-regulation has strangled the efficient functioning of financial institutions especially in emerging economies.

The most important implication of asset inflation and financialisation is rising inequality, which is evident in all high-income economies (Lin and

*Figure 4.4*  Housing price to income ratio for major cities, 2018–19.
Sources: Data from Ministry of the Interior, Republic of China for Taipei; data from Government of the Republic of Korea for Seoul. Other data from the Demographia International Housing Affordability Survey.

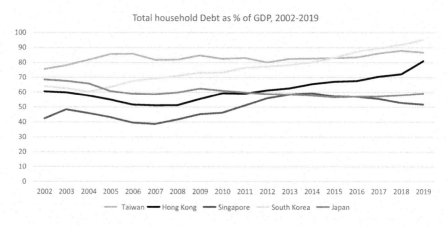

*Figure 4.5*  Total household debt as percentage of GDP in East Asia, 2002–19.
Sources: Data for Taiwan from Central Bank, Republic of China; other data from the Bank for International Settlements.

Tomaskovic-Devey 2013). As already noted, the real economic miracle Taiwan experienced during its high-growth decades was not just growth itself, but also the emergence of the middle class and a more equitable society. Today, in contrast, Taiwanese are experiencing unprecedented levels of income and wealth disparity. After integrating more with China economically and socially, Taiwan's inequality began to rise much more dramatically. Government figures show that the income of the highest 20% of households in recent years is now six times that of the lowest 20%, compared with only four times in 1976. Although Taiwan's inequality, as measured through its Gini coefficient of 0.338 in 2018, appears more moderate than Hong Kong or Singapore, the financial crises in 2001 and 2009 have worsened the plight of the low-income families which take much longer to recover from economic distress (DGBAS 2019).

Unskilled workers and young people have been most adversely affected by these symptoms of the high-income trap. Youth unemployment has been two to three times the average unemployment rate in Taiwan for the last decade. In 2019, the unemployment rate for ages 15 to 24 was 11.88%, which was three times higher than the average unemployment rate of 3.73%. With poor prospects in terms of jobs and finding affordable housing, young people are getting married later and not having children. This contributes to a demographic decline which is not reversible in the short term and extremely harmful for advanced economies in the long term. The decline in population contributes to lower productivity and consumption: compensating for such declines is difficult even with innovation and technology, which in fact may lead to further job loss and reduced demand.

Like Japan, Hong Kong, Singapore, and South Korea, Taiwan will soon face an absolute decline in population, exceeding the pace of decline in Japan or the United States. Since 2001, Taiwan's fertility has remained at or below 1.3–1.4 children per woman. Taiwan had the lowest fertility rate in the world in 2010 at a mere 0.9 and official projections show that overall population will begin to decline, starting in 2020 (Figure 4.6). Meanwhile, because of an excellent healthcare system, Taiwanese longevity for both men and women continues to improve, putting life expectancy on Taiwan among the top in Asia (Figure 4.7). With lower fertility and improved longevity, by 2026 Taiwan will have become a super-aged nation, defined as societies with over 20% of its population older than 65 years. By 2065, that

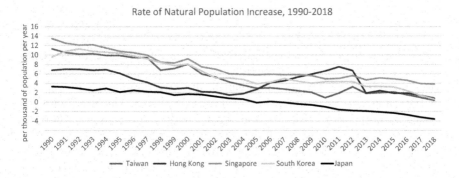

*Figure 4.6* Rate of natural population increase in East Asia, 1990–2018.
Sources: Data of Taiwan from DGBAS; the rest from World Development Indicators, World Bank. The rate of natural population increase (RNI) is calculated by subtracting the crude death rate from the crude birth rate.

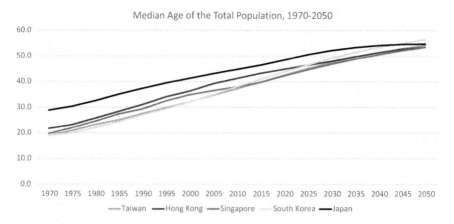

*Figure 4.7* Median age of total population in East Asia, 1970–2050.
Source: Population Division, Department of Economic and Social Affairs, United Nations (2019).

percentage will have reached 40% and overall population will have declined by 20%–30% compared with 2018. More importantly, the work force will have declined by half to 8.6 million people, constituting less than half of the total population (Liao 2018). Because of limited immigration, the key to reversing Taiwan's demographic and productivity decline may lie in having more educated women join the workforce, which in some countries actually leads to higher fertility (Cheng and Loichinger 2017 Loichinger and Cheng 2018). While women are becoming more educated in Taiwan, female labour participation, especially in the private sector, and fertility both remain persistently low. And the government has been slow to adopt a comprehensive set of policy solutions (Cheng and Hsu 2020).

Population decline will not only dampen economic growth, but also place heavy burdens on the welfare and retirement systems, which are expected to become insolvent in a few years for civil servants, military veterans, and retirees (*The Economist* 2017). Similarly, Taiwan's highly lauded and seemingly affordable single-payer healthcare system may also be unsustainable (Qi 2017). Since Taiwan's national health programme was overhauled in 1995, analysts have touted it as a model for others. However, with the projected population structure and recent increased spending on curbing COVID-19, the government will have to either cut back on the comprehensiveness of care or increase the share citizens must pay in the future (Scott 2020). This will be accentuated by the pandemic, especially given the high level of service the Taiwan government has delivered.

As a result of these negative economic and demographic developments, entitlements will have to be curtailed, which will entail sacrifices that will be hard for a democracy to accept. Slower growth, stagnating wages, growing inequality, and reduced benefits will produce political polarisation as more people see themselves as 'losers.' Many young and working-class Taiwanese blame global economic integration, especially with China, for Taiwan's growing inequality and job losses, even as they perceive business elites to have gained tremendously since China opened its economy to Taiwanese investments.

## The second half of the double bind: the emergence of a Taiwanese national identity

At the same time that Taiwan struggles with the high-income trap, consensus has been building on a distinct Taiwanese identity, in terms of both preferred national status and self-identification. This process has been underway for decades, despite first the KMT's use of national education and later Beijing's use of carrots and sticks to encourage the restoration and maintenance of a Chinese identity (Lin 2016). Since polling on the subject began more than two decades ago, support for immediate unification has never been more than in the low single digits, and the percentage of people who call themselves exclusively 'Chinese,' who are the most likely to support some form of unification, has also been in that same range for more than a decade. The latest polls show 87% in favour of autonomy, with only 5.1% favouring 'maintain status quo, move toward unification' and a mere 0.7% – an all-time low – favouring 'immediate unification.'[7] In terms of self-identification, respondents who identify as exclusively Taiwanese reached a new high at 67%, compared with a new low of 2.4% for those who say they are exclusively Chinese.[8]

Furthermore, the backlash against globalisation or economic liberalisation has been specifically directed at economic integration with China. In 2014, the largest student-led protest in Taiwan's history, the Sunflower Movement, succeeded in blocking a service trade agreement that would have promoted greater cross-Strait economic integration, but was perceived as leading to more inequality and benefiting mainly the elites. That agreement aroused anger and opposition because of the risk that it would allow massive Chinese investments to dominate many industries in Taiwan that consist primarily of small and medium businesses, including printers, hotels and hair salons. The agreement would also potentially have permitted the migration of Chinese managers and workers to staff those investments, possibly worsening the plight of Taiwanese workers by eliminating jobs and suppressing wages. But beyond these economic grievances, some also saw the prospect of immigration from the mainland as threatening Taiwanese values and paving the way for unification (Ho 2019). To many, the proposed agreement was the epitome of KMT's policy to open the economic gate to China at the expense of Taiwan's working class and younger generations.

A few months after the protest, the KMT suffered a great loss in the November 2014 local elections. The DPP won 13 out of 22 contested seats, and an independent candidate, Ko Wen-je, defeated the KMT contender to win the Taipei mayoral election. Two years later, in the 2016 national elections, the DPP gained control of both the executive and legislative branches for the first time in history. The party's presidential candidate, Tsai Ing-wen, became the first woman head of state or government in Asia who did not come from a political legacy family. A new political party, the New Power Party, elected five first-time legislators, all of whom were associated with the Sunflower Movement and embodied progressive political views and a strong Taiwanese identity. After a turbulent first term, in her second bid for presidency in January 2020 President Tsai won 8.17 million votes, the largest number ever received by any Taiwanese presidential candidate, and the DPP retained its majority in the legislature in a landslide victory. Another new party formed by Taipei Mayor Ko Wen-je, the Taiwan People's Party, won five seats as well. A younger generation, all born on Taiwan and raised in the shadow of China, was a driving force in these electoral changes. They did not believe that President Ma's proposed solution of deeper economic ties with China would create the kind of growth they desired for Taiwan: equitable, sustainable, and not dependent on China. For the youngest Taiwanese, the sense of national identity is very different from their elders. They are overwhelmingly Taiwanese with few if any identifying as Chinese, and they want to retain the way of life associated with living in a prosperous and democratic country. Moreover, many of them assert their distinctive social, economic, and political identities in ways that differentiate them from young people in China, as well as from their parents at home (Lin 2019a). Economically, they question the need to prioritise growth over equity and sustainability. Socially, they want Taiwan to become inclusive and support same-sex marriages. Politically, they mistrust existing institutions and political parties, and are generally less loyal to the major parties, compared with older generations. Furthermore, they care more about Taiwan being respected and recognised internationally and less about how it might challenge the so-called 'status quo.'

They can be called 'pragmatic idealists,' in that they remain motivated by economic opportunities and want to have the option of working or studying in China, but do not want to move to China permanently and insist on safeguarding Taiwan's democratic way of life. They are eager for Taiwan to compete in the Olympics, participate in international organisations such as the World Health Organization, and change even established brands such as 'China Airlines' to something with 'Taiwan' in the name (Chang and Holt 2014). Their support of Taiwan's legalisation of same-sex marriage – the first Asian country to do so – reflects their view that Taiwanese identity should be inclusive and pluralistic, distinct from a Chinese identity which is increasingly ethnic and state-monopolised. Indeed, when legalising same-sex marriage, Taiwan's leaders, in the judiciary, executive, and legislative branches, were responding to eager young voters who demanded that President Tsai fulfil her campaign promise.[9] While older generations remain focused on economic prosperity and have strong ideological views on China, young people prefer candidates who are firmly Taiwanese with strong commitment to progressive values, but are result-oriented in governance, and pragmatic about cross-Strait relations. Even if China is not their top choice as a place to live and work, they want to have the choice just like young people anywhere else. Politically, the experience of living and studying in China has not made them more supportive of unification, and in some cases, they have actually become more opposed to it (Lu 2018). To younger generations, there is no contradiction in working in China but supporting a more autonomous and separate Taiwan. Many of them simply regard China as another foreign country that presents a complex blend of opportunity and threat to their homeland.

As Taiwan forged this consensus over national identity, extreme versions of cross-Strait economic policy, such as extensive restriction or full liberalisation, faded from election campaigns. And as Taiwanese identity consolidated, its salience also declined from being a consideration that was explicitly present in every political debate to becoming a shared value that can normally be taken for granted but must be defended when threatened externally (Lin 2016). In recent elections, Taiwanese have rejected leaders whose cross-Strait economic policies they perceived as allowing the mainland to threaten or undermine Taiwan's identity and values. Although not wanting to be excluded from opportunities in mainland China, more voters now support the diversification of Taiwan's economy away from China as espoused by the DPP, especially under the current intense competition between the United States and China.

## DPP's response to the double bind

As soon as Tsai was elected in 2016, she began to adopt new approaches to Taiwan's high-income trap that would also show her desire to protect Taiwan's consolidated identity. Tsai's inaugural speech listed the economic challenges facing Taiwan and announced several initiatives to find other sources of economic growth. The most notable was the launch of the New Southbound Policy (NSP), aimed at diversifying Taiwan's trade and investment away from China and towards ASEAN and ten other countries in South Asia and Australasia. With a combined population exceeding two billion, these countries already constituted nearly a fifth of Taiwan's trade and outbound investment (Marston and Bush 2018). Furthermore, in recent years, many *Taishang* (Taiwanese businesses in mainland China), as well as Chinese and foreign companies, have already moved from increasingly costly coastal cities in China to inland cities or to New Southbound countries where costs are lower and growth potential is higher. The NSP was intended to encourage this trend by upgrading Taiwan's economic and political relations with these countries even in the absence of diplomatic ties. The policy differs from Lee Teng-hui's earlier 'go south' policy in 1994 in that it emphasises comprehensive relations with New Southbound countries, including not only economic ties but also public diplomacy programmes, student exchanges, and economic and technical assistance on issues where Taiwan can offer best practices, from democratic governance, public health, to women's empowerment. The policy also promotes the social integration of immigrants from these countries, although still largely limited to foreign brides (Glaser et al. 2018). While migrant workers and domestic helpers and white-collar professionals are being encouraged to work temporarily in Taiwan, there is no comprehensive immigration scheme to provide permanent residence or fully absorb them into Taiwanese society.

During the first three years of implementation, NSP has shown some notable results contributing to Taiwan's steady growth including record exports. Flows of tourists from New Southbound countries grew by 57%, which contributed to an increase in Taiwan's total tourist arrivals despite a decline in the number of Chinese tourists. Two-way trade and investments increased substantially in the first two years but have levelled off, partly due to closing off during COVID-19. Taiwan's NSP will be further enhanced by the Free and Open Indo-Pacific strategy adopted by the United States and Japan, which is expected to create more opportunities for cooperation and collaboration within the region (United States Department of Defense 2019). Overall, diversification has been driven not only by Tsai's policy, but also because of the U.S.-China rivalry, which has compelled key elements in the global supply chain to diversify away from China.

The NSP was originally viewed in tandem with other avenues for diversifying Taiwan's international economic relationships. One of these was to gain membership in the Trans-Pacific Partnership (TPP). Originally intended as a highly demanding, 'gold standard' free trade agreement linking 12 economies in the Asia-Pacific Region, negotiating the TPP was one of the biggest diplomatic accomplishments of the Obama administration and part of its 'pivot' or 'rebalancing' to Asia. Taiwan was not included among the original 12 signatories and meeting the stringent requirements and overcoming Beijing's almost certain objections to its membership would have been extremely difficult. However, Taipei still hoped to be included in a future round of negotiations when additional economies could be invited to join (Bush 2014). This avenue was dealt a major blow when the Trump administration withdrew from the TPP, as part of its general scepticism about free trade agreements. The successor agreement, the Comprehensive and Progressive Agreement for Trans-Pacific Partnership (CPTPP), which the remaining 11 economies have agreed to join, continues to offer Taiwan some hope. But Taiwan must convince all 11 remaining signatories, now led by Japan, to include Taiwan in future rounds and then to admit it to membership. Taiwan will have particular difficulties negotiating trade agreements with Japan because of Taiwan's restrictions on imports of Japanese food from five prefectures affected by the Fukushima nuclear leak. China will almost certainly try to block Taiwan's accession unless Taipei endorses the 1992 Consensus and China is able to join at the same time.

Taiwan may have a better chance of forging a separate bilateral free trade and investment agreement with the United States, given the growing sympathies in Washington for upgrading ties with Taiwan as the American relationship with Beijing deteriorates. But again, Taiwan's restrictions on imported beef and pork from the United States have impeded trade negotiations for years (Taiwan News 2019). Given the high price that some sectors of the Taiwanese economy would have to pay to meet Washington's conditions and the lack of resolve on the part of USTR to meet Taiwan half-way, the prospects for success are still dim.

In addition to these efforts to find new economic partners, Tsai has also implemented long-needed domestic reforms in order to get Taiwan out of the high-income trap. To ease the welfare burden on future generations, Tsai used much of her political capital in her first term to push through a pension reform that would reduce the payout to retired military service members, civil servants, and teachers. According to official forecasts, the pension fund for veterans and public school teachers will default by 2030, unless it is restructured (Chang 2016). Opposition to the reform was much greater than imagined and contributed to the DPP's loss in the 2018 local elections.

Taking pride in being a champion of labour rights, the DPP also rolled out a package of labour reforms that were intended to introduce a five-day workweek, limit working hours, and raise the minimum wage. But because of lack of consultation with relevant stakeholders and haphazard execution, the initial reforms were poorly designed and had to be revised soon after to appease businesses (Snyder and Lien 2018). The amended version of the reforms provoked even stronger opposition, with demands for a long list of clauses and exemptions that favoured employers. Overall, the reform did not have the effect Tsai intended and dissatisfied both employers and employees. Moreover, the reforms were badly implemented and have been widely seen as a failure. Some labour groups actually believe that the reform may have reversed decades of work to improve workers' rights (Hioe 2017).

Other well-intentioned reforms also led to controversy because the Tsai administration was unable to create a consensus over the trade-offs involved. These included efforts to develop a long-term energy policy that would phase out nuclear power by 2025 and promote environmental sustainability. The controversy led to a referendum in November 2018 that effectively retained nuclear energy rather than end its use. The DPP had campaigned for years under the promise to terminate Taiwan's nuclear programme, which generates nearly a fifth of Taiwan's power, and specifically to stop the operation of the fourth nuclear power plant, especially after the Fukushima crisis. But the proposed phase-out of nuclear power has raised several issues in recent years that cannot be easily resolved. First, Taiwan is a net energy importer and energy security is particularly important. Even though Taiwan has the potential to develop wind and solar energy, complete reliance on renewable energy is not realistic in the short term, so the only alternative to nuclear power is the greater use of carbon fuels (Freschi 2018). And the side effects of increased carbon emissions, especially air pollution, are unacceptable to businesses, environmentalists, and residents, and continue to ignite intense public disagreement even between local and central government (Chao et al. 2020). Moreover, government budgets are highly constrained, which will only obstruct solutions to the problem.

To escape the high-income trap by enhancing economic competitiveness and promoting higher value-added industries, Tsai also initiated a '5+2 Industrial Innovation Plan,' first to invest in the internet of things, the biomedical industry, green energy technology, smart machinery, and the defence industry, and then in two more sectors that were added later: high-value agriculture and the circular economy. The '5+2 Plan' was complemented by a Forward-Looking Infrastructure Development Programme that focuses on railway projects, water management, urban and rural development, the digital economy, and green energy. All these efforts are expected to create jobs and improve environmental sustainability – important priorities for young people – as well as to accelerate economic growth. But increasingly, these stimuli and restructuring plans sound like propaganda slogans with routine bureaucratic implementation and few concrete results.

Moreover, these government programmes to upgrade the economy and promote innovation must be matched by domestic and foreign investments. In the short term, there has been a significant return of investments from the mainland to Taiwan, driven by the rising costs on the mainland and the risks created by the U.S.-China trade war, and encouraged by a repatriation policy that includes subsidies for loans and favourable tax regime (Ihara 2020). Approvals for incoming investments under the 'Welcoming Taiwanese Businesses to Return to Invest in Taiwan Action Plan' have reached one trillion NTD dollars (over US$33 billion) (InvesTaiwan 2020). However, these are only commitments, some of which have not been funded, and represent only a portion of a cumulative total of over US$180 billion Taiwanese investments in China.

It is also widely recognised that there are structural constraints to upgrading Taiwan's economy that neither domestic nor foreign investment alone can remove. Attracting private investment will require further reform in financial regulation and the creation of a larger pool of talent trained to meet market needs. The latter will require several structural reforms starting with overhauling the education system to better prepare young people to contribute to a democratic society and competitive economy. Furthermore, Taiwan must attract more high-quality foreign professionals and immigrants. Tsai has introduced measures to ease restrictions on employing foreign workers but a fuller review of immigration policy is also necessary because it is perhaps the only solution to several of Taiwan's dire problems, including an ageing population, a declining labour force, and lack of innovation (Chang 2019). However, the influx of temporary migrant workers in factories that cannot attract Taiwanese workers has already created high levels of opposition. Even though Taiwan has already become a more multi-ethnic society with more than half a million foreign spouses naturalised, government agencies and politicians alike do not see the possibility of introducing large-scale immigration reforms (National Immigration Agency 2018).

Another problem is that Taiwan's financial markets are highly regulated and domestic financial institutions are severely constrained for foreign investors. Relative to other high-income economies, Taiwan has had difficulty attracting foreign investments, especially those from multinational corporations which can upgrade Taiwan's economy with jobs and know-how. Allowing Chinese investment into Taiwan would be an easier alternative solution, but it would be strongly opposed. And it has not been widely discussed since Ma Ying-jeou proposed that Taiwan become an 'Asia Pacific Financial Centre' in 2008 and further liberalised mainland investments in 100 sectors in 2009. The 2010 ECFA was intended to promote a cross-Strait financial industry with a series of Memorandums of Understanding that would have lifted restrictions and liberalised regulations on both sides. The most important of these reforms was to allow direct investment in each other's financial industry, including the banking, insurance, and securities industries. There was even the prospect that Taipei would become an RMB offshore centre (Lin 2013). But all such hopes were dashed when the 2014 service trade agreement, which would have enacted these MOUs and given Taiwanese banks preferential terms to invest in China, was shelved following the 2014 mass protests.

Due to these obstacles, the government's goals of moving Taiwan into the digital economy with more value-added manufacturing and higher-end technology in a financial dynamic environment will take years to achieve. At the same time, an increased tension between the United States and China has been challenging to navigate, especially in terms of economic and security relations between Taiwan and the superpowers.

In terms of economic relations, Taiwanese firms and *Taishang* in China have been concerned about becoming unintended victims of the increased tariffs imposed on Chinese exports, as well as global tariffs across several industries which would hurt Made-in-Taiwan products, too (Horton 2018). In the short term, the initial stage of decoupling of the global supply chain may have benefited Taiwan due to both trade diversion and the reshoring of Taiwan's overseas companies (Tan 2020). However, the U.S.-China rivalry and the softening of global demand for Taiwanese products under COVID-19 will eventually hurt Taiwan given its concentration on the export of information and communications technology industry (Feigenbaum and Smith 2020). This will especially be the case if OEM manufacturers are pressured to move out of China, refuse Chinese orders, and invest in the United States to help onshoring as TSMC has done in an ever-intensifying technology war (Sullivan-Walker 2020). Even with heavy subsidies, the cost of production in the United States is likely to be significantly higher than in Taiwan and China.

In terms of security, even as the United States appears more supportive of Taiwan than ever, Taiwan cannot rely exclusively on American intervention, but needs to spend more on defence to face rising PLA capability and assertiveness just when its fiscal resources are become more constrained. In 2019, Taiwan spent more than $10 billion in purchasing advanced weapons from the United States, and it is likely to purchase more in the future. Tsai has also initiated an indigenous defence industrial programme to produce Taiwan's own submarines and air fighters and become more self-sufficient (Axe 2020).

## KMT's response to the high-income trap

As it tries to escape from the unfamiliar status of being a true opposition party – without control of any branch of the Taiwanese government – the KMT will have to decide how to compete with the DPP in developing solutions to Taiwan's high-income trap. As a political party, the KMT has strong connections with large corporations and local interests alike and has always prided itself with well-educated and experienced leaders who understand the economy. Conversely, although far more supportive of both democratisation and Taiwanisation, the DPP has never campaigned with the economy as its priority, nor have DPP leaders demonstrated superior leadership in economic stewardship. During Tsai's first term, her administration was widely criticised for inexperience and poor judgement in carrying out domestic reforms. Furthermore, because Tsai refused to reconfirm the 1992 Consensus, Beijing ended official cross-Strait dialogue immediately and aggressively courted countries to terminate their diplomatic relations with Taiwan, ending the so-called 'diplomatic truce' that had existed during the Ma administration.[10] Economically, Beijing also began to punish Taiwan by reducing the flow of Chinese tourists, hitting the travel, hotel, and retail sectors hard.[11] With Beijing stepping up the pressure, the KMT campaigned heavily on the idea that voting for the DPP was damaging to Taiwan economically and threatened Taiwan's security. The KMT promised that it would restore stability in the Taiwan Strait and bring more prosperity to the Taiwanese people by accommodating Beijing and returning to the 1992 Consensus.

Thus in 2018, after only two years of national governance by the DPP, KMT had a strong comeback in the local elections for mayors. Not only did KMT win in a majority of the cities, but it was able to capture the mayoralty of Kaohsiung, which had been a DPP stronghold for 20 years. Much of what Taiwan's voters had given to the DPP in 2014 and 2016 they took away in 2018. The shocking victory by Han Kuo-yu in Kaohsiung is attributed by most analysts to his pledge to find a way out for the city's distressed economy by working more closely with China. And after 20 years of the DPP at the city's helm and an increasing gap between Taipei and Kaohsiung, Kaohsiung voters decided they wanted a change. There was also disappointment with Tsai's labour, pension, and energy reforms which, however necessary they may have been, had hurt many local interest groups.

Voters in Kaohsiung were therefore attracted by Han's campaign, which squarely focused on the city's economic problems (Horton 2019). As a second-generation Mainlander from New Taipei City and a KMT outsider, Han did not focus on either national identity or party identification in his campaigning. Instead, his emphasis was on the economy, with the campaign slogan 'Sell goods outside! Welcome people to Kaohsiung! Kaohsiung will prosper greatly!'[12] His platform was to bring Kaohsiung to the world, increase exports, bring in tourists, create more jobs, and make Kaohsiung great again.

Han's strategy of globalising the city's economy undeniably appealed to some voters and restoring relations with China was clearly a particular priority. Han proposed a free economic zone in order to attract more Chinese inbound investments. As soon as Han was elected mayor, in March 2019, he visited Hong Kong, Macao, Shenzhen, and Xiamen, and met with the directors of Beijing's liaison office in both special administrative regions. But with little experience, Han lacked a strategy on how Taiwan could address the double bind of taking advantage of the opportunities China offers without harming its autonomy, democracy, and freedom. Moreover, during Han's short tenure as mayor, he was unable to show immediate results in turning around the city's economic fortune. He was also seen as an opportunist since he essentially abandoned his mayoral responsibilities within six months in order to launch a presidential election campaign. Han not only lost the presidential election in January 2020, but by June, he had been removed from office in Taiwan's first successful mayoral recall (Huang et al. 2020).

For the KMT, the disastrous defeat in the 2020 general elections and Han's recall as Kaohsiung's mayor reflected the rejection of both the idea of unification and the specific "One Country, Two Systems" (OCTS) model under which Hong Kong is governed. However, the voters may not have completely turned away from KMT's policy to accommodate China in order to get Taiwan out of the high-income trap. As the opposition party, the KMT increased its representation in the legislature to 38 seats in 2020. Many KMT veterans believe that Beijing's pressure on Taiwan to accept unification as an eventual goal, and the economic benefits China is dangling in front of the Taiwanese, may eventually persuade them to recognise and accept the inevitable, if not enthusiastically embrace it as a brighter future for Taiwan. Furthermore, many KMT supporters believe the Trump Administration to be unreliable, just as previous U.S. administrations had betrayed Taiwan in the past for the sake of its relationship with China (Copper 2020). This may explain why there was a slight increase in support for unification in 2018, and why the KMT still enjoys solid support among some members of the older generations, especially when the DPP's long-term economic performance and its ability to manage cross-Strait relations remain in doubt.

Going forward, however, the KMT's challenge is not just to retain the support of the elderly, but also how to win over the younger generations. In a 2020 June poll by the Taiwan Public Opinion Foundation, not a single respondent in the age group of 20–24 supported the KMT (Chang 2020). The KMT has begun looking for a way to redefine the 1992 Consensus in order to appeal to young voters, while maintaining the reputation that it can guide with the economy better than the DPP (Drun 2020).

Meanwhile, the DPP will continue to be challenged by economic issues. Although it won in a landslide in 2020, promoting Taiwan's economic recovery from COVID-19 will be difficult. Ironically, Taiwan was shielded from the spread of the virus from China because of Beijing's punitive measures to restrict tourists to Taiwan. With hardly any Chinese tourists in 2020 and its early isolation policy, Taiwanese businesses could continue operating normally relative to other high-income economies undergoing quarantines and lockdowns. However, global demand for Taiwan's exports especially in technology has softened and the economy is projected to contract considerably. The recovery will be further complicated by an intensification of the competition between the United States and China and the decoupling of the supply chain. Thus, the KMT's solution to lean more heavily on China will continue to be relevant, but only if it can persuade voters that it can curry favour with Beijing without sacrificing Taiwan's security.

So the double bind – the choice between promoting the economy and preserving Taiwan's autonomy and identity – remains severe. It has been reflected in Han's meteoric rise and sudden fall, and in the alternating futures of the DPP and the KMT in Taiwanese politics. Even though the pendulum has swung much more in favour of safeguarding Taiwan and its values, it will be challenging for the DPP to find new economic policies that can get Taiwan out of the high-income trap. Taiwanese voters, especially younger ones, care about both sound policy design and effective implementation and can change their minds quickly to enforce accountability. Leaders will face an uphill battle to show that they understand the high-income trap issues and can find novel solutions to address them that will also preserve Taiwanese values and identity.

## Xi Jinping's carrot and sticks policy and Taiwan's response

For Beijing, pressuring countries such as South Korea and Australia economically, including reducing tourism, trade, and educational exchanges instead of relying only on diplomacy to show its displeasure on bilateral issues, is expected, but unification with Taiwan is a far more important core interest that demands bigger sticks and sweeter carrots. In the hope of winning the hearts of the Taiwanese people, Beijing has tried to offer positive incentives to selected sectors of Taiwanese society as part of Xi's carrot-and-stick approach to Taiwan. Beijing continues to believe that expanding cross-Strait economic relations can help restore a Chinese identity and renew interest in unification. Towards this end, Beijing is willing both to invest generously and to use hardline measures even if confronted with international pressure. In 2018, Beijing announced the '31 Preferential Measures for Taiwanese Compatriots,' which provided a variety of commercial, educational, and employment opportunities to young people, businesses, and professionals. National treatment in terms of medical, education, and pension benefits has been extended to Taiwanese and Hong Kong compatriots who have chosen to work on the mainland (Huang 2018). Before the 2020 general elections, Beijing doubled down by adding '26 Preferential Measures for Taiwanese Compatriots,' which allowed Taiwanese companies to participate in infrastructure projects and investments in China. During the pandemic, another '11 incentives' were provided to *Taishang* to help alleviate difficulties created by COVID-19 and to include them as beneficiaries in China's stimulus plans. In addition to the central government's incentive schemes, local governments at all levels initiated an even wider range of policies to benefit Taiwanese.

After the KMT's 2018 election victory, economic rewards such as large import orders for agricultural products were offered to cities that had thrown out the DPP and installed new KMT leaders (Maxon 2018). With attractive offers from Chinese institutions for Taiwanese, there is now a visible brain drain from Taiwan to China among professionals and young graduates who are having a hard time finding suitable employment in Taiwan. By providing those material benefits, the aim was to encourage individuals and businesses to support the KMT and against the DPP in order to shore up support for unification.

But overall, Beijing's strategy tilted more towards sticks rather than carrots. As China's military and economic power continues to rise, the resolution of the Taiwan issue on Beijing's terms has emerged as a top priority and an integral part of Xi Jinping's 'Chinese Dream.' At the 19th Party Congress in 2017, Xi again emphasised Beijing's insistence on unification and its strong opposition to Taiwan independence (Xi 2017). In 2018, as the constitutional term limits on the state presidency were lifted and Xi became the country's long-term leader, he reiterated that unification with Taiwan was essential to the 'rejuvenation of the Chinese nation' (Xi 2018). Emboldened by KMT's victory in 2018, Xi further demanded that the 1992 Consensus and the 'One China' principle must be the pre-condition for restoring cross-Strait relations. Tsai tried to mollify Beijing's demands by stating that she would honour the Republic of China's constitution and be guided by the 'Act Governing Relations between the Peoples of the Taiwan Area and the Mainland Area,' both of which imply that Taiwan and the mainland are part of the same political entity, but without saying so directly.

In January 2019, dissatisfied with Tsai's guarded response, a confident Xi stepped up the pressure and urged the people of Taiwan to circumvent their own government and work directly for unification under both the 1992 Consensus and the OCTS framework (Xi 2019). In doing so, however, Xi demanded unification on terms most Taiwanese found unacceptable and, while stating a preference for peaceful unification, again threatened the use of force if the issue were not resolved by an as yet unspecified deadline, but most likely during his term in office. Xi's assertive approach gave Tsai an unexpected opportunity to demonstrate her resolve to defend Taiwan's autonomy and its way of life. Tsai had resigned from the DPP chairmanship to take responsibility for the party's crushing defeat in the 2018 local elections and was facing increasing pressure in her party not to run for re-election in 2020. But after she forcefully rejected Xi's speech, declaring that Taiwan would never accept OCTS and emphasising that 'democratic values are the values and way of life that Taiwanese cherish,' her popularity rebounded dramatically throughout 2019 (Lin 2019b).

Beginning in June 2019, Hong Kong's mass protests against a controversial extradition law, involving a record number of two million people at one point, only reinforced the view that OCTS is a failure in Hong Kong and is unacceptable to Taiwan. The proposed bill would have facilitated sending accused people from Hong Kong to China to be tried in the Chinese legal system. The fate of the proposed law was seen as an important bellwether of whether China would keep its promise to grant Hong Kong a high degree of autonomy and to tolerate freedom of speech and press (Cheung 2019). Even after Hong Kong's Chief Executive Carrie Lam withdrew the bill in October, the protests did not stop, and there were also international reverberations highlighted by the United States adopting the 'Hong Kong Human Rights and Democracy Act.' The Taiwanese expectation of the worst in Hong Kong was coming true (Mazza 2020). Moreover, the perceived parallels between Hong Kong and Taiwan were growing, with many Taiwanese fearing that 'today's Hong Kong is tomorrow's Taiwan' (Green and Medeiros 2020). This has further boosted Tsai's popularity and made the acceptance of OCTS even more unlikely. Any economic solution to Taiwan's high-income trap that gives a central role to China has therefore become even harder to sell politically.

Furthermore, as the rivalry between the United States and China intensifies, Beijing appears to be more focused on pressuring Taiwan at all costs, perhaps because it believes time is no longer on its side especially in the weeks leading up to Taiwan's 2020 elections. Specifically, Beijing is accelerating its military investments to gain superiority in the Taiwan Strait (Work and Grant 2019). The PLA was consistently conducting drills and exercises near Taiwan, with the *Liaoning* aircraft carrier passing through the Taiwan Strait, ships frequently circumnavigating Taiwan, and aircraft even entering Taiwan's air defence identification zone (Yu and Yeh 2020). Diplomatically, Beijing lured the Solomon Islands and Kiribati to recognise Beijing and cut off ties with Taipei in the fall of 2019. Economically, Beijing further barred individual tourists from 47 cities from going to Taiwan, after first restricting group tourists. For Taiwan to navigate between the two superpowers and continue to engage with China economically while ensuring that the United

States continues to act as Taiwan's security guarantor had become increasingly difficult.

During the COVID-19 pandemic, Beijing has shown how it would only take the opportunity to make Taiwan's position untenable rather than extend an olive branch during a humanitarian crisis. Without any help from China or the WHO, the DPP administration's handling of the pandemic has won praise all around the world. But China then placed more pressure on the World Health Organization to refuse Taiwan's participation even as an observer during this crisis (Rowen 2020). In addition to leveraging hard and sticky power, Beijing has used its sharp power to influence and undermine Taiwan's democratic process through subversive policies. China has been identified to have used social media to influence the outcome of the 2018 local elections, as well as paid media outlets to continue to infiltrate Taiwanese society in the run-up to the 2020 general elections (Schmitt and Mazza 2019). However, the disinformation campaign ironically galvanised the Taiwanese people to combat disinformation and uphold freedom of speech.

Overall, the contradiction between Beijing's positive and negative incentives and the selective nature of the carrots being offered by Beijing and the risks they pose to Taiwan's security have not had the impact on Taiwanese public opinion that Beijing had hoped for. And Hong Kong's unrest has made Taiwanese even more concerned about Chinese influence and less attracted to the concept of unification than ever before. Beijing may eventually come to realise that Taiwanese are likely to continue to take the carrots without changing their minds about unification. This may exacerbate the trend for Beijing to focus more on the sticks and offer fewer carrots.

## Conclusion

In her second term, Tsai faced new challenges, such as the COVID-19 pandemic, which posed a serious test for all governments trying to navigate between the two superpowers. However, the challenge ahead in terms of reviving the economy may force Taiwan to accept more dependence on China for its future, especially if the United States like other industrialised economies suffers relatively more than China in the face of the pandemic. The outcome may be similar to how China played a more important role internationally after the global financial crisis of 2009 by assisting both Western and developing countries in their recovery (Breslin 2012). If China gains an advantage relative to the United States and Europe after the COVID-19 crisis, it could become more assertive in changing the international norms and marginalising Taiwan. Many pundits see Tsai and the DPP as playing with fire by leaning excessively on the United States given how inconsistent Donald Trump's policies towards China have been. The implications for Taiwan of any missteps in this regard will be severe.

Cross-Strait relations have always played a greater role in presidential contests than in local elections, but discussions of the issue will remain within the new context of finding the most effective way of escaping the high-income trap while preserving the autonomy that the overwhelming majority of Taiwanese want. Taiwanese voters' main concern is to find a way out of Taiwan's high-income trap without diluting their identity and fundamental values, including democracy, political autonomy, social justice, and environmental sustainability. The salience of identity, however, has increased dramatically as Beijing intensifies pressure on unification. It has become *de rigueur* for leaders to stand firm against Chinese intimidation in 2020. Such a development will put more obstacles to further economic integration with China, even if that should be a critically important strategy for escaping the high-income trap especially in the wake of the pandemic.

The double bind makes it difficult for any leader to find solutions to Taiwan's high-income trap that can also maintain Taiwan's autonomy, safeguard its values, and defend Taiwan's distinctive identity. Indeed, all the solutions to the high-income trap involve trade-offs, and it will be difficult to reach an agreement on how to prioritise competing goals and reach agreement on the best policies to achieve them. Leaders will find it difficult to mitigate the losses suffered by specific groups in the process of rebalancing Taiwan's economy, protecting its environment, and restructuring Taiwan's society, even though economic reforms are urgently needed.

In the end, the high-income trap may not have solutions that are effective, let alone easy. It may be impossible for high-income economies to grow at a steady rate and achieve rising standards of living. Rapid growth may be impossible as citizens demand greater fairness and more environmental sustainability. Small trading countries like Taiwan also face the issue of continuing competition from seemingly inexhaustible sources of cheaper goods and services, especially from a trading partner like China that is a strategic threat. With fewer resources than in the past, countries like Taiwan will find it extraordinarily difficult to adapt to slower growth and re-prioritise economic goals according to the demands of younger generations.

## Notes

1 World Bank resets the threshold for 'high-income economies' each year based on gross national income, which is $12,376 or more in 2020.
2 Most high-income economies are democracies. For a discussion of the correlation and how economic development is conducive to democracy, see Inglehart and Welzel, 2009. For Taiwan, most academic theories do not sufficiently show whether there is causality or correlation; see Wu, 2020.
3 The 13 economies are Equatorial Guinea, Greece, Hong Kong, Ireland, Israel, Japan, Mauritius, Portugal, Puerto Rico, the Republic of Korea, Singapore, Spain, and Taiwan.
4 Argentina has reached the high-income status twice but remains in the middle-income status.
5 Compare this with IMF's 2020 forecast for South Korea at −1.2%, Singapore −3.5%, Hong Kong −4.8%, and Japan −5.2%. See World Economic Outlook Database (April 2020 Edition).

6 Such negative distributional consequences of globalisation on high-income economies can be seen in the United States where wages have stagnated since 2000.

7 'Autonomy' here includes categories 'Maintain status quo, decide at later date,' 'Maintain status quo indefinitely,' 'Maintain status, quo, move toward independence,' and 'Independence as soon as possible.'

8 Another 27.5% of the respondents identify themselves as 'both Taiwanese and Chinese.' See ESC 2020.

9 For example, 80% of young people support same-sex marriage. See Jennings (2016).

10 China has convinced seven countries to sever diplomatic ties with Taiwan since the DPP returned to power in 2016.

11 In 2019, 2.7 million Chinese tourists visited Taiwan, compared with 4.18 million in 2015, as per Tourism Statistics Database (2020).

12 Han's Chinese slogan was 'Export products, welcome people in, make Kaohsiung rich' (貨出得去、人進得來，高雄發大財).

## References

Axe, David. 2020. 'Here's How Taiwan Could Still Build Its Own Submarines,' *National Interest*, January 9, 2020, at https://nationalinterest.org/blog/buzz/heres-how-taiwan-could-still-build-its-own-submarines-112156.

Breslin, Shaun. 2012. 'Paradigm(s) Shifting? Responding to China's Response to the Global Financial Crisis.' In Wyn Grant and Graham K. Wilson (eds.), *The Consequences of the Global Financial Crisis: The Rhetoric of Reform and Regulation*. London: Oxford University Press, 226–246.

Bush, Richard C. 2014. 'Taiwan and the Trans-Pacific Partnership: The Political Dimension,' Brookings Institute, February 11, 2014, at https://www.brookings.edu/research/taiwan-and-the-trans-pacific-partnership-the-political-dimension/.

Central Bank of the Republic of China. 2019. 'Financial Stability Report No. 13,' May 2019, at https://www.cbc.gov.tw/en/cp-970-101274-78a63-2.html.

Chang, Huey-por. 2020. 'KMT Lacks Message Appealing to Young Voters,' *Taipei Times*, July 5, 2020, at https://www.taipeitimes.com/News/editorials/archives/2020/07/05/2003739368.

Chang, Hui-ching and Richard Holt. 2014. *Language, Politics and Identity in Taiwan: Naming China*. London: Routledge.

Chang, Jennifer I-wei. 2019. 'Implications of Taiwan's Demographic Decline,' *Global Taiwan Brief* 4, no. 20, at http://globaltaiwan.org/2019/10/vol-4-issue-20/.

Chang, Meg. 2016. 'A Necessary Reform,' *Taiwan Today*, September 1, 2016, at https://taiwantoday.tw/news.php?unit=29&post=102493&unitname=&postname=A-Necessary-Reform.

Chao, Li-yan, Su Mu-chun and Matthew Mazzetta. 2020. 'Taichung Government, Taipower Clash over Coal-Powered Generator,' *Focus Taiwan*, June 26, 2020, at https://focustaiwan.tw/society/202006260005.

Cheng, Yen-hsin Alice and Elke Loichinger. 2017. 'The Future Labor Force of an Aging Taiwan: The Importance of Education and Female Labor Supply.' *Population Research and Policy Review* 36, no. 3, 441–66.

Cheng, Yen-hsin Alice and Hsu Chen-hao. 2020. 'No More Babies without Help for Whom? Education, Division of Labor, and Fertility Intentions.' *Journal of Marriage and Family* 82, 1270–85.

Chi, Eunju and Hyeok Yong Kwon. 2012. 'Unequal New Democracies in East Asia: Rising Inequality and Government Responses in South Korea and Taiwan.' *Asian Survey* 52, no. 5, 900–23.

Chow, Jermyn. 2016. 'A Third of Taiwan's Adults Still Live with Mum and Dad,' *Strait Times*, September 13, 2016, at https://www.straitstimes.com/asia/east-asia/a-third-of-taiwans-adults-still-live-with-mum-and-dad.

Copper, John F. 2020. 'Taiwan's 2020 Presidential, Vice Presidential and Legislative Election: Testing Election Theories.' *East Asian Policy* 12, no. 2, 45–56.

Davis, Gerald F. and Kim Suntae. 2015. 'Financialization of the Economy.' *Annual Review of Sociology* 41, 203–21.

DGBAS. 2019. 'Report on the Survey of Family Income and Expenditure, 2018,' October 2019, at https://win.dgbas.gov.tw/fies/doc/result/107.pdf.

Drun, Jessica. 2020. 'Taiwan's Opposition Struggles to Shake Pro-China Image,' *Foreign Affairs*, March 11, 2020, at https://foreignpolicy.com/2020/03/11/taiwan-opposition-kuomintang-kmt-pro-china-1992-consensus/.

ESC. 2020. 'Trends of Core Political Attitudes (1992/06~2020/6),' Election Study Center (ESC), National Chengchi University, at https://esc.nccu.edu.tw/course/news.php?class=203.

Feigenbaum, Evan A. and Jeremy Smith. 2020. 'Taiwan Was Having a Terrific US-China War Until Coronavirus Arrived,' *National Interest*, April 28, 2020, at https://nationalinterest.org/blog/buzz/taiwan-was-having-terrific-us-china-trade-war-until-coronavirus-arrived-149101.

Freschi, Nicolas. 2018. 'Taiwan's Nuclear Dilemma,' *The Diplomat*, March 14, 2018, at https://thediplomat.com/2018/03/taiwans-nuclear-dilemma/.

Glaser, Bonnie S., Derek Mitchell, Scott Kennedy and Matthew P. Funaiole. 2018. 'The New Southbound Policy: Deepening Taiwan's Regional Integration,' Center for Strategic & International Studies, January 19, 2018, at https://www.csis.org/analysis/new-southbound-policy.

Green, Michael and Evan Medeiros. 2020. 'Is Taiwan the Next Hong Kong? Hioe, Brian. 2017. 'Tsai Administration's Planned Labor Reforms Disastrous,' *New Bloom Magazine*, November 8, 2017, at https://newbloommag.net/2017/11/08/tsai-labor-reforms-2017/.

Ho, Ming-sho. 2019. *Challenging Beijing's Mandate of Heaven: Taiwan's Sunflower Movement and Hong Kong's Umbrella Movement*. Philadelphia: Temple University Press.

Horton, Chris. 2018. 'Trade War Traps Taiwan between Two Superpowers,' *Nikkei Asian Review*, December 5, 2018, at https://asia.nikkei.com/Spotlight/Cover-Story/Trade-war-traps-Taiwan-between-two-superpowers.

Horton, Chris. 2019. 'Candidate Seeks Closer China Ties, Shaking Up Taiwan's Presidential Race,' *New York Times*, June 6, 2019, at https://www.nytimes.com/2019/06/06/world/asia/taiwan-han-president.html.

Huang, Kristin. 2018. 'Taiwanese Given 'Equal Status' on China's Mainland, but Is Beijing Just Trying to Buy Their Support?' *South China Morning Post*, March 1, 2018, at https://www.scmp.com/news/china/policies-politics/article/2135291/taiwanese-given-equal-status-chinas-mainland-beijing.

Huang, Li-hsuan, and Huang Hsin-yi. 2020. 'Real Wage Stagnancy: Evidence from Taiwan.' *The Singapore Economic Review* 65, no. 2, 485–506.

Huang, Hsin-po, Hung Chen-hung, Hsu Li-chuan and Jake Chung. 2020. 'Kaohsiung Voters Recall Han Kuo-yu,' *Taipei Times*, June 7, 2020, at https://www.taipeitimes.com/News/front/archives/2020/06/07/2003737773.

Ihara, Kensaku. 2020. 'Taiwan Tech Companies' Exit from China Fuels $25bn Investment Drive,' *Financial Times*, June 11, 2020, at https://www.ft.com/content/1389cc16-bf2f-4fcd-8976-86334fc506d4.

Inglehart, Ronald and Christian Welzel. 2009. 'How Development Leads to Democracy: What We Know about Modernization.' *Foreign Affairs* 88, no. 2, 33–48.

InvesTaiwan, Ministry of Economic Affairs, R. O. C. (Taiwan). 2020. 'Three Major Programs for Investing in Taiwan,' at https://investtaiwan.nat.gov.tw/showPagecht1135?lang=eng&search=1135&menuNum=58.

Jennings, Ralph. 2016. 'Taiwan Set to Legalize Same-Sex Marriages, a First in Asia,' Associated Press, November 11, 2016, at https://apnews.com/e9c5b9c82abe4bc987f820aa104f2893.

Lee, Zong-rong and Thung-hong Lin, eds. 2017. *Unfinished Miracle: Taiwan's Economy and Society in Transition*. Taipei: Academia Sinica, Institute of Sociology.

Liao, George. 2018. 'MOI: Taiwan Officially Becomes an Aged Society with People over 65 Years Old Breaking the 14-Percent Mark,' *Taiwan News*, 10 April 2018, at https://www.taiwannews.com.tw/en/news/3402395.

Lin, Ken-hou and Donald Tomaskovic-Devey. 2013. 'Financialization and U.S. Income Inequality, 1970–2008.' *American Journal of Sociology* 118, no. 5, 1284–329.

Lin, Liang-sheng and Jake Chung. 2018. 'Ma Backs "Consensus" to Mark Xi Meeting,' *Taipei Times*, November 8, 2018, at http://www.taipeitimes.com/News/taiwan/archives/2018/11/08/2003703822.

Lin, Syaru Shirley. 2013. 'Taiwan and the Advent of a Cross-Strait Financial Industry,' Paper prepared for the Conference on Taiwan Inclusive: Trends, Opportunities and Challenges, the Miller Center, University of Virginia, November 15–16, 2013, at http://www.shirleylin.net/publicationsblog/2016/7/22/taiwan-and-the-advent-of-a-cross-strait-financial-industry.

Lin, Syaru Shirley. 2016. *Taiwan's China Dilemma: Contested Identities and Multiple Interests in Taiwan's Cross-Strait Economic Policy*. Stanford: Stanford University Press.

Lin, Syaru Shirley. 2019a. 'Analyzing the Relationship between Identity and Democratization in Taiwan and Hong Kong in the Shadow of China,' *The ASAN Forum*, December 20, 2019, at http://www.theasanforum.org/analyzing-the-relationship-between-identity-and-democratization-in-taiwan-and-hong-kong-in-the-shadow-of-china/.

Lin, Syaru Shirley. 2019b. 'Xi Jinping's Taiwan Policy and Its Impact on Cross-Strait Relations,' *China Leadership Monitor*, June 1, 2019, at https://www.prcleader.org/lin.Liu, Da-Nien and Shih Hui-Tzu. 2013. 'The Transformation of Taiwan's Status within the Production and Supply Chain in Asia,' Brookings Institute, December 4, 2013, at https://www.brookings.edu/opinions/the-transformation-of-taiwans-status-within-the-production-and-supply-chain-in-asia/.

Liu Shih-chung. 2020. 'Taiwan Faces a Changed Economic Outlook in Asia Following COVID-19,' Brookings Institution, June 29, 2020, at https://www.brookings.edu/blog/order-from-chaos/2020/06/29/taiwan-faces-a-changed-economic-outlook-in-asia-following-covid-19/.

Cheung, Anthony B.L. 2019. 'What has gone wrong in Hong Kong?.' *Public Administration and Policy: An Asia-Pacific Journal* 22, no. 2. 93–96.

Loichinger, Elke and Yen-hsin Alice Cheng. 2018. 'Feminising the Workforce in Ageing East Asia? The Potential of Skilled Female Labour in Four Advanced Economies.' *Journal of Population Research* 35, no. 2, 187–215.

Lu, Chen-wei. 2018. 'For Taiwanese Youth, Does Studying in China Lead to Changes in Political Identity?' *The Taiwan Gazette*, September 11, 2018, at https://

www.taiwangazette.org/news/2018/10/5/for-taiwanese-students-does-studying-in-china-lead-to-changes-in-political-identity.

Manyika, James Jonathan Woetzel, Richard Dobbs, Jaana Remes, Eric Labaye, and Andrew Jordan. 2015. 'Can Long-term Global Growth Be Saved?' McKinsey Global Institute, January 2015, at https://www.mckinsey.com/featured-insights/employment-and-growth/can-long-term-global-growth-be-saved.

Marston, Hunter and Richard C. Bush. 2018. 'Taiwan's Engagement with Southeast Asia Is Making Progress under the New Southbound Policy,' Brookings Institution, July 30, 2018, at https://www.brookings.edu/opinions/taiwans-engagement-with-southeast-asia-is-making-progress-under-the-new-southbound-policy/.

Maxon, Ann. 2018. 'Beijing Likely to Target KMT-Held Areas: Academics,' *Taipei Times*, November 27, 2018, at http://www.taipeitimes.com/News/taiwan/archives/2018/11/27/2003705008.

Mazza, Michael. 2020. 'Why the Hong Kong National Security Law Matters for Taiwan,' American Enterprise Institute, July 15, 2020, at https://www.aei.org/articles/why-the-hong-kong-national-security-law-matters-for-taiwan/.

National Immigration Agency. 2018. 'Interview with Director-General Jeffrey Yang of the ROC Immigration Agency,' National Immigration Agency of the Ministry of the Interior, R. O. C. (Taiwan), January 31, 2018, at https://www.immigration.gov.tw/5385/7344/7350/8887/?alias=settledown.

Newsham, Grant. 2020. 'Taiwan's Tightwad Defense Spending an Expensive Risk,' *Asia Times*, July 17, 2020, at https://asiatimes.com/2020/07/taiwans-tightwad-defense-spending-a-rising-risk/.

Ostry, Jonathan David, Andrew Berg, and Charalambos G. Tsangarides. 2014. 'Redistribution, Inequality and Growth,' *IMF Staff Discussion Note*, no. 14/02, at https://www.imf.org/en/Publications/Staff-Discussion-Notes/Issues/2016/12/31/Redistribution-Inequality-and-Growth-41291.

Palley, Thomas. 2013. *Financialization*. London: Palgrave Macmillan.

Qi, Dongtao. 2017. 'Social Welfare Expansion and National Health Insurance in Taiwan.' In Dongtao Qi and Lijun Yang (eds.), *Social Development and Social Policy: International Experiences and China's Reform*. Singapore: World Scientific Publishing, 199–231.

Rowen, Ian. 2020. 'Crafting the Taiwan Model for COVID-19: An Exceptional State in Pandemic Territory,' *The Asia-Pacific Journal* 18, no. 14, at https://apjjf.org/2020/14/Rowen.html.

Schmitt, Gary and Michael Mazza. 2019. 'Blinding the Enemy: CCP Interference in Taiwan's Democracy,' Global Taiwan Institute, October 2019, http://globaltaiwan.org/wp-content/uploads/2019/10/GTI-CCP-Interference-Taiwan-Democracy-Oct-2019-final.pdf.

Scott, Dylan. 2020. 'Taiwan's Single-Payer Success Story — And Its Lessons for America,' *Vox*, January 13, 2020, at https://www.vox.com/health-care/2020/1/13/21028702/medicare-for-all-taiwan-health-insurance.

Shirakawa, Masaaki. 2019 "The Mirage of Interest Rate Normalization," *Nikkei Asian Review*, April 10, 2019, at https://asia.nikkei.com/Opinion/The-mirage-of-interest-rate-normalization.

Snyder, Nathan and Jeffrey Lien. 2018. 'Taiwan's Latest Labor Standards Act Amendments,' *Taiwan Business TOPICS*, March 6, 2018, at https://topics.amcham.com.tw/2018/03/taiwans-latest-labor-standards-act-amendments/.

Sullivan-Walker, Kate. 2020. 'The Semiconductor Industry Is Where Politics Gets Real for Taiwan,' Lowy Institute, July 9, 2020, at https://www.lowyinstitute.org/the-interpreter/semiconductor-industry-where-politics-gets-real-taiwan.

*Taiwan News*. 2019. 'Taiwan's Ban on American Beef, Pork a Trade Barrier: US Report,' March 30, 2019, at https://www.taiwannews.com.tw/en/news/3669693.

Taiwan Tourism Bureau. 2020. 'Tourism Statistics Database.' 2020, at https://stat.taiwan.net.tw/.

Tan, Huileng. 2020. 'Taiwan's Economy Has Held Up "Extremely Well" Despite the Coronavirus, Says Economist,' CNBC, June 29, 2020, at https://www.cnbc.com/2020/06/29/taiwans-economy-has-held-up-extremely-well-despite-the-coronavirus.html.

*The Economist*. 2004. 'Unnaturally Low,' October 2, 2004, at https://www.economist.com/special-report/2004/10/02/unnaturally-dlow?FEATURE_ARTICLES_V1=0.

*The Economist*. 2017. 'Taking on Taiwan's Ruinous and Partisan Pension System,' May 18, 2017, at https://www.economist.com/asia/2017/05/18/taking-on-taiwans-ruinous-and-partisan-pension-system.

United States Department of Defense. 2019. 'Indo-Pacific Strategy Report,' June 1, 2019, https://media.defense.gov/2019/Jul/01/2002152311/-1/-1/1/DEPARTMENT-OF-DEFENSE-INDO-PACIFIC-STRATEGY-REPORT-2019.PDF.

Work, Robert O. and Greg Grant. 2019. 'Beating the Americans at Their Own Game,' Center for a New American Security, June 6, 2019, at https://www.cnas.org/publications/reports/beating-the-americans-at-their-own-game.

World Economic Outlook Database (April 2020 Edition), at https://www.imf.org/external/pubs/ft/weo/2020/01/weodata/index.aspx.

Wu, Nai-teh (吳乃德). 2020, 《臺灣最好的時刻, 1977–1987: 民族記憶美麗島》, 台灣: 春山出版.

Xi, Jinping. 2017. 'Report at the 19th National Congress of the Communist Party of China,' full text available at *China Daily*, October 18, 2017, at http://www.chinadaily.com.cn/china/19thcpcnationalcongress/2017-11/04/content_34115212.htm.

Xi, Jinping. 2018. 'Speech Delivered by Xi Jinping at the First Session of the 13th NPC,' *China Daily*, March 21, 2018, at https://www.chinadailyhk.com/articles/184/187/127/1521628772832.html.

Xi, Jinping. 2019. 'Working Together to Realize Rejuvenation of the Chinese Nation and Advance China's Peaceful Reunification: Speech at the Meeting Marking the 40th Anniversary of the Issuance of the Message to Compatriots in Taiwan,' Taiwan Affairs Office of the State Council, the People's Republic of China, January 2, 2019, at http://www.gwytb.gov.cn/wyly/201904/t20190412_12155687.htm.

Yu, Matt and Joseph Yeh. 2020. 'Chinese Military Planes Enter Taiwan's ADIZ for 8th Time in June,' *Focus Taiwan*, June 22, 2020, at https://focustaiwan.tw/cross-strait/202006220018.

# 5 Why has Taiwan not attracted much investment from mainland China? Three explanations

*Jan Knoerich and Lee Chun-yi*

## 1 Introduction

The rapid international expansion of multinational enterprises (MNEs) from mainland China over the past decade is a remarkable story that has caught the attention of many.[1] Whereas not too long ago, in 2003, mainland Chinese outward foreign direct investment (FDI) stock was a mere US$33 billion, by 2018 the accumulated assets of Chinese multinationals abroad had reached a record breaking US$2 trillion – more than 60 times the 2003 figure. Annual outward FDI flows from mainland China during this period rose from US$2.9 billion to US$143 billion. In 2016, Chinese outward FDI flows even reached a record US$196 billion, before falling to lower levels in 2017 and 2018 (MOFCOM 2006, 2019). Mainland Chinese multinationals belonging to a large variety of industrial sectors are now active as investors in almost all countries and economies of the world (Knoerich 2015a).

Yet Taiwan has to date not received a substantial share of these investments. As the Republic of China (ROC) government statistics indicate in Table 5.1, the accumulated amount of mainland Chinese direct investment (MDI) permitted in Taiwan surpassed US$2 billion only in 2018, accounting for 3.4% of all FDI in Taiwan made since 2009. Statistics on actual capital flows provided by the Ministry of Commerce (MOFCOM) of the People's Republic of China (PRC) are even more conservative, estimating the stock of direct investment from mainland China received in Taiwan by 2018 to have been just US$1.35 billion, equivalent to approximately 0.07% of the total accumulated assets owned by mainland Chinese multinationals worldwide. This figure is similar to Chinese outward FDI in Kyrgyzstan (US$1.4 billion) or Mozambique (US$1.4 billion), but much less than to Cambodia (US$6 billion) or Mongolia (US$3.4 billion), for instance (MOFCOM 2019).

These low figures for MDI in Taiwan may come as a surprise to some, especially since a good many factors ought to make Taiwan an attractive destination for multinationals from the Chinese mainland. With a GDP per capita (purchasing power parity) of approximately US$50,000, Taiwan has joined the ranks of the world's most advanced economies in terms of wealth, and its population of 24 million consumers should be sufficiently large to offer an interesting market for mainland Chinese enterprises.[2]

Some industries on the island are high-tech and internationally leading. Taiwan is geographically, culturally, and ethnically close to mainland China, which should lower transaction costs in business activities across the Strait and thereby incentivize cross-Strait investment. Similar reasons had greatly facilitated investments by Taiwanese firms in the PRC since the 1980s (Naughton 1997; Rigger 2015), and in 2018 Taiwan still ranked third as a source of direct investments in mainland China, after Hong Kong and Singapore. In that year alone, Taiwanese firms invested US$5 billion in mainland China (MOFCOM 2018). The accumulated amount of Taiwanese direct investment in mainland China since 1991 reached 182 billion in 2018, which was 57% of all Taiwanese outward direct investment, according to Taiwanese investment approval records.[3] Why should we not expect direct investment flows nowadays to expand in the other direction with similar vigour, especially given the fact that mainland Chinese outward FDI is now on a par with foreign investment in the PRC (Knoerich and Miedtank 2018)?

It could be argued that Taiwan has lagged as an investment destination for mainland Chinese multinationals because of Taipei's prohibition, until 2009, of such investments for political reasons. However, a decade has passed since 30 June 2009, when Taiwan officially reversed this policy and began to welcome investments by mainland Chinese multinationals. Since then, both sides have engaged in unprecedented efforts of economic integration, strengthened through the conclusion of the Economic Cooperation Framework Agreement (ECFA) on 29 June 2010 and, most notably, the signing of a Cross-Strait Bilateral Investment Protection and Promotion Agreement (Cross-Strait BIA) on 9 August 2012. Such an investment agreement normally signifies commitment to the promotion of investment in both directions by the signatory parties. But while mainland Chinese outward FDI to other parts of the world has expanded at a rapid pace in the decade since 2009, MDI in Taiwan is still very modest and somewhat below expectations.

In this chapter, we explore three possible explanations for why the level of investments by mainland Chinese multinationals in Taiwan is still so modest. The first explanation is that official statistics still underreport the true level of investment from the mainland, either due to political sensitivity or because capital tends to flow via Hong Kong or other tax havens, thereby concealing the fact that the original source of the investment is mainland China. The second explanation we offer is that Taiwan, as a small island economy with no adjacent regional markets, or for other reasons, may not be – whether viewed from an economic or business perspective – an attractive investment destination for mainland Chinese multinationals. Third, we analyse how regulatory hurdles still hinder the expansion of mainland Chinese multinationals on the island, and how this links to the unique political and security dimensions that characterise the relationship between mainland China and Taiwan. In sum, while MDI offers economic opportunities for mainland Chinese companies and the Taiwanese economy, these are in many ways outweighed by economic and diplomatic challenges.

To judge the plausibility of each of these explanations, we draw on a variety of sources, including relevant statistics, accounts from specific cases of mainland investments in Taiwan, and official documents such as laws and regulations. We also draw on fieldwork interviews, undertaken from April 2014 until August 2015, with Chinese investors in Beijing, Shanghai, and Kunshan, and with consultants from a Taiwanese semi-official institute for the promotion of industrial development.[4]

## 2  Background: ECFA and the Cross-Strait BIA

Although restrictions on MDI in Taiwan began to loosen with the decision of 30 June 2009, a more significant milestone in the development of cross-Strait economic and political ties was the signing of the ECFA almost exactly a year later and its coming into effect on 12 September 2010 (BBC 2010). The ECFA not only reflected the political will of the Ma Ying-jeou government to improve relations with the mainland; it was also an attempt to save the Taiwanese economy from further decline in a post-2008 financial crisis era. There were expectations that signing the ECFA would yield strong economic benefits for Taiwan in terms of GDP growth and trade expansion. It promised to further strengthen the already intensive trade relations between Taiwan and mainland China, in which the former had become increasingly dependent on trade with the latter.

Discussions about concluding the ECFA commenced in late February 2009, one year after Ma Ying-jeou came to power. Although the ECFA negotiations resulted in some immediate concessions on reducing trade barriers between both sides, it should be understood as a framework within which more detailed agreements on more complex matters of economic cooperation were to be negotiated. These included matters concerning further liberalisation of trade in goods, a trade-in-services agreement, and investment across the Strait.

Bearing in mind the controversies currently surrounding negotiations of investment agreements in other parts of the world, Taiwan and mainland China were surprisingly quick in concluding one of their own. The apparent prioritisation of the Cross-Strait BIA can be explained by the strong demand among Taiwanese businesspeople for better protection of their numerous investments on the mainland. Less attention was given to the fact that, as a bilateral agreement, the Cross-Strait BIA would equally apply to mainland investments in Taiwan. In its information material, the ROC Ministry of Economic Affairs marketed the Cross-Strait BIA as an important tool to protect the investment rights and interests of Taiwanese companies on the mainland, but did not explicitly mention that it would provide the same for mainland Chinese investments in Taiwan (MOEA 2012). The preamble of the agreement was, however, very explicit in stating that its key objective was to 'promote mutual investments,' with the term 'investor' defined as a natural person or an enterprise of a party that makes an investment in 'the other party.'[5]

In most parts, the Cross-Strait BIA follows the typical format and content of an international investment treaty, of which more than 3,000 have been concluded globally. In accordance with standard practice, the Cross-Strait BIA incorporates provisions on fair and equitable treatment, full protection and security, national treatment, most-favoured nation (MFN) treatment, expropriation, transfer of funds, and dispute settlement. At the same time, the agreement – which also covers investments made via Hong Kong or off-shore financial centres (Article 1, paragraph 2, (1)-(2)) – is unique, since it does not constitute a 'treaty' between two states, but an 'agreement' be-tween two economic entities that enjoy *de facto* sovereignty over their in-ternal affairs. It therefore incorporates some unique features to address the specific context of this agreement.

The governments on both sides of the Taiwan Strait have pledged in the agreement to offer to investors from Taiwan and mainland China, respec-tively, treatment equivalent to that offered to domestic companies (but only once the investment is made: Article 3, paragraph 3) and third parties (includ-ing in relation to matters concerning the preparatory stages of an investment: Article 3, paragraph 4). Such post-establishment national treatment and pre-establishment MFN treatment provisions should serve to open the Taiwanese economy to investors from the mainland, offering them the same conditions as those enjoyed by Taiwanese companies themselves and investors from other parts of the world. Yet, there are several restrictions on the nature and pace of such investment liberalisation, which will be discussed in greater detail below.

The Cross-Strait BIA also regulates the settlement of disputes in a unique way. There is no explicit discussion of how disputes between mainland China and Taiwan as the parties to the agreement (so-called 'state-state dis-pute settlement' in international treaties) should be resolved. Instead, Ar-ticle 12 refers to the ECFA's own dispute settlement provision (Article 10 of the ECFA) for this purpose. Investors who find themselves in a dispute with a government can, among other options, refer the case to a specific 'Cross-Strait Investment Dispute Settlement Institution.' This is also dif-ferent from international treaties, in which investor-state dispute settlement clauses commonly allow cases to be referred to established international arbitration institutions, such as the International Centre for Settlement of Investment Disputes under the World Bank. Strong emphasis appears to rest on the use of alternatives to arbitration for the settlement of investment disputes (Joubin-Bret and Knoerich 2010), such as mediation (see the An-nex), instead of arbitration. In addition, a very unusual provision is Article 14 on the resolution of investment-related commercial disputes. While no such clause exists in international investment treaties, its purpose appears to have been to enhance the legal rights of Taiwanese investors on the main-land in commercial disputes with mainland Chinese companies.

*Table 5.1* ROC investment permits granted to
mainland Chinese, 2009–18 (US$ million)

| Year | Number of MDI projects | MDI | FDI inflows |
|------|------------------------|-----|-------------|
| 2009 | 23 | 37 | 4,798 |
| 2010 | 79 | 94 | 3,812 |
| 2011 | 105 | 52 | 4,955 |
| 2012 | 138 | 332 | 5,559 |
| 2013 | 138 | 349 | 4,933 |
| 2014 | 136 | 335 | 5,770 |
| 2015 | 170 | 244 | 4,797 |
| 2016 | 158 | 248 | 11,037 |
| 2017 | 140 | 266 | 7,513 |
| 2018 | 141 | 231 | 11,440 |
| Total | 1,228 | 2,188 | 64,614 |

Source: Ministry of Economic Affairs (Republic of China)
Investment Commission, Monthly Report (December 2018).

A final special feature of the agreement is the strong emphasis on security issues (Lo 2013). This includes both personal freedom and safety (Article 3, paragraph 2) as well as the 'essential security interests' of the parties concerned (Article 2, paragraph 4), reflecting both the need for Taiwanese investors on the mainland for enhanced personal security, and the desire of the Taiwanese government to be able to legislate in favour of its own security interests whenever this is seen to be necessary.

Given the importance of the Cross-Strait BIA for Taiwanese business interests on the mainland, and the emphasis on such interests in its actual provisions, it does not come as a surprise that no significant opposition formed to prevent it, despite controversies that surrounded ECFA from the moment when it was concluded. However, the next agreement on the agenda – the Cross-Strait Service Trade Agreement (CSSTA) – did encounter such difficulties. This agreement exacerbated concerns over ECFA that had been voiced in 2010 – that the ECFA would give mainland China too much access to the Taiwanese market, would threaten employment of industrial workers and those employed in agriculture, and would make Taiwan overly dependent on the mainland (Chou 2010: 11). Despite the growing opposition, the CSSTA was signed in Shanghai on 21 July 2013 by representatives of the Taiwanese Straits Exchange Foundation (SEF) and its mainland counterpart, the Association for Relations across the Taiwan Strait (ARATS). Under the agreement, mainland China was to open 80 sectors to Taiwanese investments, while in return Taiwan pledged to open 64 sectors to mainland investment, including hotels, tourism, printing, and medical services (Rowen 2015: 6). Although it appears that the mainland made larger concessions in the negotiations of the CSSTA, scepticism about the CSSTA mounted when the Kuomintang (KMT) began its attempt to push the agreement, widely seen to have been negotiated in secrecy, through the parliamentary process without prior public consultations. Following the occupation of the assembly hall of the Legislative Yuan on 18 March 2014 by student protesters, which lasted for 24 days, and the strengthening of the 'Sunflower Movement' as a response to these concerns, the ratification of the CSSTA had to be suspended.

## 3 Explanation 1: errors in statistical reporting of cross-Strait investments

Estimates of cross-border investments in the Greater China region are prone to miscalculation and underreporting, which – beyond the generally questionable nature of all FDI data – has its origins in the political economy and geographic particularities of the region. Historically, sensitivities – especially in Taiwan – about the issue of facilitating capital flows across the Taiwan Strait have minimised or even prevented the direct flow of investment between the two sides. With MDI in Taiwan officially prohibited until 2009, statistics on investments from the mainland were inevitably close to zero up to that point, after which approvals of MDI gradually increased (see Table 5.1). Yet this does not mean that there were no companies from the mainland operating in Taiwan prior to 2009. One account suggests that before 2009, Taiwan received at least US$170 million worth of investments from the mainland, counting only investments by non-state–owned firms made after 1997 (Brown, Hempson-Jones and Pennisi 2010). Another source estimates the amount of mainland investment in Taiwan until the early 2000s to have totalled 'billions of Taiwanese dollars' (Cheng and Mo 2008: 107). There were special cases like Lenovo, which obtained approval from the Ministry of Economic Affairs of Taiwan to keep IBM's personal computer operations in Taiwan when it acquired IBM's PC business in 2005 (Cheng and Mo 2008: 106). Another account suggests that, as of 2010, 20 cross-border Mergers and Acquisitions (M&As) had been made by mainland Chinese firms in Taiwan (Yang 2014). Nevertheless, such cases are likely to have been exceptional.

Probably quite common has been the circumvention of existing restrictions by investing via holding companies in Hong Kong, offshore financial centres, or even third countries. Such trans-shipping investments help conceal that the original source of investment is the mainland. However, to extract any insights on FDI trans-shipped through offshore financial centres from available statistics is notoriously difficult. Data for 2018 show that around 56% of mainland Chinese outward FDI – US$1.1 trillion in outward FDI stock – was destined for Hong Kong, while approximately another 20% went to offshore financial centres, with US$398 billion having targeted the British Virgin Islands, the Cayman Islands, and the Bermuda Islands (MOFCOM 2019). While there is general agreement that a substantial part of these funds does not remain in these tax havens, there are no data specifying the ultimate destinations of these investments. Round-tripping has been very common, with mainland Chinese capital in Hong Kong and offshore financial centres being re-invested in the PRC to take advantage of tax incentives and other benefits offered exclusively to foreign investors there. Most inward FDI in mainland China comes from Hong Kong. One can only speculate about any other destinations for trans-shipped FDI originating from mainland China, and Taiwan could be one of them. As shown in Figure 5.1, Taiwan has received considerable amounts of investments from Hong Kong and the British Overseas Territories in the Caribbean. But compared to the huge amount of outward FDI from mainland China going to offshore tax havens, statistics on investments entering Taiwan from these economies appear to be more modest – a few hundred million US dollars from Hong Kong each year, and a little more than one billion US dollars annually from other offshore financial centres. It is impossible to say what proportion of these funds originates from mainland China, but it is unlikely to be all of it.

Thus, while statistical underreporting of cross-Strait investments has occurred over the years, and despite several companies from mainland China having used various means to dodge barriers to investment in Taiwan, the magnitude of unaccounted investments is unlikely to be sufficiently large to invalidate our observation that MDI in Taiwan has been low. At the very least, available evidence is simply insufficient to uphold such a claim. If we assume that at least some proportion of MDI that would previously have used obscure channels to enter Taiwan has been shifting to officially sanctioned forms of entry since 2009, then we might expect the magnitudes of previous underreporting to be revealed, at least partially, in official statistics on mainland investments entering Taiwan after 2009. Yet as we have demonstrated in Table 5.1, these are very low, giving no reason to believe

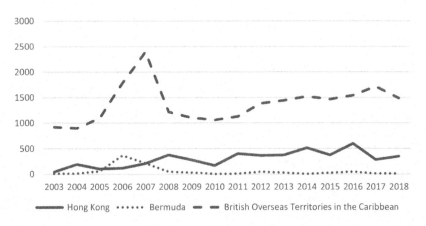

*Figure 5.1* Investment in Taiwan from Hong Kong and offshore financial centres, 2003–18.

Source: Ministry of Economic Affairs (Republic of China) Investment Commission, Monthly Report (December 2018).

that underreported MDI from mainland China has ever reached a significant magnitude. Similarly, we would expect a larger amount of investments to have used the direct route from mainland China to Taiwan in more recent years, and a smaller amount to have been undertaken via tax havens. Since no changes of note after 2009 in FDI into Taiwan from Hong Kong and offshore financial centres appear in Figure 5.1, we conclude that the use of these channels by mainland Chinese firms to invest in Taiwan has never been widespread. In sum, there are likely to be other explanations for the low amount of MDI in Taiwan beyond statistical underreporting. To these we turn in the next two sections.

## 4 Explanation 2: Taiwan is not an attractive investment location for mainland firms

In FDI theory, firms invest overseas for four distinct reasons: to seek foreign markets, to seek (natural) resources, to seek efficiency (especially cost reduction), and to seek strategic assets, such as various kinds of know-how and firm-specific capabilities (Dunning and Lundan 2008: 325). In this section, we review to what extent these economic determinants of FDI have encouraged mainland Chinese firms to expand their operations to Taiwan.

Studies and surveys of mainland Chinese outward FDI have found market-seeking to be the predominant motivation for mainland Chinese firms to invest overseas (Knoerich 2015a). It is quite common for such investments to be made in more advanced economies than that of China, where the world's largest markets exist. With a GDP of almost US$600 billion in 2018, Taiwan ranks among the top 25 largest economies in the world, and its high GDP per capita points to a high degree of affluence among consumers. Given the cultural similarities across the Strait, Taiwanese consumers should be particularly attractive to mainland firms, being more likely to have tastes and preferences similar to those of mainlanders. With the wholesale and retail industry being the dominant sector of mainland Chinese investment in Taiwan (Knoerich 2015b: 103), gaining access to the Taiwanese market appears to be a motivation behind many mainland Chinese investments. For illustrative purposes, Table 5.2 provides a list of mainland Chinese companies that have undertaken investment in Taiwan since 2002. Market-seeking is likely to have been a motivation in a number of these investments.

Yet Taiwan may still be viewed as a small market, and it is an isolated market, with no opportunities for mainland Chinese firms to seek other nearby markets or serve third markets from within a customs union – behaviour that has, for instance, been observed for mainland Chinese FDI in member states of the European Union (Knoerich 2012). As a CEO from one of the mainland Chinese companies we interviewed stated: 'We didn't consider investing in Taiwan because Taiwan's domestic market is not big enough' (Interview K3). Taiwan's proximity to mainland China may, in

*Table 5.2* Examples of MDI in Taiwan

| Mainland Chinese firm | Taiwanese (target) firm | Year | Entry mode |
|---|---|---|---|
| Shenzhen Liande Automation Equipment | Huayang Precision Machinery | 2017–18 | Acquisition of 51% stake |
| Fenghua Advanced Technology | Viking Tech | 2016 | 40% acquisition via tender offer |
| Xiaomi | | 2015 | Stores |
| China Yingke Law Firm | | 2015 | Office |
| Auhua Clean Energy | Taiwan Ziolar Technology | 2014 | Acquisition |
| Bank of China | | 2012 | Branch office |
| Bank of Communications | | 2012 | Branch office |
| Sanan Optoelectronics Co. | Formosa Epitaxy | 2012 | Purchase of 20% stake |
| BCD Semiconductor Manufacturing Limited | Auramicro Corporation | 2011 | Acquisition |
| BOE Technology Group | Jean Co. Ltd | 2010 | Purchase of assets |
| China Southern Airlines | | 2009 | Branch office |
| Lenovo | IBM's operations in Taiwan | 2005 | Purchase |
| Tsingtao Brewery Group | San Yo Pharmaceutical Industrial Co. | 2002 | Joint venture |

Source: Knoerich (2015b), Li (2015), Xinhua (2017), Chung, Han and Huang (2015), Liande (2018).

many cases, still make it feasible to serve this market from the mainland without the need for an investment. Furthermore, our interviewees from mainland Chinese enterprises indicated that there would be no need to invest in Taiwan as a 'pre-test' for an eventual investment in American or European markets (Interviews K1 and K2). In sum, Taiwan is a potentially interesting destination for market-seeking investments from mainland China, although there is not always a convincing business case for making an investment in Taiwan.

The global quest for natural resources by state-owned enterprises (SOEs) from the PRC is among the most widely discussed aspects of mainland China's investments abroad. But Taiwan is hardly an attractive destination for such investments. Even though Taiwan does of course possess some natural resources, such as minerals, limited amounts of coal and natural gas, agricultural products, and aquatic products, as a small island, it does not offer scope for large-scale exploitation of natural resources. Moreover, any claims on offshore resources (potentially) available in the broader South China Sea would be contested by the mainland. Similarly, given Taiwan's relatively small size of approximately 36,000 km$^2$, it is less geographically attractive for large-scale infrastructure projects, which is another activity in which Chinese SOEs are involved in many other parts of the world, especially in the context of the Belt and Road Initiative.

Efficiency-seeking is not yet a major motivation for mainland Chinese investments, given mainland China's own pre-eminent role as the world's factory and a low-cost production location. Despite recent rises in labour costs, it remains more efficient to maintain production in mainland China rather than moving to somewhere like Taiwan, where production costs are much higher. If anything, countries like Cambodia or Bangladesh are becoming more attractive low-cost destinations for mainland Chinese outward FDI in order to overcome rapid cost increases in the mainland's coastal cities. However, labour costs in Taiwan are too high to compete in this area. To the contrary, during the past 30 years most of Taiwan's manufacturing industries have themselves formed industrial clusters in the coastal areas of mainland China to save costs, and Taiwanese firms are also increasingly investing in Southeast Asian countries for efficiency-seeking purposes.

A final motivation for mainland Chinese investment in Taiwan is the pursuit of strategic assets, such as technological know-how, managerial or marketing skills, brands, and other intangible capabilities. Some mainland Chinese firms are interested in penetrating Taiwan's leading high-technology industries in order to upgrade their own firm-specific capabilities, especially in areas where they are still deficient. In this context, cultural and linguistic commonalities might be important in facilitating relevant organisational learning processes. Some if not all of the acquisitions and purchases listed in Table 5.2 have been made – at least to some extent – with strategic asset-seeking objectives in mind. That mainland firms do invest in Taiwan to gain exposure to intangible assets was further confirmed by one of our interviewees at a mainland Chinese IT firm: 'Taiwan's service industry is much more advanced than in China. I think China already has the "hard-ware," but Taiwan's service attitude is the key point that I think makes it worthwhile for me to invest in Taiwan' (Interview SH1).

But the level of technology and the innovative capacity of Taiwanese firms still fall short of the world's leaders, and hence the 'learning space' for mainland Chinese companies may therefore be quite narrow. Science and technology hubs in other countries, such as California's Silicon Valley, may be better choices for mainland Chinese strategic asset-seeking investments. A CEO from a mainland Chinese IT company confirmed that 'although we have little cultural and language differences with Taiwanese firms, we didn't consider investing in Taiwan because … Taiwan's core technology is not that mature' (Interview K3). Another mainland Chinese interviewee expressed the same view more directly: 'To cooperate with Taiwanese factories has not been our main focus in the past ten years. The innovation capacity of Taiwanese factories has slowed down; therefore, we would prefer to work with German, Japanese or American companies' (Interview K4). Moreover, mainland China had already benefited since the 1980s from Taiwanese investors transferring skills and know-how to the mainland, reducing the additional gains to be made through MDI in Taiwan today.

The extent of the 'learning gap' is therefore an important consideration in the investment decisions of companies from mainland China. A narrow gap between the level of technology and innovation capacity at Taiwanese and mainland Chinese firms could be overcome by means other than strategic asset-seeking FDI, such as by head-hunting for key Taiwanese engineers or even hiring entire teams from the R&D departments of Taiwanese companies. Mainland Chinese companies may find these less costly alternatives sufficiently effective in providing the desired boost in organisational learning, especially in view of the economic, political, and social challenges and risks commonly associated with direct investment activities. Uncertainties about the general feasibility of strategic asset-seeking activities and the difficulties and risks of seeking such assets in a highly regulated environment such as Taiwan (see below) may make other avenues of organisational learning even more attractive.

For the past decade at least, competition for high-technology human capital in mainland China has been fierce, and mainland China offers increasingly attractive employment opportunities for highly skilled engineers from Taiwan. 'You can't blame those Taiwanese skilled engineers who came to the Chinese market. We offer a much wider career development vision and to be very realistic, the salary is much better than in Taiwan' (Interview B1), explained an interviewee from a mainland Chinese company. Another interviewee from the Industrial Technology Research Institute (ITRI) in Hsinchu, Taiwan made the following observation: 'We are quite powerless in preventing colleagues leaving for jobs in China, when they [the mainland Chinese companies] offer the same numerical salary, but in Chinese Renminbi. It is a real challenge to keep skilled human capital in Taiwan' (Interview H1). At the Hsinchu Science Park and the ITRI, a decline of human capital is observable, with higher salaries and better opportunities for promotion and career development attracting key talent to the mainland Chinese magnet across the Strait.

## 5  Explanation 3: regulatory hurdles in Taiwan

Since the policy shift in 2009, Taiwan has opened individual sectors step by step to investments from the mainland. On the face of it, liberalisation appears to have been decisive, with approximately 97% of manufacturing sectors and about 50% of services and public construction sectors now open to MDI, as shown in Table 5.3. However, restrictions on the degree of ownership and managerial control over a company in Taiwan often remain stringent, in some cases limiting participation to a mere 10% and requiring investors to disclose their business strategies. High-technology sectors such as telecommunications and networks, semiconductors, and machinery are particularly affected by such restrictions, and investments in sensitive sectors, such as

*Table 5.3* Liberalisation in Taiwan towards investment from the mainland since 2009

| Stage | Year | Total | Manufacturing | Services | Public (infrastructure) construction |
|-------|------|-------|---------------|----------|--------------------------------------|
| 1 | 2009[a] | 205 | 64 | 130 | 11 |
| 2 | 2011 | 42 | 25 (42%) | 8 (42%) | 9 (24%) |
| 3 | 2012 | 161 | 115 (97%) | 23 (51%) | 23 (51%) |

Source: Mainland Affairs Council, Republic of China (Taiwan), 2013; Taipei Times, 2012.
Note: Figures in parentheses indicate the percentage of the total sector opened by that time.
a   Initially, these were 192 categories in 2009; a further 12 were added in 2010 and another one category in early 2011

the media, continue to remain partially restricted or even fully prohibited. The Investment Commission of the Ministry of Economic Affairs has put in place strict investment screening and approval procedures, and several mainland Chinese investments have been blocked or have not gone forward as intended (Knoerich 2015b). In addition, Taiwanese regulations are very strict towards people from the mainland who want to visit Taiwan, let alone reside there (National Immigration Agency), providing an additional hurdle to mainland companies planning investments in Taiwan. Following the failure of the CSSTA and the election and subsequent re-election of Tsai Ing-wen from the Democratic Progressive Party (DPP), the prospects for relaxing investment restrictions, let alone further liberalisation, have moved into the distant future.

These restrictions on investments and investors from the mainland are discriminatory, since they do not apply equally to companies from other countries. The political sensitivities in the relationship between mainland China and Taiwan, and uncertainties about the security threat emanating from mainland Chinese investors, are the main reasons for this discriminatory approach. Not only are these investors from a country that threatens to invade Taiwan if it declares formal independence, but many of them are also SOEs with strong links to the government and privileged access to financing channels. The government of the PRC has launched a series of favourable policies and incentives to promote outward investment and especially projects conforming to the national and economic interests of China, which applies in the case of many strategic asset-seeking investments. While these concerns in Taiwan mirror anxieties over investments from the PRC in other countries, they are exacerbated by Taiwan's unique geopolitical status and the particular problems it faces in its relationship with mainland China. Some worry that enhanced economic and investment liberalisation across the Strait will increase Taiwan's dependence on the mainland and offer a stronger rationale for eventual unification. Large-scale capital investments from the mainland could increase mainland China's economic and political leverage and exert cultural and ideological influence on the island. High-tech investments could provide a platform for malicious activities, such as espionage or hacking, and there is concern that strategic asset-seeking investments might move valuable technology to the mainland and compromise Taiwan's technological edge over its main rival. It is not possible to rule out political motivations behind some mainland investments.

Taiwan has been able to uphold a discriminatory approach towards investments from mainland China despite being a member of the World Trade Organization (WTO) and having signed the Cross-Strait BIA which seeks to reduce investment restrictions. Mainland China considered negotiating within the WTO framework to be undesirable, since it would have elevated Taiwan to an equal player in international diplomacy. The Cross-Strait BIA, in turn, left a variety of loopholes on the degree and pace of investment liberalisation. More specifically, Article 3, paragraph 5 of the agreement, states that existing laws and regulations which do not conform with the principles of national and MFN treatment can be maintained, offering the Taiwanese government a lot of flexibility on the pace with which it reduces its existing restrictions on mainland Chinese investments. National treatment applies only at the post-establishment phase, providing Taiwanese authorities with leverage when reviewing newly proposed investments by mainland Chinese companies prior to granting official approval. Article 5 does require the gradual reduction of restrictions on the basis of 'reciprocity and mutual benefit,' yet there is no specified timeframe. Given the still largely one-directional nature of direct investment flows across the Strait, primarily involving Taiwanese investors on the mainland, and the fact that mainland China has already welcomed Taiwanese investments through a more open legal framework, this was a concession made to Taiwan in the agreement.

Taiwanese authorities have used the scope for discriminatory treatment towards mainland investments, screening and monitoring them more thoroughly than investments from other economies and applying stricter approval procedures to MDI, involving the Mainland Affairs Council and potentially other ministries in the assessment of investment projects. The system is especially rigid towards larger investments from the mainland, whereas approval of smaller investments, such as the establishment of representative offices to promote Taiwanese exports to the mainland, is relatively easy to obtain. Yet the only way in which to genuinely overcome these additional barriers towards MDI is by investing via an offshore financial centre, as discussed in Section 3.

Policies regulating foreign investment play an important part in a company's decision to invest in a particular location. Our interviews confirm that the numerous restrictions still in place on Taiwan, and the limited prospects for improvement following the Sunflower Movement, have minimised the extent to which mainland Chinese firms have been willing or able to make investments on the island. For some interviewees, the policy uncertainty and lack of guarantees about the stability of the investment environment became major issues of concern following the Sunflower Movement (Interviews SH1, K1, and K2). One mainland Chinese investor made further remarks about the difficulties of investing in Taiwan:

I can only get a 15-day visitor's visa each time. This is extremely difficult for me as an investor in Taiwan. Fifteen days is a very short period for me to go through every small detail of my business in Taiwan. From last April [2013] until now [April 2014], I have been to Taiwan at least seven times. If my company only had me as the CEO to set up the company, it would be very troublesome, because I can only stay in Taiwan for 15 days each time I visit – that is a very limited timeframe to set up a business in any given country.

Interview SH1

The case of Tsinghua Unigroup is an illustrative example of the difficulties faced by mainland Chinese investors in Taiwan, especially when strategic assets are being sought in industries of strategic importance. Towards the end of 2015, Tsinghua Unigroup – a mainland Chinese chipmaker – unveiled its plans to purchase stakes of 25% in two Taiwanese chip testing companies, Siliconware Precision Industries Co. (SPIL) and ChipMOS Technologies Inc. As part of the SPIL deal, Unigroup pledged adherence to Taiwanese regulations on investment from the mainland by producing an industry co-operation plan and declaring its intention not to gain control over SPIL. Tangible benefits to SPIL were also expected in terms of better access to the mainland's increasingly important semiconductor market (Culpan and Browning 2015). But despite such assurances by the mainland side and potential benefits for the Taiwanese counterpart, the deal has been viewed by the government as a national security issue, not least because the semiconductor industry is a sensitive sector in Taiwan with a key role in assuring its industrial competitiveness (Chao 2015). As a result of these complications, both deals were eventually withdrawn within the year after their announcement (Wu 2017). As for the possibility that the Taiwanese government might prevent such investments, the CEO of Unigroup, Mr Zhao Weiguo, referred in an interview to the option of head-hunting human capital from Taiwan as a viable alternative (Huang, Chen and He 2015). This comment echoes the views of our own interviewees. It leads us to speculate that readier acceptance of mainland investments in Taiwan might facilitate the retention of Taiwanese human capital on the island and thereby minimise some of the emigration of talent to the mainland.

## 6 Conclusions

This chapter has sought to explain why investments made by mainland Chinese companies on Taiwan have been so limited. The US$2.2 billion in investment stock received by Taiwan by the end of 2018 is modest in comparison to mainland China's overall overseas financing capacity, and unexpected in view of Taiwan's geographical and cultural proximity to the mainland. Taiwan's policy shift to open its economy to mainland investors in 2009 and the conclusion of a bilateral investment agreement between both sides a few years later should have further promoted and facilitated the expansion of mainland Chinese companies into Taiwan.

In this chapter, we have identified three distinct explanations for the modest and unexpectedly low amount of MDI in Taiwan. The first is that MDI is not fully reported by official statistics from which we have derived our figure of US$2.2 billion. Rather, investments might have either bypassed official statistical reporting, or been trans-shipped through Hong Kong or other offshore financial centres, in part to overcome the consistently rigid regulatory restrictions towards mainland investments. MDI in Taiwan is thus likely above officially reported levels. Nevertheless, no evidence has been found to suggest that such circumvention of formal channels has significantly distorted the reality of MDI in Taiwan offered by recorded statistical figures. Other 'real-world' explanations for the low amounts of mainland investments in Taiwan are likely to be more compelling.

Our second explanation refers to the business rationale for investing in Taiwan. Certainly, a large number of mainland Chinese companies do not even consider investing in Taiwan, simply because they operate in an industry or business activity – for example, natural resources or low-cost manufacturing – for which Taiwan does not offer any appropriate opportunities. In other areas, such as those where Taiwan offers a potential market or opportunities to seek strategic assets, there is often still no viable business case for an actual investment. For example, the Taiwanese market may simply be too small or may easily be directly served from the mainland. Luring Taiwanese talent to mainland China may be a more credible alternative to strategic asset-seeking activities.

Finally, the unfavourable and discriminatory treatment of MDI and the unpredictable policy environment related to such investments are further factors that have prevented mainland Chinese firms from investing in Taiwan. Policy uncertainty and associated risks have no doubt deterred some mainland Chinese investors who might have otherwise seriously considered making an investment. Other firms have made concrete attempts to invest but failed to receive timely approval by the Taiwanese government.

Figure 5.2 summarises our three explanations in graphical form. In terms of their relative importance, we believe the policy environment and investment restrictions to be the most serious factor limiting investments from the mainland. This is followed by the lack of a viable business case to make an investment, although we do believe that if Taiwan were to open up fully to MDI on a non-discriminatory basis, the magnitude of mainland investments in Taiwan would be more substantial. There are of course statistical anomalies, but these are unlikely to have led to significant distortions.

Looking ahead, the Taiwanese government is unlikely in the foreseeable future to loosen its firm grip over investment inflows coming from mainland China. In particular, after the election of Tsai Ing-wen of the DPP, the subsequent cooling of cross-Strait relations and communications, and Tsai's re-election in 2020, the prospects for further liberalisation of cross-Strait

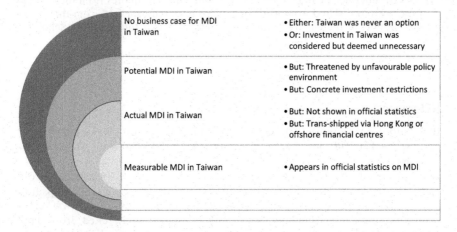

*Figure 5.2* Explanations for the modest amount of mainland investments in Taiwan.

*Appendix 5.1* Interviews conducted for this study

| Location | Date | Code |
| --- | --- | --- |
| Beijing | 6 December 2015 | B1 |
| Kunshan | 29 July 2015 | K1 |
| Kunshan | 29 July 2015 | K2 |
| Kunshan | 30 July 2015 | K3 |
| Kunshan | 3 August 2015 | K4 |
| Hsinchu | 7 July 2015 | H1 |
| Shanghai | 30 April 2014 | SH1 |
| Shanghai | 21 April 2014 | SH2 |

trade and investment look bleak. Meanwhile, mainland China has the option of exerting pressure on the Taiwanese government in relation to the commitments it made in the Cross-Strait BIA, although the effectiveness of such an approach remains questionable. In all likelihood, the pace of further genuine policy relaxation on investment matters will be very slow. As a result, we should expect MDI in Taiwan to remain subdued in the years to come.

## Notes

1 Within this chapter, the terms 'mainland China' and 'Taiwan' are used for the two entities on the two sides of the Taiwan Strait, for want of any other terminology acceptable by all the actors involved.
2 These statistics on Taiwan are from the CIA World Factbook.
3 See Table 10 in Mainland Affairs Council, Republic of China (Taiwan), Cross Strait Economic Statistics Monthly No. 310, Taiwan Institute of Economic Research.

4 A list of interviews can be found in the Appendix. The quotes from these interviews were translated from Mandarin. This research benefited from the generous support of the Chiang Ching-kuo Foundation for International Scholarly Exchange.
5 See Cross-Strait Bilateral Investment Protection and Promotion Agreement, Preamble and Article 1(2).

## References

BBC. 2010. 'Historic Taiwan-China Trade Deal Takes Effect', BBC News Asia-Pacific, 12 September 2010, http://www.bbc.co.uk/news/world-asia-pacific-11275274 (accessed 24 October 2015).

Brown, Kerry, Justin Hempson-Jones and Jessica Pennisi. 2010. 'Investment across the Taiwan Strait: How Taiwan's Relationship with China Affects Its Position in the Global Economy', Chatham House, November 2010, http://www.kerry-brown.co.uk/files/website-8.pdf (accessed 3 August 2014); cited from Jane Macartney, 'Taiwan Opens Up to Mainland Chinese Investors', *The Times*, 1 May 2009.

Chao, Stephanie. 2015. 'Tsinghua Investment a Security Issue: Cabinet', *The China Post*, 16 December 2015, http://www.chinapost.com.tw/taiwan/national/national-news/2015/12/16/453616/p1/Tsinghua-investment.htm (accessed 12 January 2016).

Cheng, Joseph Y. S. and Shixiang Mo. 2008. 'The Entry of Mainland Chinese Investment into Taiwan: Considerations and Measures Adopted by the Taiwan Government', *China Information*, Vol. 22, No. 91, 103–7.

Chou, Chi-an. 2010. 'A Two-Edged Sword: The Economic Cooperation Framework Arrangement between the Republic of China and the People's Republic of China', *Brigham Young University International Law and Management Review*, Vol. 6, No. 2, 1–20

Chung, Jalen, Ting-ting Han and Frances Huang. 2015. 'China Firm Seeking to Acquire Stake in Taiwan's Viking Tech', *Focus Taiwan*, 23 September 2015. http://focustaiwan.tw/news/aall/201509230030.aspx (accessed 18 February 2019).

CIA World Factbook, https://www.cia.gov/library/publications/the-world-factbook/geos/tw.html (accessed 21 December 2018).

Culpan, Tim and Jonathan Browning. 2015. 'China's Tsinghua to Spend $2.1 Billion on Taiwan Chip Testers', *BloombergBusiness*, 11 December 2015. http://www.bloomberg.com/news/articles/2015-12-11/tsinghua-unigroup-to-buy-1-7-billion-stake-in-siliconware (accessed 14 February 2016).

Dunning, John H. and Sarianna M. Lundan. 2008. *Multinational Enterprises and the Global Economy*. Cheltenham: Edward Elgar.

Huang, Yijun, Liangrong Chen and Yunting He. 2015. 'If You Do Not Open Up for Mainland Chinese Investments, I Can Only Go to Taiwan to Grab Talent – An Interview with the CEO of Unigroup, Zhao Weiguo' [「你不對大陸開放投資, 我只能去台灣挖人」《天下》專訪紫光集團董事長趙偉國], *Tianxia Magazine*, 1 November 2015. http://www.cw.com.tw/article/article.action?id=5072030 (accessed 6 March 2016).

Joubin-Bret, Anna and Jan Knoerich. 2010. *Investor-State Disputes: Prevention and Alternatives to Arbitration.* UNCTAD Publication. New York and Geneva: United Nations.

Knoerich, Jan. 2012. 'The Rise of Chinese OFDI in Europe', in: Ilan Alon, Marc Fetscherin and Philippe Gugler (eds.), *Chinese International Investments*. Basingstoke: Palgrave MacMillan, 175–211.

Knoerich, Jan. 2015a. 'China's Outward Investment Surge', in: David A. Dyker (ed.), *World Scientific Reference on Globalisation in Eurasia and the Pacific Rim, Volume 1 – Foreign Investment.* Singapore: World Scientific Publishing, 273–97.

Knoerich, Jan. 2015b. 'The Role of High Technology in Mainland China's Outward Investment into Taiwan: Economic, Security and Cultural Dimensions', in: Paul Irwin Crookes and Jan Knoerich (eds.), *Cross-Taiwan Strait Relations in an Era of Technological Change: Security, Economic and Cultural Dimensions.* Basingstoke: Palgrave Macmillan, 96–117.

Knoerich, Jan and Tina Miedtank. 2018. 'The Idiosyncratic Nature of Chinese Foreign Direct Investment in Europe', *CESifo Forum*, Vol. 19, No. 4, 3–8.

Li, Shangjing. 2015. 'China's Yingke Opens in Taipei', *Asian Legal Business*, 28 January 2015. https://www.legalbusinessonline.com/news/china%E2%80%99s-yingke-opens-taipei/68013 (accessed 18 February 2019).

Liande Equipment. 2018. 'Announcement on the Issue of Foreign Investment Increase' [联得装备：关于对外投资增资事宜的公告], Sina.com.cn, 27 August 2018. http://vip.stock.finance.sina.com.cn/corp/view/vCB_AllBulletinDetail.php?stockid=300545&id=4696851 (accessed 18 February 2019).

Lo, Alex. 2013. 'The Investor-State Dispute Settlement Mechanism under the Cross-Strait Bilateral Investment Agreement to Address the Protection of Personal Freedom and Safety', *Contemporary Asia Arbitration Journal,* Vol. 6, No. 2, 275–98.

Mainland Affairs Council, Republic of China (Taiwan). 2013. 'Policy and Promotion Status on Allowing Mainland Investment in Taiwan', http://www.mac.gov.tw/ct.asp?xItem=104267&ctNode=5945&mp=3 (accessed 3 August 2014).

MOEA. 2012. 'Cross-Strait Bilateral Investment Protection and Promotion Agreement'. Department of Investment Services, Ministry of Economic Affairs, R.O.C.

MOFCOM. 2006. *2005 Statistical Bulletin of China's Outward Foreign Direct Investment.* Beijing: China Commerce and Trade Press.

MOFCOM. 2018. 'News Release of National Assimilation of FDI from January to December 2018.' http://www.fdi.gov.cn/1800000121_49_4859_0_7.html

MOFCOM. 2019. *2018 Statistical Bulletin of China's Outward Foreign Direct Investment.* Beijing: China Commerce and Trade Press.

National Immigration Agency Document No. QD0504. http://www.immigration.gov.tw/immigr-law/cp.jsp?displayLaw=true&lawId=8a8a99f139c407590139d224c5f40007 (accessed 14 February 2016).

Naughton, Barry. 1997. 'The Emergence of the China Circle', in: Barry Naughton (ed.), *The China Circle: Economics and Technology in the PRC, Taiwan, and Hong Kong.* Washington, DC: Brookings Institution Press, 3–37.

Rigger, Shelley. 2015. 'Taiwanese Business in Mainland China: From Domination to Marginalization?' in: Paul Irwin Crookes and Jan Knoerich (eds.), *Cross-Taiwan Strait Relations in an Era of Technological Change: Security, Economic and Cultural Dimensions.* Basingstoke: Palgrave Macmillan, 61–76.

Rowen, Ian. 2015. 'Inside Taiwan's Sunflower Movement: Twenty-Four Days in a Student-Occupied Parliament, and the Future of the Region', *The Journal of Asian Studies*, Vol. 74, No. 1, 5–21.

'Taiwan Readies for Third Wave of Chinese Investment', *Taipei Times*, 20 March 2012, http://www.taipeitimes.com/News/biz/archives/2012/03/20/2003528196 (accessed 13 February 2016).

Wu, J. R. 2017. 'Chinese Tech Giant's Taiwan Deals Unravel as Powertech Calls off Share Pact', *Reuters*, 13 January 2017, https://www.reuters.com/article/us-powertech-tech-tsinghua/chinese-tech-giants-taiwan-deals-unravel-as-powertech-calls-off-share-pact-idUSKBN14X1BA (accessed 18 February 2019).

'Xiaomi Opens Two More Offline Stores in Taiwan', *Xinhua*, 19 November 2017, http://www.xinhuanet.com//english/2017-11/19/c_136763836.htm (accessed 18 February 2019).

Yang, Monica. 2014. 'Cross-border Mergers and Acquisitions between China and Taiwan 1997–2010', in: Ming-Chin Monique Chu and Scott L. Kastner (eds.), *Globalization and Security Relations across the Taiwan Strait: In the Shadow of China*. Abingdon: Routledge, 118–34.

# 6 Review and look ahead

## Taiwan's New Southbound Policy in the case of Vietnam

*Lee Chun-yi*

## Introduction

Since the late 1980s, Taiwanese investment in Southeast Asian countries has increased significantly; according to Kung, Taiwanese businesses became one of the largest groups of investors in the region in the late 1980s and early 1990s (Kung, 2003: 146). The Taiwanese government officially initiated the 'Go South' policy in 1994, under President Lee Teng-hui, but companies had in fact begun investing in Southeast Asian countries in 1959, when a Taiwanese firm set up a cement factory in Malaysia (Chen, 1996: 454). The reason for the Taiwanese government's the 'Go South' policy initiative in 1994 was to balance the 'Go West' investment trend to China. However, the 1994 'Go South' policy was more of a government-led strategy, while the majority of Small and Medium Enterprises (SME) still went west because of the familiarity of language and culture, and, more importantly, the Chinese government's warmly welcoming policies in terms of tax benefits (Lee, 2012). Recent research by Yang and Hsiao (2016) also indicates that Taiwanese businesses in the Southeast Asian countries have contributed to the transnational network of profits, which in their analytical framework refers to the bilateral gains of Taiwanese businesses in Southeast Asian countries (Yang and Hsiao, 2016: 214). From Yang and Hsiao's perspective, even more important than the profits accruing from Taiwanese investment in Southeast Asia was the opportunity it offered to bring reciprocal investment and civil involvement by relevant Southeast Asian countries in Taiwan itself.

The Belt and Road Initiative (BRI) project initiated by China's President Xi Jinping was unveiled in October 2013. The aim of the BRI is to build networks of connectivity. The first step is to create the necessary infrastructure to facilitate trade: enormous financial input is required for this initial infrastructure construction. It has to be noted that the geographical connections of 'belt' and 'road' are manifold. There are two road routes, namely the 21st Century Maritime Silk Road and the Maritime Silk Road Continental extension; three main corridors embedded in the Silk Road Economic Belt, respectively, the Northern, Central, and Southern corridors; and two main railway routes, the Silk Road Rails and the Trans-Siberian Railway (Summers, 2016: 1631). In the maritime belt, China is heavily involved with

Southeast Asian countries' infrastructure investment, including bidding against Japan in order to gain the Singapore-Malaysia high-speed railway track construction contract. After Mahathir Mohamad was elected as Prime Minister in May 2018, the Malaysian government halted the construction of this high-speed railway with Singapore, although this was a postponement, not a cancellation (Jaipragas, 2018).

The rationale for this chapter's inclusion of research observations on both Taiwan's New Southbound Policy (NSP) and China's BRI is not for the purpose for comparison, but more with the intention of observing to what extent the BRI has impacted upon Taiwanese investors/businessmen in Southeast Asian countries, in the face of the overwhelming influence of China's rising economic strength in those countries, especially since 2013 under the flag of the BRI; conversely, I also try to explore whether existing Taiwanese investment has influenced Southeast Asian countries' receptivity to the Chinese government's proposed construction projects. Hsu (2017) has provided a comprehensive policy report on how Taiwan's NSP will meet China's BRI. At a macro-level, Hsu's report examines the trading volume between Taiwan and the main NSP targeted countries, including not only ASEAN member states but also India, New Zealand, and Australia. Her study offers a panoramic view of NSP and highlights the differences and/or competitive strengths between NSP and BRI. This chapter supplements Hsu's policy paper by providing an in-depth understanding of the situation in Vietnam, through interview data and secondary resources.

With regard to methodology, between March and June 2018 12 interviews were conducted in Vietnam. The selected interviewees include not only Taiwanese businessmen in Vietnam but also local Vietnamese officials who are responsible for encouraging foreign investment, who deal with both Taiwanese and Chinese investors. The first part of this chapter provides a brief history of Taiwanese investment in Southeast Asian countries (Chinese investment in the region is rather a latecomer compared to Taiwanese), comparing it with Taiwanese investment in China. This is followed by an analysis of the motivations for Taiwan's investment in Vietnam. The third section of this chapter explores the complications associated with playing the 'China card' in Southeast Asian countries (those countries seen here through the prism of Vietnam). The last two sections examine, respectively, the Southbound and New Southbound policies in Taiwan, and the potential impact of NSP in the face of the Chinese government's promotion of its Belt and Road Initiative (BRI) in the region.

In short, the aim of this chapter is to provide an initial and empirical understanding of Taiwan's NSP in Vietnam.

## Taiwanese investment in China and Southeast Asian countries

In the literature on Taiwanese investment abroad, a large part of existing findings has focused on Taiwanese investment in China. Alongside the traditional economic scholarly literature about trade and investment across the Strait and in Greater China (Ash and Kueh, 1993), scholars working on the cross-Strait relationship have begun to pay attention to the civic influence of Taiwanese businesses (Taishangs) on the cross-Strait relationship (Wu, 1997; Hsing, 1998; Cabestan, 2002; Tung, 2003). Some have emphasised the importance of sub-governmental interaction in the process of cross-Strait integration (Keng, 2007). Others assert that Taiwanese businesses have been able to exert their strength as economic leverage to constrain the Chinese government in its cross-Strait policy-making activities (Tung, 2003). Differing from Tung's research, Lee indicates that the interaction between Taiwanese businessmen and local Chinese governments has been influenced by both central and local Chinese governments' strategic interests. Thus, Taishangs in China have been more conditioned by the Chinese government, rather than vice versa (Lee, 2012). Though there are different viewpoints about the extent to which (if at all) Taiwanese businesses are able to constrain the Chinese government's decision-making, the role of Taiwanese businesses in the cross-Strait relationship, especially viewed from their political attitudes, has gradually attracted scholarly attention (Schubert, 2010). Recent research related to Taiwanese investment in China focuses on the changing identity and political thinking of Taishangs on the Chinese mainland (Keng and Schubert, 2011).

In comparison to this considerable corpus of literature, the literature about Taiwanese investment in Southeast Asia is somewhat smaller. Ku's seminal work (1995) on Taiwan's relationship with Southeast Asian countries was the first to provide an overview of Taiwan's political economic engagement with those countries. Chen's comparative framework applied useful quantitative data to compare Taiwanese investment in China and Southeast Asian countries, on the basis of which Vietnam emerged as the most popular country for Taiwanese investment in Southeast Asian countries (Chen, 1996: 456). However, Chen's research failed to explain *why* Vietnam should have been the most popular destination for Taiwanese investment compared with other Southeast Asian countries. Chan and Wang's work (2004/2005) on the working conditions of Taiwanese factories in China and Vietnam specifically compares Taiwanese investment in China and Vietnam. Though the analysis in this chapter does not cover the working conditions of Taiwanese factories, later in the analysis I offer some remarks about Taiwanese factories' management style which reflect Chan and Wang's work.

This brief literature review of Taiwanese investment in China and Southeast Asia highlights the small number of researchers who have conducted comparative research in this area. Furthermore, most of this research was conducted from the mid-1990s to the early 2000s: there is therefore a need for updated comparative research in this area, including in relation to the conceptual question of whether economic statecraft can be considered as the backbone of the Taiwanese government's NSP.

## Motivations for Taiwanese business to invest in Vietnam

In the late 1980s, few Taiwanese investors were active in Southeast Asian countries. Although Yang and Hsiao (2016) documented that Taiwanese businesses started to invest in Southeast Asian countries in the late 1980s, their number and investment scale were still quite modest. The reason for Taiwanese businesses to choose Vietnam, for instance, is partly cultural affinity. A Taiwanese businessman who owned a bicycle factory in Vietnam for more than two decades said: 'At least in Southeast Asian countries, the culture in Vietnam is closer to the Chinese culture; most of the workers eat rice and use chopsticks, they also have similar holidays as we do, for instance the Chinese New Year' (Interview V2). This interviewee's answer underlines the role of Vietnam as certainly the second best choice after China. Why is cultural affinity important for business practice? As the interviewee informed me: 'It is because of the annual leave that workers can take' (Interview V2). From a business perspective, if there are too many national holidays, as for instance in Muslim countries, it will slow down manufacturing factories' production. This is one of the issues that influence business owners, especially in labour-intensive manufacturing industries, in terms of choosing the most cost-effective location for investment. Two reasons contributed to the later arrival (post-2008) of Taiwanese businesses in Southeast Asian countries: the first was the realisation of the challenge of Chinese markets; the second related to the buyer and the market.

Most of the businessmen went first to China to investigate the market, then decided to start their business in either Vietnam or Malaysia. One of my interviewees in Ho Chi Minh City informed me:

> I have been to China in the early 90s, but I didn't like the Chinese government's attitudes towards us (Taiwanese people): we had to go through under the division of "Chinese citizen" at customs and it stated Taiwan is part of China on the entry card. I also didn't like local Chinese government's attitudes, they were very arrogant.
>
> (Interview V1)

Compared with China, the Vietnamese government treated Taiwanese businesses more as investors, rather than political agents. For Taiwanese businesses, there are pros and cons. If we examine the development of Taiwanese business associations (TBAs), we can see this more clearly. The development of TBAs in China is viewed as much more controversial in the eyes of local and central Chinese governments (Lee, 2014; Schubert et al., 2017), mainly because local Chinese governments initially regarded TBAs as potential anti-governmental agencies, organised by the Taiwanese government. By contrast, TBAs' development in Vietnam is much less controversial in the eyes of local government. However, since the TBAs were not seen as a potential agent to organise anti-government activity, as they were in China, they were not as valued as their counterparts in China. Here, attention from lo-cal governments is a double-edged sword. On the one hand, the TBAs were tightly scrutinised in China, to the extent that it became a normal practice in every case that the local Taiwanese Affairs Office (TAO) assigned a dele-gate to each TBA as its vice chairman. On the other hand, local TAOs also responded to TBAs' requests efficiently because they monitored all TBA activities.

Without the governments' political interest, the Taiwanese business asso-ciations in Vietnam are freer than their counterparts in China: there were no Vietnamese officials as vice chairmen in the TBAs. On the other hand, because they lacked this 'privilege' of being closely followed by the local officials, Taiwanese businesses in Vietnam have been more regulated, since they are treated as normal business people, rather than potential political agents. Another textile factory owner informed me: 'We have to pass all the environmental regulation checks, there are no convenient ways for us to pass the local officials' examinations' (Interview V3). This situation is dif-ferent from that of Taiwanese investors in China: since both local and cen-tral Chinese governments viewed Taiwanese investors as potential political agents, Taiwanese investors face more flexible business conditions in China compared with those in Vietnam in terms of all the investment barriers, in-cluding labour recruitment, environmental checks, and tax benefits.

Having said that, in Vietnam large group meetings still elicited local government's attention. 'Vietnamese local government would send someone to "supervise" our meetings' (comment by a Taiwanese consultant to the TBA in Ho Chi Minh City, V4). Not only do Taiwanese businesses not offer political added value to the Vietnamese government, but furthermore,

> It is difficult for us (Taiwanese businesses) to negotiate with the Viet-namese government because our government cannot offer the Viet-namese government any political bonus, the Vietnamese government doesn't even acknowledge the Taiwanese government ... There is no government-to-government level dialogue. Compared with Chinese in-vestors, their government is much stronger, which can open many "con-venient doors" for the Chinese investors.
>
> (Interview V5)

From this quote, we can see the difficult position of the Taiwanese govern-ment in relation to the conditions Taiwanese investors face in Vietnam. If Taiwanese investment in Vietnam (or elsewhere in the world) does not de-pend on Taiwan's official diplomatic relationship with the local government, it probably will be difficult for the Taiwanese government to use the busi-ness community to build a bridge between Taiwan and any Southeast Asian countries in diplomatic or semi-diplomatic terms.

A second reason for Taiwanese businesses to invest in Vietnam after 2008 relates to market forces and buyers' decision-making. After 2008, when China started to implement the New Labour Contract Law (Baker and McKenzie, 2013), labour costs started to increase quite substantially in China. For most Taiwanese businesses, which concentrated on labour-intensive manufacturing, this trend certainly threatened to erode their profits. The Chinese government also started to impose harsher environmental regulations; again, this increased investment costs for Taiwanese factories in China. However, statistical indicators (Taiwanese business net, 2018, in Chinese) do not show any increase in Taiwanese investment in Southeast Asian countries after 2008. One of my interviewees explained:

> in China, the industrial chain has already firmed up, therefore it is relatively difficult for those businesses who already invested in China to relocate to other countries. We moved to Vietnam because the whole production chain moved with us, although this is not so easy.
>
> Interview V3

The supply chain in fact is the main reason why, although investment conditions have become harsher in China, a relatively small number of Taiwanese businesses considered moving to other Southeast Asian countries. Taiwanese businesses in China either closed down or struggled on, making smaller profits but still staying; few of them considered relocating. Besides, Taiwanese businesses in Vietnam also pointed out: 'Those late comers in fact have not much profits to share, the long-standing ones are the businesses that arrived here [Ho Chi Minh city] before 2000' (Interview V3). However, after 2015, some more Taiwanese low-end manufacturing factories moved to Vietnam at the request of buyers. One of my interviewees informed me: 'We are one of the processing factories for an international textile brand, our brand company encouraged us to move to Vietnam in order to increase the prosperity of the local economy' (Interview T1). In short, relocating was motivated more by the brand companies' requests, based on their own strategic considerations, than by the business interests of Taiwanese investors themselves.

## The anti-Chinese riots in Vietnam

In 2014, in Ho Chi Minh City, some Taiwanese factories were burned down in anti-Chinese riots (*The Guardian*, 2014). The reasons for the anti-Chinese riots are complicated. On the surface it was because of competition over the South China Sea oil rigs; however, information from the interviewees suggests that other factors were at work. There are two reasons why most of the burnt-down factories were Taiwanese. First of all, in the eyes of Vietnamese, Taiwanese are the same as Chinese – or to be more precise, Taiwan is considered as a part of China (Interviews V3 and V5). From officials to general society, there is not seen to be much difference between Chinese and Taiwanese people. Therefore, anti-Chinese and anti-Taiwanese means essentially the same for Vietnamese workers. The second reason is that, as can be seen from the interviews with factory owners and employees, most Taiwanese factories hired Chinese rather than Taiwanese managers, so that the shop-floor Vietnamese workers dealt directly with Chinese managers instead of the Taiwanese owners. It was certainly these shop-floor workers, who were responsible for burning down those factories that were managed by Chinese. The reasons why Taiwanese factories in Vietnam prefer to hire Chinese managers lie mainly in wage costs and language skills. A Taiwanese factory owner informed me that 'the Chinese managers are much cheaper than Taiwanese employees, and Chinese managers are also much more dili-gent when it comes to learning the local language' (Interview V3). Chan and Wang's paper claims that the management methods in Taiwanese factories were much harsher in China than in Vietnam (Chan and Wang, 2004/2005: 632). Nevertheless, my own fieldwork suggests that Taiwanese factories' management style in Vietnam is similar to their counterparts in China: the upper management level failed to engage with local Vietnamese communi-ties. Many Taiwanese businessmen among those who came to Vietnam in the first wave still do not speak Vietnamese.

It is difficult to say whether the misunderstanding and/or hatred between Vietnamese workers and Taiwanese investors in 2014 has been resolved. The launch of the NSP came only two years afterwards, and it can be argued that the 2014 incident in Vietnam established an unfortunate starting point for the new policy.

## The Southbound Policy and New Southbound Policy

From Taiwan's perspective, exploring links with Southeast Asian coun-tries was first promoted in the mid-1990s by then President Lee Teng-hui. The purpose of directing Taiwanese economic links to this region was to avoid the huge and increasing volume of investment going west, to China, where it was in danger of being over-committed. Apart from the heavy investment bias towards China, the Taiwanese government also worried that such high economic dependency would hollow out Taiwan's economy and therefore incurred security risks. In 1998, the value of Taiwan's indi-rect investment in mainland China was $21.4 billion (Deng, 2000). In June 2008, under Ma's government, Taiwan opened the three direct links with China, and by 2016, Taiwanese investment in China had reached $88.5 bil-lion, which was 44% of Taiwan's total investment abroad that year (Main-land Affairs Council, 2018). Between 1952 and 2013, Taiwanese investment in Southeast Asian countries, including Cambodia, Indonesia, Malaysia, Singapore, Thailand, the Philippines, and Vietnam, amounted to $813.9 billion (Yang and Hsiao, 2016: 221). Given that the total sum invested over 60-plus years was less than ten times investment in mainland China in a single recent year, Taiwan's investment in Southeast Asian coun-tries might seem to be insignificant; however, concealed in these figures is steady growth of Taiwan's Southbound investment, which in fact was already under way before the new government's NSP was initiated.

Since President Tsai entered the presidential office in 2016, the aim of the NSP has focused on expanding Taiwan's presence across the Indo-Pacific, with increased connections with the ten countries of ASEAN and six states in South Asia (India, Pakistan, Bangladesh, Nepal, Sri Lanka, and Bhutan). The policy also extends to Australia and New Zealand (Glaser et al., 2018). Interestingly enough, in promoting this policy Tsai's government did not emphasise business links, but focused more on cultural and educational exchanges. A notable feature has indeed been the increasing number of bilateral tourists. Between 2016 and 2017 the number of Taiwanese tourists visiting Vietnam increased by 121.4% to reach 616,000; Vietnamese tourist visits to Taiwan also surged by 94.94% compared with 2016, reaching 380,000 (DeAeth, 2018, *China News*). In addition, Taiwan gained from many students from Southeast Asian countries enrolling in degree programmes in Taiwanese universities (*ICEF Monitor Report*, 2019). The two biggest sources of foreign students are Vietnam and Indonesia. With hindsight, this is indeed a significant achievement, especially against the background of China having prohibited individual travellers from 47 provinces to Taiwan on 31 July 2019 (*The Times*, 2019). The achievement of NSP therefore can be seen in terms of the boost that it has given to tourism and foreign students' enrolments, but perhaps not in terms of business investment.

Taiwanese businesses in Vietnam told me that

> We don't feel there are any benefits for us under this policy, except that on the National Day, the Taipei Representative office asked us to return to Taiwan to attend the Double Ten Day ceremony. The government needs a certain number from Ho Chi Minh city to return to Taiwan, but in fact that is quite a disturbance to us because we have to stop our production work.
>
> (Interview V3)

It can be argued that the NSP has succeeded in expanding the connection to more civic organisations; however, for Southeast Asia countries investment is still the most vital connection with Taiwan. It is already far from easy to maintain this link: as this chapter explained earlier, investment in Southeast Asian countries has been much smaller than in China. Nevertheless, according to Yang's research (2017: 16), the NSP placed much more emphasis on people-to-people connections and connectivity, through education and tourism. Business groups in Southeast Asian countries are important, but they are not the only group that the Tsai government has targeted as the enactors of the NSP. As Yang rightly pointed out (2017: 25), the Tsai government has realised that is it not easy simply to 'command' the Taiwanese businessmen: the incentives offered by the Taiwanese government are the business investment agreements (BIAs) and taxation agreements with

NSP target countries. It can certainly be suggested that the Tsai government learned the lesson of Lee Teng-hui's 1996 Go South Policy that the business sector cannot be commanded, but must rather be induced to relocate from the magnetic Chinese market. The question here is, to what extent can the Tsai government's good intentions be thoroughly implemented? As we discussed earlier in this chapter, Taiwanese businesses are not much different from Chinese businesses in the eyes of local Vietnamese officials. Furthermore, Taiwan and Vietnam do not have any 'official'-level contact through which to negotiate investment details. More to the point, how does Taiwan's NSP deal in Southeast Asian countries with the Chinese government's unavoidable grand geo-political scheme of the Belt and Road Initiative?

## Taiwanese investment in Southeast Asia, compared with the Chinese investment

The BRI project initiated by the Chinese President Xi Jinping took shape in March 2015. It is envisaged to connect the vibrant East Asian region and developed Europe via a Silk Road Economic Belt running through Central Asia, linking China with Asian and other countries via the 21st Century Maritime Silk Road. Its ultimate goal is to facilitate trade and investment in Eurasia and promote economic growth. In the middle of 2016, the official English translation changed from One Belt, One Road (OBOR) to the Belt and Road Initiative (BRI). It should be noted that the geographical connections of 'belt' and 'road' are multiple. They include two routes for silk road routes, namely the 21st Century Maritime Silk Road and the Maritime Silk Road Continental Extension, and three main corridors embedded in the Silk Road Economic Belt. These are respectively the Northern corridor, Central corridor, and Southern corridor. Finally, there are so far two main railway routes – the Silk Route trains and Trans-Siberian Railway (Summers, *Ibid*). As Ferdinand (2016: 949) indicates, the main repository of China's hard power, the PLA, now places much greater importance on fulfilling the goal of 'winning victoriously' rather than just focusing on modernising its force. From the perspective of the maritime belt, for instance, in 2017 the PLA Navy Third Fleet carried out seven training exercises and also military manoeuvres in the Western Pacific. Apart from military hard power, strong Chinese capital is another important backbone for China's BRI. With the launch of the Asian Infrastructure Investment Bank (AIIB) in 2015, China envisages completing the whole BRI project within 35 years (Ferdinand, 2016).

The maritime belt, which links Southeast China with Southeast Asia, Bangladesh, India, the Persian Gulf, and the Mediterranean, reaches its ultimate destination in Germany and the Netherlands, passing through the territory of the ASEAN countries. The maritime belt comprises many large-scale new infrastructure routes, such as the China-Pakistan Economic Corridor (CPEC), the Trans-Asia railway that connects Kunming to Thailand,

China-Bangkok-Laos and Kunming-Vietnam-Cambodia, the Mekong River Development Initiative, the China-India-Bangladesh-Myanmar Economic Corridor, and the multilateral Greater Mekong Sub-region Economic Cooperation Program (Blanchard and Flint, 2017: 227). That means that China not only needs these countries as staging posts to reach its European destinations, but also envisages investing in their infrastructure to support those pathway countries' economic development. China has also bid against Japan in order to win the Singapore-Malaysia high-speed railway track construction project, a sign of how much it seeks to use fast train technology: it has built up some of the world's most advanced knowledge of how to build links with other countries.

The BRI maritime belt is important to Taiwan because the countries that define the maritime belt of China's BRI are identical to Taiwan's targeted NSP countries, embracing most of the countries in the Association of Southeast Asian Nations (for instance Malaysia, Singapore, Vietnam, the Philippines, and Indonesia). It is still too early to evaluate the results of both China and Taiwan's economic diplomacy towards Southeast Asian countries, but a few preliminary points may be made.

First of all, the construction of infrastructure in the maritime belt countries is steered and funded by the Chinese government, but not by private companies. The scale and amount of investment is therefore proportionally vast. By contrast, Taiwan's NSP emphasises people-to-people interaction, involving private entrepreneurs rather than state actors, as well as bilateral visitors between those countries and Taiwan. This makes it a very different strategy from China's. Second, from a strategic perspective we can view BRI as an indirect means whereby China seeks to prevent Taiwan's participation in the region. To be clear, the primary aim of China in the region is to consolidate its power through both monetary buy-out and military strength in order to monopolise the pathways from the region to European and other markets. But by doing so, China also squeezes Taiwan's diplomatic space in the region. However, it can be argued that Taiwan's engagement in the region is through track-two diplomacy or, as the NSP's statement puts it, people-to-people interaction. It is early days, and hard to evaluate just how successful the Chinese strategy will be. But one should not underestimate the determination, and commitment, that lie behind it.

Samuel C.Y. Ku divides cross-Strait relations into four stages: December 1949 to October 1971, October 1971 to July 1987, 1987 to 1997, then from the financial crisis of 1997 onwards (Ku, 2017). His main argument is that the change in the cross-Strait relationship impacted on China's and Taiwan's relationships with Southeast Asian countries. Accordingly, it is difficult to understand Taiwan's relationship with South Asian countries without understanding those countries' engagement with China. In the case of Taiwanese investment, the players in the field therefore are Taiwanese investors, Southeast Asian countries' governments, and Chinese government or investors – or most of the time, the combination of these two in the form of Chinese state-owned enterprises. Furthermore, as I mentioned previously, the criteria of NSP success lie less in business investment than in people-to-people's exchange in terms of tourism and foreign students' enrolment in Taiwanese universities. These are different points of emphasis from those of China's construction-oriented outward investment. Although the targeted countries of NSP and BRI overlap in Southeast Asia, because of different emphases in terms of economic diplomacy, and also – as the next section shows – the complexity of 'China card,' acceptance of NSP may not exclude acceptance of BRI (and vice versa).

## The difficulty of playing the 'China card' for Taiwanese business in Southeast Asian countries

Understanding what is meant by the 'Chinese community' in Southeast Asian countries is impossible without reference to the Taiwanese communities there. The 'Chinese community' in this context refers mainly to investors from Taiwan and China.

Taiwanese and Chinese investment activities are characterised by two main distinctive differences. The first relates to timing: Taiwanese investors came to Southeast Asian countries in the late 1980s – earlier than their mainland counterparts. This reflects the different stages which each had reach in the evolution of its external investment trajectory. Taiwanese businesses began to invest abroad in the late 1980s, whereas Chinese investment started to appear in Southeast Asian countries in the mid-1990s. Indeed, the real take-off period of Chinese investment may be dated from 2000, since when Chinese Overseas Direct Investment (OFDI) has played a disproportionate role in the region (Lee and Yin, 2017: 44–45). The second difference is that most Taiwanese overseas investments have focused on small and medium-sized enterprises (with fewer than 1,000 employees), concentrated in traditional manufacturing industry, such as textiles, shoemaking, and plastic rubber manufacturing. By contrast, Chinese investment in Southeast Asian countries has to a greater extent been undertaken by State-Owned Enterprises (SOEs), focusing more on real estate, infrastructure, and energy supplies. Liu and Lim (2018: 3–4) have pointed out that the Beijing government uses its diplomatic instruments and policy tools to help its national firms secure better access to recipient countries' natural resources (for instance the oil and gas fields of Russia, Central Asia, Africa, and South America). In fact, state policy assistance not only applies to important energy fields, but also extends to SMEs' day-to-day business activities. A Taiwanese businessman informed me that it is much easier for his Chinese competitors to secure advantageous terms from local Vietnamese government, because 'the Chinese government offers more policy benefits to the Vietnamese government, not just in terms of economic activity' (Interview V1).

According to Liu and Lim (2018: 11), China has become the biggest investor there in 2016, contributing investment totalling US $1.6 billion

(equivalent to 17.5% of the country's total FDI inflow). But Chinese investment in Malaysia has not met with a uniformly positive response: an obvious example is the suspension of the East Coast high speed railway and
the cancellation of the high-speed rail link with Singapore (*The Straits
Times*, 1 June 2018). After the general election in May 2018, the Malaysian
government completely changed its attitude towards Chinese infrastruc-
tural investment. Although this change is not reflected in Liu and Lim's
paper, they rightly highlight the Malaysian government's long-standing
'Pro-Malay' policy (Liu and Lim, 2018: 9–12). This policy mainly refers
to the government's support for Malay families and children's education.
For instance, the government distributes children's tuition fee allowances
to Malay families but not to Chinese families. Furthermore, only Malay
students can enter the public universities. Although in 2019, the Malaysian
government changed its attitude towards the Chinese constructed high-
speed railway (for instance, cf. the restart of the East Coast rail link in
2019) (Terengganu, 2019), initial reservations about China's high-speed
railway construction reflected doubts about China's debt diplomacy –
although issues relating to Malaysia's domestic elections were a further
complicating factor.

Government protection of national interests was also an important factor
at work in Vietnam. Though the Chinese diaspora was established in Vietnam much earlier than in any other Southeast Asian countries, the complicated relationship between Vietnamese and Chinese communities also
restrained the Vietnamese government from extending more wholehearted
support to Chinese investment or the BRI project. The Vietnamese impression of Chinese communities is rather mixed, and Vietnam has given a cautious welcome to Chinese investment. The planned North-South railway
between Hanoi and Ho Chi Minh City is an example (Chin, 2018). China's
potential involvement in railway construction notwithstanding, cost considerations have led Vietnam to considering whether to accept Japan's rather
than China's bid. Therefore, in terms of BRI-related construction projects,
the strength of the Chinese diaspora in Vietnam is not necessarily a winning
card. Reference to the complexity of the 'China card' here touches on the
fact that for Vietnamese government, there is no difference between China
and Taiwan. That is, the official position of the Vietnamese government
is that Taiwan is part of China. What is the impact of this official understanding? According to an interviewee from the Taiwan representative office at Ho Chi Min City (V5), it has created many difficulties for Taiwanese
businesses in their efforts to engage with the Vietnamese officials through
official channels. In society, Vietnamese people clearly understand the differences between Chinese and Taiwanese investors, and yet the previous discussion (see above) indicated that in 2014 anti-Chinese riots in Ho Chi Min
City, Taiwanese factories were burnt down. Certainly, one can argue that
Taiwanese factories were established in Vietnam earlier and were also more
numerous than their Chinese counterparts, and therefore were easy targets

for the rioters. However, the question remains: if Vietnamese workers/people were able clearly to differentiate between Taiwanese and Chinese factories, why under the guise of *anti-China* demonstrations, did they choose mainly to burn down Taiwanese factories?

In short, for Taiwanese businesses in Vietnam, the dilemma is, officially they are recognised as Chinese, whether in the wish of Taiwanese businesses or not, the mixed feelings of Vietnamese society towards the Chinese government and investors, to a certain extent, is also shared by the Taiwanese business groups in Vietnam.

## Conclusion

Let me return to the answer to the original research question: using NSP as an example, what form has Taiwan's economic statecraft towards Vietnam assumed? The answer is that although 'money can talk,' comparing Taiwanese business investment in China and Southeast Asia, the scale of such investment has been much greater in China than in Southeast Asian countries, and Taiwanese firms have had much more institutionalised interaction with Chinese local governments than with the governments of Vietnam or Malaysia. However, Taiwanese firms' close interaction with Chinese government is not only a reflection of the scale of investment; even more importantly, Chinese central and local governments regard Taiwanese firms as a strategic asset that can be mobilised in order to win over Taiwanese people's hearts and minds for reunification. Can then Taiwan's NSP really succeed in Southeast Asian countries? The answer to this depends on the perspective from which an evaluation of the NSP is made. If we use the number of bilateral tourists and foreign (Vietnamese) students' enrolments in Taiwanese universities as the criteria, the NSP is seen to have achieved considerable success. If, however, we judge the NSP by the criterion of the increasing scale of investment, perhaps more time is needed before we can talk in terms of success.

In terms of the overlapping of the NSP and BRI in Southeast Asian countries, money is – but at the same is not – the most powerful vehicle for building relationships. The nature and scale of Taiwanese and Chinese investment are very different. Taiwanese investments in Southeast Asian countries are mainly in the form of SMEs, whereas the BRI project has mainly involved Chinese SOEs from China and has tended to focus on infrastructure construction projects.

An obvious limitation of this chapter is that its main geographical focus is just a single country in Southeast Asia – Vietnam. Although it is the most popular Taiwanese investment destination, Vietnam may not be sufficiently representative to provide a full explanation of the impact of the implementation of the NSP. It is therefore important to keep in mind that the purpose of this chapter is not to evaluate NSP in its entirety, but rather to use Vietnam as a single case in the hope of providing a more nuanced and deeper analysis of the NSP (as well as throwing light on the current status of Taiwanese investment in Vietnam).

## Postscript

In January 2020, the Democratic Progressive Party (DPP) won a landslide victory in the presidential election, with President Tsai Ing-wen taking 57.1 of the vote, compared with 38.6% for her KMT opponent (van der Wees, 2020). What are the likely implications of this for the NSP? As a DPP initiative, the impact on the NSP should be positive, although it will take time for the effects of many aspects of the policy to make themselves felt – and thereby be properly evaluated. A case in point is the establishment of the Taiwan-Asia Exchange Foundation (TAEF), which was founded only in 2018. TAEF serves as a new think tank, designed to facilitate government policy and promote civil society connectivity between Taiwan and ASEAN, as well as Southeast Asian countries (TAEF webpage). The complications of 'China factors' addressed in this chapter do indeed suggest that it is much easier to facilitate people-to-people policies through a quasi-governmental think tank than by a governmental bureau. In any case, it will need time to monitor, assess, and evaluate such activities. The continued implementation of policy under the same government for another four years will allow provide the time that is needed for the hard work of think tanks, such as TAEF, to bear fruit.

At the time of writing (June 2020), the global pandemic caused by COVID-19 is still at its peak. What is likely to be the impact of COVID-19 on Taiwan's NSP? According to Chiang, the pandemic has significantly strengthened Taiwan's image in Southeast Asian countries (Chiang, 2020). With only seven deaths and 441 infections reported (June 2020), Taiwan has coped very successfully with COVID-19. In addition, it has been proactive in exporting protective masks not only to Southeast Asian countries, but also to European countries. The 'mask diplomacy' (Horton, 2020) that Taiwan has pursued in an attempt to assist the global battle against the pandemic – that is, the large-scale production of surgical masks for shipment overseas, including to Southeast Asian countries – may be said to have exerted a more subtle effect than the usual 'chequebook diplomacy' – 'subtle,' because it has demonstrated not only Taiwan's capacity to produce the masks, but also through its success in controlling the virus at home to help other countries in their efforts to combat the pandemic. Moreover, recognition of Taiwan's role in these regards has transcended targeted South bound countries and been recognised globally. Nevertheless, prudence demands that we note that even allowing for global appreciation of Taiwan's mask diplomacy apart, it will require much more consistent work by both government and civil societies in Taiwan to ensure that this positive impression lasts beyond the pandemic and into the longer-term future, thereby facilitating the successful fulfilment of the major goals of Tsai Ing-wen's NSP and Taiwan's regional strategy.

## References

Ash, RF and Kueh, YY. 1993. 'Economic Integration with Greater China: Trade and Investment Flows between China, Hong Kong and Taiwan.' *The China Quarterly* 136: 711–45.

Baker & McKenzie. 2013. 'China Employment Law Guide, 2013.' Available at: https://digitalcommons.ilr.cornell.edu/cgi/viewcontent.cgi?referer=https://www.google.co.uk/&httpsredir=1&article=1071&context=lawfirms (accessed 10 December 2018).

Blanchard, JF and Flint, C. 2017. 'The Geopolitics of China's Maritime Silk Road Initiative.' *Geopolitics* 22(2): 223–45.

Cabestan, JP. 2002. 'Integration without Reunification.' *The Cambridge Review of International Affairs* 15(1): 95–103.

Chan, A and Wang, HZ. 2004/2005. 'The Impact of the State on Workers' Conditions: Comparing Taiwanese Factories in China and Vietnam.' *Pacific Affairs* 77(4): 629–6.

Chen, X. 1996. 'Taiwan Investments in China and Southeast Asia: "Go West, But Also Go South."' *Asian Survey* 36(5): 447–67.

Chiang, Jeremy Huai-che. 2020. 'How Covid-19 Challenges Taiwan's New Southbound Policy,' *The Diplomat*, 18 May 2020. Available at: https://thediplomat.com/2020/05/how-covid-19-challenges-taiwans-new-southbound-policy/?utm_source=BenchmarkEmail&utm_campaign=TAEF_Brief_No._43&utm_medium=email (accessed 5 June 2020).

Chin, S. 2018. 'Vietnam Plays Catch Up with High Speed Rail,' *The ASEAN Post*, 2 September 2018. Available at: https://theaseanpost.com/article/vietnam-plays-catch-high-speed-rail (accessed 20 January 2019).

DeAeth, D. 2018. 'Tourism between Taiwan and Vietnam Surged in 2017,' 13 April 2018. Available at: https://www.taiwannews.com.tw/en/news/3404648 (accessed 27 August 2019).

Deng, P. 2000. 'Taiwan's Restriction of Investment in China in the 1990s: A Relative Gains Approach.' *Asian Survey* 40(6): 958–80.

Ferdinand, P. 2016. 'Westward ho—The China Dream and "One Belt, One Road": Chinese Foreign Policy under Xi Jinping.' *International Affairs* 92(4): 941–57.

Glaser, B, Kennedy, S and Funaiole, MP. 2018. 'The New Southbound Policy—Deepening Taiwan's Regional Integration,' Centre for Strategic and International Studies. Available at: https://www.csis.org/analysis/new-southbound-policy (accessed 30 November 2018).

Horton, C. 2020. 'Taiwan Counters China's Isolation Campaign with Mask Diplomacy,' *Nikkei Asia Review*, 23 April 2020. Available at: https://asia.nikkei.com/Politics/International-relations/Taiwan-counters-China-s-isolation-campaign-with-mask-diplomacy (accessed 5 June 2020).

Hsing, Y. 1998. *Making Capitalism in China: The Taiwan Connection*. New York: Oxford University Press.

Hsu, TK. 2017. 'A Review of Taiwan's Old and New Go South Policy: An Economic Perspective.' *Prospect Journal* 18: 63–88. Available at: https://www.pf.org.tw/files/5976/20F5B418-F25E-469F-B347-F564B17D433B (accessed 27 August 2019).

ICEF Monitor Report. 2019. 'Taiwan's Foreign Enrolment Getting a Boost from Southeast Asia.' Available at: https://monitor.icef.com/2019/02/taiwans-foreign-enrolment-getting-a-boost-from-southeast-asia/ (accessed 27 August 2019).

Jaipragas, B. 2018. 'Singapore High-Speed Rail Delayed in Mahathir U-Turn,' *South China Morning Post*, 5 September 2018. Available at: https://www.scmp.com/week-asia/geopolitics/article/2162841/malaysia-singapore-high-speed-rail-delayed-mahathir-u-turn (accessed 30 January 2019).

Keng, S. 2007. 'Understanding the Political Consequence of People-to-People Relations across the Taiwan Strait: Towards an Analytical Framework.' *Chinese History and Society* 32: 63–80.

Keng, S and Schubert, G. 2011. 'Agents of Unification? The Political Role of Taiwanese Businessmen in the Process of Cross-Strait Integration.' *Asian Survey* 50(2): 287–310.

Ku, SCY. 1995. 'The Political Economy of Taiwan's Relations with Southeast Asia: The "Southward Policy."' *Contemporary Southeast Asia* 17(3): 282–97.

Ku, SCY. 2017. 'Strategies of China's Expansion and Taiwan's Survival in Southeast Asia.' In: Dittmer, L (ed.), *Taiwan and China, Fitful Embrace*. Oakland: University of California Press, pp. 249–83.

Kung, IC. 2003. 'Taiwanese Business in Southeast Asia.' In: Gomez, ET and Michael Hsiao, HH (eds.), *Chinese Business in Southeast Asia: Contesting Cultural Explanations, Researching Entrepreneurship*. London: Taylor and Francis, pp. 146–64.

Lee, CY. 2012. *Taiwanese Business or Chinese Security Asset? A Changing Pattern of Interaction between Taiwanese Business and Chinese Local Governments*. London: Routledge.

Lee, CY. 2014. 'From Being Privileged to Being Localised? Taiwanese Businessmen in China.' In: Fell, D, Ping, L and Chiu, K (eds.), *Migration to and from Taiwan*. London: Routledge, pp. 57–72.

Lee, CY and Yin, MX. 2017. 'Chinese Investment in Taiwan: A Challenge or an Opportunity for Taiwan?' *Journal of Current Chinese Affairs* 46(1): 37–59.

Liu, H and Lim, G. 2018. 'The Political Economy of a Rising China in Southeast Asia: Malaysia's Response to China's "Belt and Road Initiative."' *Journal of Contemporary China*. Online publication. DOI: 10.1080/10670564.2018.1511393 (accessed 10 November 2018).

Mainland Affairs Council. 2018. 'Cross-Strait Economic Statistics Monthly.' Available at: www.mac.gov.tw (accessed 10 March 2018).

Schubert, G. 2010. 'The Political Thinking of the Mainland *Taishang*. Some Preliminary Observations from the Field.' *Journal of current Chinese Affairs* 1: 73–105.

Schubert, G, Lin, R and Tseng, JYC. 2017. 'Are Taiwanese Entrepreneurs a Strategic Group? Reassessing Taishang Political Agency across the Taiwan Strait.' *Asian Survey* 5795: 856–84.

Summers, T. 2016. 'China's "New Silk Roads": Sub-national Regions and Networks of Global Political Economy.' *The Third World Quarterly* 37(9): 1628–43.

TAEF. Available at: https://www.taef.org/about (accessed 5 June 2020).

Taiwanese business net. 2018. Available at: https://twbusiness.nat.gov.tw/old/pdf/1071113%E5%BD%99%E6%95%B4(%E5%88%8A%E7%99%BB).pdf (accessed 21 November 2018).

Terengganu, D. 2019. 'China, Malaysia Restart East Coast Rail Link Project after Year-Long Suspension,' *Channelnewsasia*, 25 July 2019. Available at: https://www.

channelnewsasia.com/news/asia/china-malaysia-restart-belt-road-east-coast-rail-link-11752570 (accessed 27 August 2019).

*The Guardian.* 2014. 'At Least 21 Dead in Vietnam Anti-China Protests over Oil Rig.' Available at: www.theguardian.com/world/2014/may/15/vietnam-anti-china-protests-oil-rig-dead-injured (accessed 11 November 2018).

*The Times.* 2019. 'China Bans Citizens from Traveling to Taiwan as Individual Tourists,' 31 July 2019. Available at: https://time.com/5639832/china-bans-travel-taiwan-tourists/ (accessed 27 August 2019).

Tung, CY. 2003. *Cross-Strait Economic Relations in the Era of Globalization.* Taipei: Yang Chih Reading Club.

Van der Wees, G. 2020. 'President Tsai and the DPP Win an Overwhelming Victory: A Strong Rejection of China's Encroachment,' *Taiwan Insight*, 15 January 2020. Available at: https://taiwaninsight.org/2020/01/15/president-tsai-and-the-dpp-win-an-overwhelming-victory-a-strong-rejection-of-chinas-encroachment/, (accessed 5 June 2020).

Wu, JM. 1997. 'Strange Bedfellows: Dynamics of Government-Business Relations between Chinese Local Authorities and Taiwanese Investors.' *Journal of Contemporary China* 6(15): 319–46.

Yang, AH. 2017. 'Strategic Appraisal of Taiwan's New People-Centered Southbound Policy: The 4Rs approach.' *Prospect Journal* 18: 1–34.

Yang, AH and Hsiao, HHM. 2016. 'Tai-Shang (Taiwanese business) in Southeast Asia: Profile and Issues.' In: Kim, YC (ed.), *Chinese Global Production Networks in ASEAN: Understanding China.* Switzerland: Springer, pp. 213–29.

### Interview data

Interview T1: A Taiwanese textile factory owner who has just opened his factory in Ho Chi Minh City in 2018 (he still keeps his factory in Shanghai), interview date: 29 December2018.

Interview V1: A Taiwanese textile factory owner in Ho Chi Minh City, interview date: 22 March 2018.

Interview V2: A Taiwanese factory which makes bicycles in Ho Chi Minh City, interview date: 22 March 2018.

Interview V3: A second Taiwanese textile factory owner in Ho Chi Minh City, interview date: 21 March 2018.

Interview V4: A Taiwanese consultant to TBA in Ho Chi Minh City, interview date: 18 March 2018.

Interview V5: A member of the Taipei economic section in Ho Chi Minh City, interview date: 19 March 2018.

# 7 Facing the Pacific

## An Eastbound strategy for Taiwanese maritime commerce in the 21st century

*Lin Kun-chin and Charles I-hsin Chen*

When political analysts and policymakers talk about the 'Pacific Age,' or China 'ruling the waves,' or the strategic notion of the Indo-Pacific, they are imposing a spatial and conceptual construct that runs counter to the fundamental geo-economic reality of global container traffic flows. From East Asia, trade via inter-continental container traffic follows one of two directions in reaching the European and East Coast United States (hereafter US) market destinations – Westbound through the Malacca Strait, or Eastbound via the Pacific Ocean. While China has designed a Westbound, land- and sea-based connectivity as the main thrust of its economic expansion via the *Belt and Road Initiative* (BRI), Taiwan has been constrained by its dependence on Sino-centric global supply chains, and from the early 2000s to 2016 it was swept along by the momentum of major shipping liners to the Westbound route. With the expansion of the Panama Canal in 2016, Taiwan has gained the economic option of privileging Eastbound maritime shipping routes that service continental US. In turning away from shipping routes dominated by Chinese goods and companies, Taiwan could find itself in a better position to hedge against likely disruptions from trade disputes and emerging trade blocs centred on China, and to gain political currency in joining the Indo-Pacific strategic cooperative space defined by the US. We call this geo-economic approach the 'New Eastbound Strategy' (NES).

## Taiwan's New Southbound Policy

Taiwan's President Tsai Ing-wen launched the New Southbound Policy (NSP) at the inauguration of her first presidency on 20 May 2016, when she promoted closer cooperation between Taiwan and 18 countries in the Association of Southeast Asian Nations (ASEAN) and South Asia, as well as New Zealand and Australia. The main objective of the NSP is 'to elevate the scope and diversity of our external economy, and to bid farewell to our past over-reliance on a single market,' as President Tsai declared on her first day in office (Office of the President 2016). Though she avoided explicitly identifying 'People's Republic of China' (hereafter PRC) as the 'single market,' the dilemma is clear and acute. In 2015, the final year of Ma Ying-jeou's administration, the export share to the PRC market was 39.4% of the island's total exports (see Table 7.1). Tsai's grand strategy sought to reduce this figure by redirecting more exports to South and Southeast Asian markets. However, the NSP was launched against the background of two powerful trends over the past four years, which have complicated policy choices of smaller countries in Asia: first, China's politically driven, multi-billion dollar promotion of its foreign economic interests via the BRI in the same region; and second, the US-PRC trade war and initial disruption of regional supply chains. The COVID-19 pandemic in 2020 has added new variables to these trends, which will be discussed later.

Preliminary data reveal a mixed progress report for the NSP policy. It appears to have stimulated greater commercial flows and people mobility between Taiwan and Southeast Asia. In a three-year comparison before and after the policy was initiated, the number of tourists coming from the 18 NSP countries to Taiwan grew by 56.6% (Office of Trade Negotiations 2019). Trade expanded by 3.4%, while Taiwan's investment increased by US $0.6 billion (Ibid). However, other statistics cast doubt on the policy effect on market diversification (Chen 2018). Taiwan's export share to the NSP 18 was 21.2% in 2015. While the policy goal was to increase this share, it actually

*Table 7.1* Taiwan's export reliance on major countries

|  | *Taiwan export percent to Hong Kong and Mainland China (%)* | *Taiwan export percent to NSP 18 countries (%)* | *Taiwan export percent to ASEAN 10 countries (%)* |
| --- | --- | --- | --- |
| 2000 | 24.4 | | |
| 2001 | 26.6 | | |
| 2002 | 32.2 | | |
| 2003 | 35.7 | | |
| 2004 | 37.9 | | |
| 2005 | 39.2 | | |
| 2006 | 39.8 | | |
| 2007 | 40.7 | | |
| 2008 | 39.0 | 18.6 | 15.2 |
| 2009 | 41.2 | 18.1 | 15.0 |
| 2010 | 41.8 | 18.4 | 15.2 |
| 2011 | 40.2 | 20.0 | 16.7 |
| 2012 | 39.6 | 21.8 | 18.6 |
| 2013 | 40.2 | 22.2 | 19.0 |
| 2014 | 40.2 | 21.8 | 18.8 |
| 2015 | 39.4 | 21.1 | 18.1 |
| 2016 | 40.1 | 21.2 | 18.3 |
| 2017 | 41.0 | 21.2 | 18.5 |
| 2018 | 41.3 | 20.4 | 17.4 |
| 2019 | 40.2 | 19.2 | 16.4 |

Source: Cross-Strait Economic Statistics Monthly, No. 325, May 2020. Summary of Exports and Imports for October 2020, Ministry of Finance, ROC, 8 May 2020.

dropped in both 2018 and 2019 against a stronger policy stimulus. The corresponding percentage in 2019 was 19.2%, and 19.0% for the first quarter in 2020 – the lowest figure yet of the decade (Ministry of Finance 2020). Even as Taiwan's export reliance to the NSP 18 decreased to a significant degree, its export reliance on PRC increased in the same period, rising from 39.4% in 2015 to 41.3% in 2018, and reaching a new peak at 44.8% in March 2018. A slight drop of one percentage point in 2019 is likely to have been caused by the trade war between the US and China. In short, the NSP has not been a sufficient remedy to reduce Taiwan's trade dependence on PRC. Another level of geo-economic and strategic thinking is needed to expand the options.

## China's Westbound initiative

Chinese President Xi Jinping's Maritime Silk Road is predicated on a Westbound strategy. It focuses on establishing international port networks and logistics on shipping routes starting at ports in China's coastal provinces, across the Indian Ocean and via the Suez Canal to reach the European and US East Coast markets. These Westbound shipping routes have experienced significant growth in the past two decades due to the Suez Canal's inherent capacity to accommodate supersized tankers and container ships that the Panama Canal could not match until its recent expansion. For example, during the 2000s, shipping liners switched about 30% of their Asia-US East Coast traffic from the Eastbound to the Westbound route (Wright 2016). Of the total container shipments from Asia-Pacific to the US East Coast, the share of voyages via the Suez Canal increased from 36% to 54% between 2011 and 2015, while those via the Panama Canal dropped from 55% to 44% (Institute of Transportation 2016).

China's rapid growth and Asia's rising trade dependency since the Asian Financial Crisis have driven both the rise of Asian ports and their intensified competition, resulting in China capturing the lion's share of the expansion of container traffic. In the first decade of the 2000s, approximately 65% of the world's container traffic came from Asian ports, with the top eight Chinese ports alone accounting for about a quarter of all container traffic. Of the top 25 seaports in the world port traffic league, ranked by containers handled between 1999 and 2003, 15 formed what has been called 'a string of pearls' stretching from Singapore to Tokyo. Of these 15 ports, seven are located in China (Funke and Hao 2011). In 2015, 13 Chinese seaports were ranked in the global top 20 ports. In this context, Taiwan's major ports, particularly Kaohsiung, have faced limited growth opportunities, further challenged by significant policy constraints from cross-Strait relations and the prospect of a massive pull of trade flows driven by Beijing's BRI. The medium-term risk of policy inaction is that Taiwan might be locked into Chinese BRI's Westbound approach in maritime trade orientation. Fortuitously, a potentially transformative opportunity arrived on its doorstep in the massive capacity upgrading of the Panama Canal in 2016 and President Trump's launch of America's Indo-Pacific strategy the year after.

## America's Indo-Pacific strategy

The 'Indo-Pacific' as a region includes over 40% of global economic output, but the so-called 'Indo-Pacific strategy' was not a clear idea when it was first proposed by President Donald Trump during his Asia trip in November 2017. In the summit with Japanese Prime Minister Shinzo Abe, he addressed new foci in the Indo-Pacific region (which he used to describe an expanded version of the Asia-Pacific region): viz., (1) promotion and establishment of fundamental values; (2) pursuit of economic prosperity; (3) and a commitment to peace and stability (Koga 2018, 133). The strategic goal is a 'free-and-open Indo-Pacific (FOIP),' as the then US Secretary of Defense James Mattis stressed to his ASEAN counterparts in the Shangri-La Dialogue in June 2018 (McDonald 2018). A month later, Secretary of State Mike Pompeo revealed the economic vision of this new regional order by making a pledge to keep this region 'free from coercion or great power domination' in order to 'enhance the security of our partners and to assist them in developing their economies and societies in ways that ensure human dignity' (Cossa and Glosserman 2018, 5).

Some ideas in this new doctrine are old. In 1995, the Department of Defense issued a *US Security Strategy for the East Asia-Pacific Region*, listing its major goal in Asia as 'to enhance security by maintaining a strong defense capability and promoting cooperative security measures; to open foreign markets and spur global economic growth; and to promote democracy abroad' (Auslin 2018). Two decades later, the new version retains some core elements: for example, peace and stability, promotion of democracy, and development of trade relations (Ibid). Only one element is new – the targeting of the PRC.

This policy goal has been further clarified in a National Security Council report released in May 2020, which stresses that US-China relations fall within the Indo-Pacific strategy whose aim of a free and open Indo-Pacific region includes the PRC (National Security Council 2020). The US would ally with the ASEAN, Japan, India, Australia, South Korea, and Taiwan to preserve their geopolitical interests from the status-quo in the post-Cold War order, which are under threat from the PRC (Ibid). The Indo-Pacific strategy sets three practical priorities: first, to deny Beijing's control of the South China Sea; second, to leverage Indo-Pacific economic integration to balance against Chinese economic power; and third, to integrate India as a regional security partner against the PRC (Carlisle 2018, 3). Countering Chinese regional hegemony has become the main theme in the Indo-Pacific strategy, gathering bipartisan support in the US, and supported by economic and security measures taken as part of the US-PRC trade war.[1]

In a significant way, the US has striven for a whole-of-government response to China's grand strategy in this region. As Mr Mattis remarked in the ceremony renaming the US Pacific Command to the US Indo-Pacific Command in May 2018, his department intended to achieve 'a shared vision of an Indo-Pacific region of "many belts and many roads,"' a term apparently against Beijing's BRI (Carlisle 2018, 6). To date, American efforts have fallen short of decisively convincing regional leaders to forego hedging between the superpowers in preference of band-wagoning with the US (McDonald 2018). The $113 million US budget set initially for this plan, in comparison with China's $126 billion in the BRI, was mocked by analysts as 'overwhelming.' In due time, the US may commit more resources in the economic warfare, but the pandemic in 2020 has stalled the effort for the foreseeable future, leaving many countries with no option but to maintain 'debt diplomacy' with Beijing.

## Expanded Panama Canal

Back in the 1860s, Secretary of State William H. Seward understood the value of a transport waterway in Central America for promoting American trade in Asia. He suggested building the Panama Canal in order to shorten the shipping route between America's East Coast and Asian ports, which at that time had taken a long route via the Cape Horn (Auslin 2018, 4). When the construction of Panama Canal was initiated by the French in 1879, President Rutherford B. Hayes warned that 'the US should control this great highway,' since it was required for 'our prosperity and safety' (LaFeber 1993, 73). President Benjamin Harrison emphasised in 1891 that 'the canal is the most important subject now connected with the commercial growth and progress of the US' (LaFeber 1993, 74). The US finally gained rights over the land of the Panama Canal in *The Hay–Bunau-Varilla Treaty* in 1903 and committed a budget of $352 million over the next ten years to complete the construction in 1914. The benefit was immediate – US exports to Asia and Oceania rose from 6% to 9% from 1897 to 1917, and peaked at 21% of US exports before the Second World War (Schoonover 2003, 120). The completion of the Panama Canal brought the first structural change in maritime trade relations between the US and the Asia Pacific, and provided the logistics basis for the post-WWII transformation of this region into what is now the top destination of US exports.

A similarly critical structural change in global logistics took place with the massive expansion of the Panama Canal, which was completed in June 2016. The widening of the canal enabled the Panama Canal to accommodate larger vessels – up to 14,000 20-foot equivalent units (TEUs) (Schwarz 2017). The expansion has doubled the overall capacity of the Canal (Panama Canal Authority 2018). New locks have enlarged the maximum vessel size from 4,400 TEUs to 13,000–14,000 TEUs. On 22 August 2017, the Canal welcomed the largest ever vessel – CMA CGM Theodore Roosevelt, carrying 14,863 TEUs – to transit the new locks on its voyage from Shanghai to New York (Panama Canal Authority 2017, 18). This record remained for two years until the transit of the CMA CGM Magellan, carrying 15,442 TEUs in September 2019 (Panama Canal Authority 2019, 21). In the three fiscal years after the expansion (October 2016 to September 2019), the Canal saw record increases in annual tonnage of cargo – 402.8 million tons PC/ UMS (Panama Canal/Universal Measurement System) with an increase of 22% in 2017, 442.1 million tons with an increase of 10% in 2018, and 469.6 million tons with a further increase of 6.2% in 2019. In 2018, 18 out of 30 liner services deployed Neopanamax vessels, which contributed 52% of the transits, 76% of the TEU capacity, and 75% of the total revenue in traffic statistics.

The expanded Panama Canal quickly overtook the Suez Canal as the preferred logistic choice for container traffic from and to Asia. The Panama Canal option saves 5,302 nautical miles – that is 11 fewer days at vessel speed of 19.5 knots – for a Neopanamax vessel to sail from Japan to the Caribbean Sea. Holding constant exogenous factors such as fuel prices, disruptions in regional production networks, and dramatic and lasting consumer demand changes in the US and Europe, analysts expected shipping liners to see sizeable benefits in using the Panama Canal to avoid the US West Coast ports and railway transit across the US, and the longer shipping time via the Suez. Within a year of the Canal's reopening, it had won back all its market share of Asia-US east coast container traffic lost to Suez in the preceding decade (Barnard 2016). Network details published by global shipping alliances in late 2016 reveal that more carriers are pledging allegiance to the Panama waterway, with 12 weekly services compared with only four confirmed loops via the Egyptian waterway (Barnard 2016). The data also indicate that Suez lost out more than the West Coast option in the first year. The 2M Alliance (Maersk Line and Mediterranean Shipping Co.), which gave up on the Panama Canal in 2013 in favour of strictly Suez Canal routeing, returned in 2016 to a round-the-world service with the Eastbound routeing through the widened Panama Canal. This shift has prompted 2M's global rival, Ocean Alliance – comprising CMA CGM, COSCO Container Lines, Orient Overseas Container Line, and Evergreen Line – also to lean towards a Trans-Pacific network (Szakonyi 2016).

With the re-routeing of container traffic, the domestic supply chain in continental US reorganised around the East Coast ports. The allowance of larger ships will lower the per unit slot cost of containers, and drive cascading competitive effects that will generally lower the cost of transport for the Eastbound route. Key effects include the upgrading of US East Coast ports (such as NY/NJ, Charleston, Savannah, and Miami) and linked logistics centres in the Midwest and South, in particular Texas; the probable lowering of US railway costs to bolster the relative appeal of the West Coast ports; and a significant reduction in sailing time from Asia to US East Coast, where around 80% of American consumers live (Edmonds 2012, 43).

In 2018, 14 out of 16 Neopanamax liner services via the Panama Canal were from Asia to the Caribbean, the US Gulf, or its East Coast, while the other two services were from West America to the Europe (Panama Canal Authority 2018, 17). None of them terminates at the US West Coast. More TEU volumes moved to East Coast ports. The share of TEU unloaded in West Coast ports in 2016 was 4.9% higher than that in East Coast ports, but the gap was reduced to 2.2% in 2018. The trend predicts a golden cross in the near future. The amount of Asian imports from the Charleston port (South Carolina) enjoyed rapid growth of 17.2% in the first 11 months of 2017; likewise the Savannah port (Georgia), 10.9% (Mongelluzzo 2017). Most US East Coast ports recorded similar growth in 2017, with an average annual increase of 9.7%, compared with an increase of 4.6% in 2016 (Ashe 2018). The growth trend continued in 2018 – Asian imports to Huston port (Texas) increasing by 19.6%, Savannah port by 11%, Charleston port by 10%, and New York and New Jersey ports by 8.2% (Mongelluzzo 2019).

Anticipating further interests from shipping liners and traders, the Panama government has proposed further expansion for the Canal to accept ships of upwards of 18,000 TEU within 15 years (Gardner and Moreno 2015). The COVID-19 pandemic has introduced considerable uncertainties in fulfilling this plan, with a short-term effect of reducing overall global container traffic and steering shipping liners towards the Suez route. With the US-PRC trade war brewing and the Chinese economy suffering extended factory shutdowns from the pandemic, US and EU retailers have increased sourcing in Southeast Asia. Due to the closer distance, the Westbound Suez route is preferred by Southeast Asian exporters (Mongelluzzo 2020). Another example of route uncertainty is US-Asia liquefied natural gas (LNG) and liquefied petroleum gas (LPG) trade, which gained significant attention as a commercial priority of President Trump in 2017–18. The expanded Panama Canal was predicted to play a major role in global LNG/LPG trade for American firms (for example, Cheniere Energy) to feed thirsty Asian markets. By April 2020, some LNG/LPG shippers were avoiding the Panama Canal to take more than a month longer to reach the Asian market, in hope of netting better offers in the process of transit.[2]

## A new hedging strategy for Taiwan

Taiwanese ports and shipping liners are in a position to benefit from the advantages of the Eastbound options via the expanded Panama waterway. The port of Kaohsiung was once a mega-hub in trans-Pacific shipping routes, but during this century it has seen its role gradually displaced by Chinese ports. Kaohsiung's place in the World Container Ports Ranking receded from fourth in 2001 to 15th in 2018, with a current annual capacity of 10.4 million TEUs (Ministry of Transportation and Communications 2020). Forced into a sub-hub status specialising in regional and cross-Strait transits, Kaohsiung has seen a re-adjustment of its composition of shipping routes to accommodate more Westbound routes. In 2011, seven out of eight routes from the Asia-Pacific to the US East Coast via Kaohsiung were East-bound routes via the Panama Canal, compared with one Westbound route via the Suez Canal. By 2015, the relative numbers were four versus four routes (Institute of Transportation 2016, 67–68). By 2016, Kaohsiung was evidently less integral to the Eastbound route than the Westbound route. Among ten major China-US East Coast shipping routes, Kaohsiung is a port of call for most Westbound routes, but for none of the Eastbound routes (Callahan 2016). The new Panama Canal offers an urgent opportunity to reassess Kaohsiung's options if the Taiwanese government is committed to reversing the fortune of its global ports.

To capitalise on this Eastbound strategy, the Taiwan government could adopt a series of mutually reinforcing policies and incentive schemes that would draw global shipping liners into Kaohsiung on their way to Eastbound routes. The Eastbound policy framework would be based on two basic premises: first, under the intensely competitive world of shipping, liners pick the ports for a set of advantages extending beyond shipping cost savings. Second, intermodal and spatially integrated port development offers numerous positive spillover benefits if ports are seen as more than distribution points and logistics hubs, but are built up as commercial centres with related industries and services including maritime finance and tourism, launching pads for urban and regional development strategies, and testing ground for new industrial policies, trade and investment, and tax regimes. It follows from the above premises that policy priorities should include the following.

### (1) Rebuild production bases in Southeast Asia

Taiwan had already launched two waves of Southbound policies in order to reduce the island's export reliance on PRC. The first wave by President Lee Teng-hui began from 1994 to around the outbreak of Asian financial crisis in 1998, while the second wave by President Chen Shui-bian lasted from 2002 until the end of his presidency. As a result, before 2008, the total amount of Taiwanese foreign direct investment (FDI) going to Southeast Asia was US $12.9 billion (see Table 7.2). During Ma Ying-jeou's presidency, Taiwan tripled its investments in Vietnam and achieved significant increases in Singapore and Australia without a declared policy targeting the region. The first three years under President Tsai Ing-wen's NSP saw clear increases in Australia, Thailand, India, and other smaller NSP countries. However, the present level of $8.8 billion under Tsai's period was only half of the $19.7 billion under Ma's period. The policy effect of the NSP is clearer for the relocation of investment than for the trend of growth.

The favourite destination for Taiwan's FDI in NSP countries is Singapore, which has accumulated $14.2 billion since 1952, mainly in advanced sectors such as computers, electronics, and optical products, or the financial and insurance sectors (see Table 7.3). The next is Vietnam, which accumulated $10.9 billion in

*Table 7.2* Taiwan's FDI to NSP 18 countries (US$1,000)

| Area | | 1952–2008 | 2009–16 | 2017–19 | 1952–2019 |
|---|---|---|---|---|---|
| Asia | Singapore | 5,439,434 | 7,095,633 | 1,717,318 | 14,252,385 |
| | Vietnam | 2,103,122 | 6,377,058 | 2,499,373 | 10,979,553 |
| | Thailand | 1,946,796 | 1,087,287 | 1,032,344 | 4,066,427 |
| | Malaysia | 1,736,957 | 1,090,810 | 468,797 | 3,296,564 |
| | Philippines | 753,875 | 908,132 | 482,154 | 2,144,161 |
| | Indonesia | 622,126 | 615,845 | 405,666 | 1,643,637 |
| | India | 63,708 | 280,394 | 462,158 | 806,260 |
| | Others[a] | 137,352 | 386,734 | 629,186 | 1,153,272 |
| Oceania | Australia | 159,942 | 1,860,332 | 1,166,985 | 3,187,260 |
| | New Zealand | 6,295 | 331 | 10,000 | 16,626 |
| Total | | 12,969,606 | 19,702,557 | 8,873,981 | 41,546,145 |

Source: Authors' calculations from data published in 'Taiwan FDI Statistics Summary Analysis (May 2020),' Department of Investment Service, Ministry of Economic Affairs, 20 June 2020.
a   Others in Asia includes Lao, Myanmar, Cambodia, Brunei, Sri Lanka, Nepal, Bangladesh, Bhutan, and Pakistan.

*Table 7.3* Taiwan's FDI in major NSP countries by sectors (1952–2019)

| | Cases | Main sectors |
|---|---|---|
| Singapore | 649 | • Computers, electronic, and optical products<br>• Financial and insurance<br>• Real estate and rental and leasing<br>• Wholesale and retail trade<br>• Petroleum and chemical products |
| Vietnam | 747 | • Textile mills, wearing apparel, and clothing accessories<br>• Shoe products<br>• Food processing<br>• Rubber and plastic products<br>• Furniture |
| Thailand | 579 | • Electrical equipment<br>• Rubber products<br>• Basic metal products<br>• Petroleum and chemical products<br>• Motor vehicles and parts<br>• Machinery and equipment<br>• Chemical products<br>• Textile mills |
| Malaysia | 454 | • Machinery and electrical equipment<br>• Petroleum and chemical products<br>• Food processing<br>• Furniture<br>• Chemical products<br>• Fabricated metal products<br>• Rubber and plastic products |
| Philippines | 245 | • Machinery and electrical equipment<br>• Wholesale and retail trade<br>• Food<br>• Chemical material<br>• Finance |

| | | |
|---|---|---|
| Indonesia | 318 | • Aquaculture<br>• Furniture<br>• Textile mills, wearing apparel, and clothing accessories<br>• Shoe products<br>• Mining<br>• Machinery equipment<br>• Motor vehicles and parts<br>• Electronic parts and components<br>• Fabricated metal products |
| India | 108 | • Machinery and electrical equipment<br>• Basic metal products<br>• Shoe products<br>• Medical equipment<br>• Information and communication products |
| Australia | 117 | • Mining<br>• Sugar manufacturing<br>• Bio-medical manufacturing<br>• Eating-drinking places<br>• Wholesale and retail trade |
| New Zealand | 10 | • Education<br>• Real estate<br>• Travel<br>• Food<br>• Computer repairing<br>• Retail trade |

Source: *Homepage for New Southbound Policy*, Bureau of Foreign Trade, Ministry of Economic Affairs, https://newsouthboundpolicy.trade.gov.tw (last accessed 24 June 2020).

light manufacturing sectors such as textiles, shoes, food, and rubber or plastic products. Australia has risen in importance, attracting $3.1 billion in Taiwanese capital in the past decade in mining, sugar, bio-medical manufacturing, etc. India has received $8.0 billion, mainly in the past three years and mainly embracing traditional manufacturing and ICT products.

The regional value chain is in place for Taiwan to upgrade its economic ties with Southeast Asia and also to extend it to South Asia and Oceania. For the past two and a half decades, Taiwan has maintained strong economic complementarity and corporate interests in expanding trade relations in this region, and established industrial agglomeration in Singapore, Vietnam, Thailand, and Malaysia (see Tables 7.2 and 7.3). Existing ties could support new strategies, partly in response to the disruptive effects of the trade war between the US and China, which is altering the global value chain and the supply chain networks in Asia-Pacific. Taiwan's economic policy could emphasise a stronger regional agenda – such as supporting Taiwanese enterprises to establish presence in these overseas regions as part of industrial upgrading and risk management.

Furthermore, to take full advantage of the cost and time savings of the increasing Eastbound routes, the Taiwanese government may encourage its producers to build new and advanced production bases that facilitate processing exports from the region back to the island, and forward to the final US market. One option would be to offer government guidance in a collective investment strategy. Another would be to pursue outward direct investment (ODI) policies that provide business incentives in the form of government loans, economic diplomacy, and comprehensive trade and investment support incorporated in new bilateral and regional agreements.

### *(2) Upgrade Taiwan as a high value-added innovative processing centre*

After the first export processing zone was established in Kaohsiung in 1966, Taiwan achieved a period of miraculous economic growth for three decades long. The island's industrialisation strategy was to first promote labour-intensive export processing and later shift to technology-intensive products. Nowadays, an advanced version of the same strategy may still work.

The new pattern of export processing may need an upgrade from the simple-processing to the deep-processing model, which would allow the extension of the value chain in the product line. In practice, Taiwan could import raw materials and components – presumably in agriculture or manufacturing sectors – from Southeast Asia, India, or Australia, before applying high valued-added processing manufacture on the island and then re-exporting the finished products to global markets, especially to North America. Taiwan's existing supply chains in the region would be valuable in providing expanded bases. Its upgrading project would require more logistic links with their home factories back in Taiwan, which could be expedited by government actions.

In addition, Taiwan maintains comparative advantages in human capital, information technology, and biotechnology in the region. Government agencies should be encouraged to consult with and coordinate innovative business interests in moving Taiwan upwards in global value chain. The aim is thereby to wage a new marketing agenda to promote and polish the brand 'Made in Taiwan (MIT)' in the global arena. More likely, these regional upgrades will endow Taiwan's processing industries with a better place to accommodate – if not take advantage of – the impact of expected trade restructuring in the Indo-Pacific region resulting from the US-China trade war.

### *(3) Make Kaohsiung port a free and smart mega-hub*

The first proposal in history suggesting turning Kaohsiung into a free port was made by Japanese colonial consuls in 1935, who at the time were looking for ways to enhance the trade route between Japan and Southeast Asia (Lin 2010, 1070). However, the idea fell by the wayside as the Japanese military launched the invasion of China. The potential for Kaohsiung to play a pivotal role in the regional economy was largely forgotten until 1993, when another Japanese strategist, Kenichi Ohmae, advised Taiwan to make the

Chinese mainland and Southeast Asia Kaohsiung's hinterlands. His idea was to turn this global port into a major shipping centre under the name of the 'Asia-Pacific Regional Operations Centre,' which was later accepted by the government as a new development strategy for this second biggest city in Taiwan (Sun 2015, 5). The new role designed for Kaohsiung was as a regional mega-hub in the hope of managing transnational logistics on a free-trade basis across the Taiwan Strait and the South China Sea. However, the connection to China was dropped from the government's plan when President Lee Teng-hui tried to reduce Taiwan's capital outflows to the PRC in order to enhance the island's economic security. At the same time, more serious challenges came from ascending Chinese ports that drew regional shipping traffic to the Westbound routes.

With a more relaxed approach to cross-Strait relations, this pivot scheme was re-introduced in 2011, when the Ma administration proposed a new wave of economic reform seeking greater liberalisation of the island economy. The programme – under the name of *Free Economic Pilot Zone* (FEPZ) – sought to liberalise Kaohsiung on an even greater scale in an attempt to make this city the 'Second Singapore.' It was planned that Kaohsiung could take a pioneer role to be the first port in Taiwan to upgrade its simple-processing model to a deep-processing one.[3]

A sizeable budget was set to upgrade the port's facilities with the aim of accommodating Neo-Panamax vessels. Five deep-water docks (with 18 metres water depth and the capacity to accommodate vessel size up to 22,000 TEUs) were scheduled to be completed in 2019, while the annual capacity was expected to increase a quarter to over 18 million TEUs (Port of Kaohsiung n.d.). The expansion plan is incomplete as of June 2020.[4] When finished, the hugely improved capacity promises to enable Kaohsiung to attract new trans-Pacific liner services. Smaller ports in Taiwan would also share benefits by providing dedicated regional liner services. With advanced ICT capabilities, Taiwan would develop an island-wide smart logistics system with cloud platforms supporting digital and multiple integration that can manage complicated logistics required by the newly established product chains in the global or regional scale. The system also promises to anticipate the objectives of marine ecological protection and climate change mitigation of ships and ports recently formulated by the International Maritime Organization.

### (4) Facilitate access to the American markets, particularly the East Coast

In the late 19th century, it took a 65-day trip for Taiwan's oolong tea to arrive in New York via the Suez Canal. The trans-Pacific shipping lines established by Japan in the beginning of the 20th century reshaped the trade relationship between East Asia – particularly Taiwan – and North America (Lin 2010, 1059). Taiwan's shipping route was replaced by a 27-day trip to Seattle, followed by overland shipment to New York (Lin 2010, 1062). Taiwan's trade ties with the US were hugely expanded thereafter, with the island's exports to the US rising from less than 1% in 1899 to more than 20% in 1907 (Lin 2010, 1061).

This first-ever 'Eastbound strategy' for Taiwan of a century ago may inform the upgraded version today. Taiwanese industries could capture the economic benefits of an Eastbound global product chain that places production bases in South or Southeast Asia, processing centres in Taiwan, and consumer markets in Northeast America, through the expanded Panama Canal. Taiwan may thereby endeavour to remove trade barriers with the US by initiating high-standard bilateral or multilateral economic agreements, such as the US-Taiwan Free Trade Agreement and the Comprehensive and Progressive Agreement for Trans-Pacific Partnership (Bush 2004). Several notable American former diplomats formerly in charge of Taiwan affairs voiced their support for the negotiation of a bilateral trade agreement with Taiwan (Burghardt 2019). They see a window of opportunity as both governments have displayed a strong political will to resolve some long-standing trade issues.

A new trade deal between the US and Taiwan will not only forge a stronger strategic partnership but will also help the US reorganise its Asian supply chains away from the PRC. Taiwan's envoy, Morris Chang, to the APEC 2018's leader summit proposed this idea to the US Vice President, Mike Pence, who agreed to carry back this case but promised nothing in the meeting. *The newly passed Taiwan Allies International Protection and Enhancement Initiative (TAIPEI) Act* of 2019 mandates the US Trade Representative to strengthen bilateral trade and economic relations between the US and Taiwan. Considering the broader interests at stake, however, Taiwan may need to reassess its resistance to US imports of beef and pork – a sticking point that has caused the suspension of the regular economic talks between the US and Taiwan since October 2016.[5]

### *(5) Double down on developing a comprehensive maritime strategy*

Taiwan's coastline of over 1,500 kilometres (including the Pescadores Islands) had supported a prosperous maritime economy for the island, which reached its peak in the 1980s. Its champion shipping company – Evergreen – in 1984 ranked first globally in terms of the number and size of container ships. Meanwhile, Kaohsiung port ranked global third in container traffic from 1986 until the end of the 1990s. Taiwan's deep-sea fisheries joined the global top three from that time. However, the trend turned downwards from the 2000s. The share of maritime output to the GDP dropped from 2.5% in 1991 to 1.4% in 2011 (Huang and Chang 2015, 34). Between 2006 and 2011, the value of the island's international water freight was reduced by 30%, (Ibid) while Kaohsiung's global port ranking fell from sixth to 12th place.[6] The output of deep-sea fishing also shrank 10 percentage points from 2001 to 2011.

It is apparent that the challenge ahead is twofold. The traditional maritime industries require significant upgrading in response to the global structural changes ahead. New maritime industries – such as maritime tourism, bio-technology, or renewable energy – are in urgent need of further development and policy guidance. A new cabinet-level agency in charge of maritime affairs was set up in April 2018, but unfortunately a comprehensive maritime strategy is for the time being nowhere in sight.

Recognising that port competitiveness stems from a broader supportive policy environment for outward orientation, the Taiwanese government at all levels should provide appropriate financial, infrastructure, and urban planning policies to foster a more comprehensive maritime policy. Options could include expanding the existing Free-Trade Ports, and reviving earlier measures aiming at greater liberalisation reform proposed in the FEPZ, a policy scheme abolished in October 2016 (Executive Yuan 2013). An island-wide deregulation of the mobility of goods, talents, capitals, information, and knowledge with more domestic markets opening to foreign investors could be a critical precondition for this strategy to become a success.

## Enhanced energy and food security

This new Eastbound strategy has additional benefits of enhancing the energy and food security of Taiwan by increasing the capacity and reliability of supply chain from the Western Hemisphere.

The expanded Panama Canal enables 90% of current LNG/LPG tankers to pass through its new locks, compared with a meagre 30% through the old locks (Energy Information Administration 2016). The LNG-carrying capacity has increased more than fivefold from 0.7 billion cubic feet (BCF) to 3.9 BCF (Ibid). The travel time is also significantly reduced. For example, sailing a large LNG/LPG tanker from the Gulf of Mexico to Japan now only takes 25 days, compared with 41 days previously (Moryadee and Gabriel 2017, 3). It makes the LNG/LPG of the Gulf area more accessible to Asian markets. It has been speculated that nearly all US LNG/LPG exports could go to East Asia by around 2035 (Ibid). Given Northeast Asia's long-term interest in a regional gas hub, Taiwan could be positioned to benefit from supply diversification. Taiwanese ports could be configured to accept LNG/LPG imports, including regasification facilities.

Taiwan has long sought to reduce its reliance on nuclear energy, requiring it to increase the consumption of thermal (gas or oil) energy – which accounted for 38.6% of the island's energy composition in 2017, but is expected to rise to 50% in 2025 (Ministry of Economic Affairs 2017). More imports would be required to help fulfil this energy ambition. Taiwan currently imports LNG/LPG from five countries: Qatar, Malaysia, Indonesia, Nigeria, and Australia. Many of these suppliers place an 'Asian Premium' to raise the gas price. Except for a tiny share from Australia, 99% of Taiwan's gas imports need to pass through disputed waters in the South China Sea. Hence, the risk of supply disruption is significant – either from conflict or tension suddenly rising in the South China Sea or the Taiwan Strait. In particular, the US LNG/LPG import may turn out to be more economical, and certainly more politically secure for Taiwan's needs.

Likewise, Taiwan's food security may also be strengthened by cheaper and more reliable supply lines from East Coast America, especially the US and Brazil. In 2016, 83% of Taiwan's domestic cereal supplies – mainly corn and wheat – were imported, with 55% coming from the US and 27% from Brazil (Council of Agriculture 2018). Taiwan also imports 95% oilseeds and pulses, with 58% from the US and 37% from Brazil (Ibid). The increased capacity of the Panama waterway would considerably reduce transportation cost of dry bulk carriers, making East Coast American grains – particularly of Brazilian and Argentinian origin – more competitive in Asian markets.

### Stronger Taiwan-US ties

Taiwan's economic ties with the US were strongly driven by the growing Pacific shipping lines established by the Japanese in early 20th century. Taiwan's trade dependence on the US was less than 1% at the end of 19th century, but this figure soared to 20% in 1907, and peaked at 23% in 1915, a similar level to figures in the 1990s (Lin 2010, 1061–2).

We expect that this growing Eastbound strategy for Taiwan would make a major contribution in aligning Taiwan's expanding economic space with US national interests as articulated recently in the Trump administration's 'Indo-Pacific' strategy (Majumdar 2018). While, like most Asian economies, Taiwan will see disruptions from a trade war between the US and China, its Eastbound orientation could at the minimum serve as an insurance policy or hedging strategy in the scenario that trade diversion from competitive regionalism and political conflicts put pressure on Taiwan.

In the face of the current diplomatic impasse and future uncertainties hanging over cross-Strait relations, Taiwan should proceed to forge a stronger economic partnership with the US and its economic alliances in this region and across the Atlantic. The Eastbound trade route will form the transport backbone for these partnerships.

### Notes

1 This anti-China approach is new and opposite to the previous one based on engagement and integration. After Washington shifted its official recognition from Taipei to Beijing in 1978, the US policy had remained that of integrating China into the global economy and international politics in the hope that China would become a responsible stakeholder in the global system. See Auslin 2018, p. 7.
2 Low fuel cost and rebates by the Suez Canal Authority for LNG/LPG passage render this 'floating storage' option viable.

3 Other than Kaohsiung, six more ports – including Keelung, Taipei, Taichung, Suao, Anping seaports, and Taoyuan airport – were included in the programme. See National Development Council 2014.
4 According to the formal information provided by the Ministry of Transportation for the Legislator Charles Chen's Office on June 20, 2020.
5 This series of regular economic talks are set by the US-Taiwan Trade and Investment Framework Agreement (TIFA) signed in 1994, while the first talks began in the following year.
6 The global rank of Kaohsiung port in 2018 was No.15. Lloyd List (2018).

# References

Ashe, Ari. 2018. 'US Southeast Ports Attract New Asia Services, Larger Ships,' *Journal of Commerce*, 2 March 2018, https://www.joc.com/port-news/us-ports/port-savannah/southeast-us-ports-attract-new-asia-services-larger-ships_20180302.html (last accessed 20 May 2018).

Auslin, Michael R. 'The Question of American Strategy in the Indo-Pacific,' Hoover Institute, Stanford University, 17 July 2018, p. 7, https://www.hoover.org/research/question-american-strategy-indo-pacific (last accessed 27 December 2018).

Barnard, Bruce. 2016. 'Panama Canal Overtakes Suez on Asia-US East Coast Route,' *Journal of Commerce*, 22 November 2016, https://www.joc.com/maritime-news/trade-lanes/panama-canal-overtakes-suez-asia-us-east-coast-route_20161122.html (last accessed 24 April 2018).

Burghardt, Raymond F. 2019. 'NCAFP Trip to Taipei, Beijing, Seoul and Tokyo November 27 – December 11, 2018,' *National Committee on American Foreign Policy*, 14 January 2019, p. 12, https://www.ncafp.org/2018-ncafp-asia-trip-report/ (last accessed 25 January 2019).

Bush, Richard C. 2004. 'The United States, Taiwan and an FTA,' *Brookings Op-Ed*, https://www.brookings.edu/opinions/the-united-states-taiwan-and-an-fta/ (last accessed 5 May 2018).

Callahan, Amanda. 2016. 'Ocean Shipping from China to US East Coast: Carriers and Routes Reviewed,' *Lilly and Associates International Transportation*, 21 January 2016, http://www.shiplilly.com/blog/ocean-shipping-from-china-to-miami-carrier-review-and-routes/ (last accessed 24 April 2018).

Carlisle, Herbert H. Fall 2018. 'Advancing US Strategic Priorities in the Indo-Pacific Region,' *Journal of Indo-Pacific Affairs*, Vol. 1, No. 1, pp. 1–11.

Chen, Charles I-hsin. 2018. 'After Election, Taiwan's Grand Strategy Is in Doubt,' *The National Interest*, 27 November 2018, https://nationalinterest.org/feature/after-election-taiwan's-grand-strategy-doubt-37277 (last accessed 28 November 2018).

Cossa, Ralph A. and Brad Glosserman. 2018. 'The Pivot Is Dead, Long Live the Pivot,' *Comparative Connections*, Vol. 20, No. 2, pp. 1–12.

Council of Agriculture. 2018. Executive Yuan R.O.C., 'Agricultural Statistics.' http://agrstat.coa.gov.tw/sdweb/public/trade/tradereport.aspx (last accessed 23 April 2018).

Edmonds, James T. 2012. '"Panama Canal: Game Change" Depends on Who Provides the "Playing Fields,"' *Economic Development Journal*, Vol. 11, No. 2, pp. 42–47.

Energy Information Administration of the United States. 2016. 'Expanded Panama Canal Reduces Travel Time for Shipments of US LNG to Asian Markets,' *Today in Energy*, 30 June 2016, https://www.eia.gov/todayinenergy/detail.php?id=26892 (last accessed 15 March 2018).

Executive Yuan. 2013. 'Free Economic Pilot Zones a New Wave of Economic Liberalization,' Executive Yuan, Republic of China (Taiwan), 16 January 2013, https://english.ey.gov.tw/News_Content2.aspx?n=8262ED7A25916ABF&sms=DD07AA2ECD4290A6&s=C001CBEFFE5E743A (last accessed 24 April 2018).

Funke, Michael and Hao Yu. 2011. 'The Emergence and Spatial Distribution of Chinese Seaport Cities,' *China Economic Review*, Vol. 22, No. 2, pp. 196–209.

Gardner, Simon and Elida Moreno. 2015. 'Panama Canal Sets Sights on New $17 Billion Expansion Project,' *Reuters Business News*, 26 March 2015, https://www.reuters.com/article/us-panama-canal/panama-canal-sets-sights-on-new-17-billion-expansion-project-idUSKBN0MM24I20150326 (last accessed 24 April 2018).

Huang, Yo-yi and Chang Shu-man. December 2015. 'A Study on the Linkages and Cluster Effect of the Taiwan Ocean Sector,' *Maritime Quarterly*, Vol. 24, No. 4, pp. 29–52.

Institute of Transportation. 2016. '2016 Analysis on Global Liner Shipping Database,' Institute of Transportation, Ministry of Transportation and Communication of the Republic of China (Taiwan), pp. 67–68, ir.lib.ncku.edu.tw/bitstream/987654321/175804/1/3010603002-000003.pdf (last accessed 15 March 2018).

Koga, Kei. 2018. 'Redirecting Strategic Focus in the Age of the Indo-Pacific,' *Comparative Connections*, Vol. 20, No. 1, pp. 129–37.

LaFeber, Walter. 1993. *The Cambridge History of American Foreign Relations: The American Search for Opportunity, 1865–1913*. Cambridge: Cambridge University Press.

Lin, Man-houng. 2010. 'Taiwan, Hong Kong, and the Pacific, 1895–1945,' *Modern Asian Studies*, Vol. 44, No. 5, pp. 1053–80.

Lloyd's List. 2018. 'One Hundred Ports 2018.' https://lloydslist.maritimeintelligence.informa.com/one-hundred-container-ports-2018 (last accessed 12 February 2019).

Majumdar, Dave. 2018. 'Trump Has Big Plans for Asia. Well, More Like the "Into-Pacific" Region,' *The National Interest*, 3 April 2018, http://nationalinterest.org/blog/the-buzz/trump-has-big-plans-asia-well-more-the-indo-pacific-region-25204 (last accessed 20 April 2018).

McDonald, Scott D. 2018. 'Wanted: A Strategy for the Indo-Pacific Region,' *The National Interest*, 7 August 2018, https://nationalinterest.org/print/feature/wanted-strategy-indo-pacific-region-28182 (last accessed 12 November 2018).

Ministry of Economic Affairs. 2017. 'Road Map for Energy Transformation,' Ministry of Economic Affairs, Executive Yuan, Republic of China (Taiwan), 13 June 2017, p. 6, https://www.google.com/url?q=https://www.ey.gov.tw/DL.ashx%3Fs%3D08CDAD84C3FB3B752234ED2054834D409A9FAB090DD737D4BB2793E2D1357C2BCBC610B3782C1FB1BAF5A49A7F46CF3138AB054172DCBE10E007DBC593EB66BF%26u%3D%252FUpload%252FRelFile%252F3524%252F751735%252F2289cdde-c659-49f4-ab4f-f6abc69c2b8a.pdf&sa=U&ved=0ahUKEwj3q76lydjaAhWoh6YKHRooDOsQFggEMAA&client=internal-uds-cse&cx=017432093606973510952:u6v95vqvv6o&usg=AOvVaw0XhdLcSwaYWmjWa8YMHbdM (last accessed 26 April 2018).

Ministry of Finance. 2020. 'Summary of Exports and Imports for May 2020,' Ministry of Finance, Republic of China (Taiwan), 8 May 2020, https://www.

mof.gov.tw/singlehtml/384fb3077bb349ea973e7fc6f13b6974?cntId=651e3f5ae 85f42eea62874923f6d3851 (last accessed 26 June 2020).

Ministry of Transportation and Communications of the Republic of China. 2020. 'Container Ports World Ranking Top 20,' *International Transportation Statistics*, https://www.motc.gov.tw/uploaddowndoc?file=compare/e5080.pdf&filedisplay= e5080.pdf&flag=doc (last accessed 20 June 2020).

Mongelluzzo, Bill. 2017. 'Savannah, Charleston Drive Coastal Asia Import Gains,' *Journal of Commerce*, 21 December 2017, https://www.joc.com/port-news/ us-ports/port-charleston/savannah-charleston-drive-east-coast-asia-import-gains_20171221.html (last accessed 15 March 2018).

Mongelluzzo, Bill. 2019. 'Savannah, Houston Drive Asia Import Shift to East, Gulf Coasts,' *Journal of Commerce*, 21 March 2019, https://www.joc.com/port-news/us-ports/savannah-houston-drive-asia-import-shift-east-coast_20190321. html?utm_source=Eloqua&utm_medium=email&utm_campaign=CL_JOC%20 Daily%203%2F22%2F19_PC9156_e-production_E-29251_BM_0322_0617 (last accessed 19 July 2019).

Mongelluzzo, Bill. 2020. 'COVID-19 Changes Big Ship, Asia Focus for US Ports,' *Journal of Commerce*, 22 April 2020, https://www.joc.com/maritime-news/trade-lanes/covid-19-changes-big-ship-asia-focus-us-ports_20200422.html (last accessed 20 June 2020).

Moryadee, Seksun and Steven A. Gabriel. 2017. 'Panama Canal Expansion: Will Panama Canal Be a Game-Changer for Liquefied Natural Gas Exports to Asia?' *Journal of Energy Engineering*, Vol. 143, No. 1. Article 04016024.

National Development Council. 2014. 'The (Amended) Program of the Free Economic Pilot Zone,' January 2014, p. 37, https://www.ndc.gov.tw/News_Content. aspx?n=9D32B61B1E56E558&sms=9D3CAFD318C60877&s= 0130A47699EA56D4 (last accessed 11 January 2019).

National Security Council. 2020. 'United States Strategic Approach to the People's Republic of China,' 26 May 2020, p. 7, https://www.whitehouse.gov/wp-content/ uploads/2020/05/U.S.-Strategic-Approach-to-The-Peoples-Republic-of-China-Report-5.20.20.pdf (last accessed 4 June 2020).

Office of the President. 2016. 'Inaugural Address of ROC 14th-term President Tsai Ing-wen,' Republic of China (Taiwan), 20 May 2016, https://english.president.gov. tw/NEWS/4893 (last accessed 14 December 2018).

Office of Trade Negotiations. 2019. 'Achievements for the New Southbound Policy,' Office of Trade Negotiations, Executive Yuan, Republic of China (Taiwan), 6 September 2019, p. 7, https://www.ey.gov.tw/File/2B746482758B9A5B (last accessed 2 June 2020).

Panama Canal Authority. 2017. *Annual Report 2017*, https://www.pancanal.com/ eng/general/reporte-anual/2017-AnnualReport.pdf (last accessed 12 March 2018).

Panama Canal Authority. 2019. *Annual Report 2018*, https://www.pancanal.com/ eng/general/reporte-anual/2018-AnnualReport.pdf (last accessed 12 March 2019).

Panama Canal Authority. 2018. *Frequently Asked Questions*, http://micanalde panama.com/expansion/faq/ (last accessed 15 March 2018).

Panama Canal Authority. 2019. *Annual Report 2019*, https://www.pancanal.com/eng/ general/reporte-anual/2019-AnnualReport-Rev02.pdf (last accessed 7 June 2020).

Port of Kaohsiung, Taiwan International Ports Corporation. n.d. 'The Execution of Public Construction,' *Open Information*, https://kh.twport.com.tw/chinese/cp. aspx?n=0BDC6CAF354A3A57 (last accessed 8 May 2018).

Schoonover, Thomas David. 2003. *Uncle Sam's War of 1898 and the Origins of Globalization*, Lexington: University Press of Kentucky.

Schwarz, Elaine. 2017. 'Why the Panama Canal Is Bigger and Better,' *Econlife*, 13 October 2017, https://econlife.com/2017/10/panama-canal-expansion/ (last accessed 24 April 2018).

Sun, Her-feng. 2015. 'The Political Economy of the Taiwan's Free Economic Pilot Zone Program,' Master Thesis, Department of Political Science, National Taiwan University.

Szakonyi, Mark. 2016. '2M Service Reroute from Suez to Panama to Speed US Import Transits,' *Journal of Commerce*, 21 July 2016, https://www.joc.com/maritime-news/container-lines/2m/2m-service-shift-suez-panama-routing-give-us-importers-faster-transits_20160721.html (last accessed 24 April 2018).

Wright, Robin. 2016. 'Panama Canal Banks on $5.3bn Locks: Gates Swing Open to Bigger Ships Riding out Capacity Storm in Container Sector,' *Financial Times*, 26 June 2016, https://www.ft.com/content/245cd7a2-38df-11e6-a780-b48ed7b6126f

# 8 A new westbound policy? The case for increasing EU-Taiwan engagement

*Michael Reilly*

From a cursory glance at official websites and statements, bilateral trade between the European Union (EU) and Taiwan appears to be flourishing. As of mid-2020, the website of the European Commission states *Trade between the EU and Taiwan has increased more than eightfold over the past two decades.* Taiwanese statements are less dramatic in their content but still describe the two as 'important economic partners' (European Commission 2020). But the statistics tell a rather different story. Four EU member states – Germany, the Netherlands, the UK, and France together – account for more than 60% of all the EU's bilateral trade with Taiwan. Two-way trade between Taiwan and these four grew just 17% between 2000 and 2015. Three quarters of the increase – $3.6 billion of $4.79 billion – was accounted for by an increase of 78% in German exports to Taiwan. By contrast, EU trade with South Korea grew 168% in the same period and with China more than tenfold (IMF 2018). It is a far cry from the late 1990s when the trade of most EU countries with Taiwan exceeded that with China and, in their determination to win big contracts there, they were willing to engage politically with Taiwan at a hitherto unprecedented level. After the Chiang Kai-shek government was expelled from the United Nations in 1971, European countries broke all diplomatic and political links with Taiwan. Then, as trade grew, Cabinet level ministerial visits were followed by the opening of quasi-non-governmental 'trade offices,' staffed by diplomats, euphemistically described as being 'on secondment,' or 'retired.' Some countries went further, France and the Netherlands incurring the wrath of China through the sale of submarines, frigates, and fighter aircraft. By 2001, Taiwan was the EU's third largest bilateral trading partner in Asia and the message seemed to be clear: European countries were very ready to run the supposed risks of engaging with Taiwan provided they saw enough benefits for themselves from doing so (Reilly 2017, 18).

The heady days did not last. By 2011, Taiwan had dropped to the EU's seventh largest Asian trading partner, accounting for a smaller share of total EU trade than both Hong Kong and Singapore despite its much larger size. As of 2018, Taiwan is only the EU's 15th largest trading partner overall, while the EU – the world's largest single market – is Taiwan's fourth largest market, behind China, the USA, and Japan.

The obvious explanation for this change is the rise of China, more particularly its impact on global trade patterns since its accession to the World Trade Organisation (WTO) in 2001. For both Taiwan and the EU, China is now a much more important trade partner than is the other: China is now the EU's second largest export market, taking nearly 10% of all EU exports, and, at more than 20% of the total, its biggest source of imports. For Taiwan, the figures are much larger, China and Hong Kong together taking over 40% of all its exports in 2019.

This latter figure is, in large measure, a direct consequence of the policies pursued by Taiwanese companies in offshoring much of their production to China. The full significance of the impact of this on the growth of China's economy remains understated, not least for political reasons. In 2015, the top three, and no fewer than eight of the top 11, exporters from China were Taiwanese-owned companies (MOFCOM 2015). The largest, Honhai Precision (Foxconn), is also China's largest private sector employer with more than 800,000 employees (it has been reported to be more than one million), equivalent to over 7% of the entire Taiwanese labour force. This domination of Chinese exports is concentrated in the electronics and information and communications technology (ICT) sector where the top three exporters – Honhai, Quanta, and Asustek – set the pattern for the rest of the industry by exporting either under their own name or that of wholly owned subsidiaries, frequently as contract manufacturers on behalf of companies such as Apple, HP, and Dell.

While China's exports are dominated by Taiwanese-owned companies, the impact of Taiwanese investment in China extends further. Middle-class shoppers in first-tier cities such as Beijing and Shanghai shop at department stores owned by a Taiwanese-Japanese joint venture and take their families to eat at the Taiwanese dim-sum restaurant chain *Din Tai Fung*. In what is by far the world's largest instant noodle market, just two companies account for almost 60% of all sales, both Taiwanese owned (Wang 2015). One of them, Uni-President, is a major retailer and while almost unknown outside East Asia, it regularly features in lists of the most highly regarded foreign brands in China (Rapoza 2012).

But it is in exports from China, those of the ICT industry above all, where Taiwanese investment has had the greatest impact. The worldwide slump in the ICT sector in 2000 after the bursting of the 'dotcom bubble' led in Taiwan to a 55% fall in demand for semiconductor production equipment. By contrast, despite the global slowdown, the Chinese semiconductor industry grew by 40%, and by around 25% annually over the next five years, much of it driven by Taiwanese investment (Wu 2006). One result is that today the overseas production ratio for Taiwanese ICT manufacturers is 91.3%, most of this due to production in China. Another consequence is that intermediate goods and services account for over 86% of Taiwan's exports to China, principally components and sub-components for assembly into finished products and subsequent export, usually by the mainland-based factories of Taiwanese-owned companies. Between 2008 and 2015, China's imports of electronic goods and components from Taiwan grew by 114% and Taiwanese companies increased their share of this segment of the overall market to over 20%. But this was entirely due to the growth of exports of integrated circuits. By 2015, these comprised over 75% of Taiwan's electronics exports and almost 50% of *all* its exports to China (Reilly 2017).

The full significance of Taiwanese investment in the sector becomes apparent when one looks at the role of the country in industry supply chains. According to the WTO, in 2018 China's top four exports by value were all in the electronics and ICT sectors and totalled some $455 billion (over $75 billion of which was accounted for by just three Taiwanese-owned companies), or more than 18% of all China's merchandise exports. But China's top import in the same year was in the same sector – integrated circuits. At $261 billion, these represented around 15% of all China's imports and were equivalent in value to almost 60% of the country's four main exports combined. Although Taiwan's exports to China have been growing more slowly than those of the rest of the world since the bilateral Economic Co-operation Framework Agreement (ECFA) was signed between the two countries in 2010, the electronics sector has been an exception. Here, Taiwan has successfully increased its market share of Chinese imports by more than one-third, to over 20%. This is mainly on the back of rapid growth in its export of integrated circuits. Around one-third of all those imported by China now come from Taiwan, with most ultimately destined for export from China in a finished product (Reilly 2018).

Many in Taiwan worry that this has created an unhealthy, even dangerous, dependence on China. Like Taiwan, Korea has also increased its share of China's electronics imports but not at the expense of its exports in other sectors. Despite the huge success of companies like Samsung and to a lesser extent LG, electronics equipment comprised under 50% of Korea's exports to China in 2015. And whereas Korean exports include higher value-added branded final products, such as mobile phones, tablets, and laptops, the integrated circuits which comprise the core Taiwanese export are an almost entirely commoditised business: margins are cut to the bone and profits are dependent on volume. Taiwan's exports are also heavily dependent on a small number of major purchasers: among listed companies on the Taiwan stock market, 35% of total market value is attributable to companies in Apple's supply chain, while Taiwan's semiconductor giant TSMC currently receives around 14% of its total earnings from supplying Huawei (Hille 2020b).

Many reasons have been advanced to explain this reliance on a niche sector, not just for export success but for the country's economic growth generally, ranging from the continued predominance of first-generation owners in many of Taiwan's small and medium enterprises (SMEs), which are reluctant to adapt their hitherto successful business models to a changing world, to the level of regulation and state interference in the economy hampering initiative (Reilly 2017, ch.3). Not surprisingly, the consequences are causing growing concern among Taiwan's policy makers given the growing dependence on China that has resulted. The concern is understandable, not least given regular bellicose remarks and threats emanating from China towards Taiwan. For good measure, Chinese companies have been quick to learn from their Taiwanese counterparts and are increasingly powerful competitors: China's fourth largest exporter by value is now Huawei Technologies, while other ICT companies such as ZTE, Lenovo, and Xiaomi have risen to global prominence almost as quickly.

In response, the Tsai Ing-wen government has two trade priorities: one is the *New Southbound Policy*, through which it is trying to encourage exporters to look for opportunities in South and South East Asia rather than China, the second is its stated objective of trying to join the Comprehensive and Progressive Agreement for Trans-Pacific Partnership, or CPTPP. Originally known as the TPP until Donald Trump's decision to withdraw the USA from it, Taiwan's desire to join was originally and primarily driven by the importance of its bilateral trade and wider relationship with the USA. Even without the USA as a member, however, the CPTPP members led by Japan will still account for over 25% of Taiwan's total trade, making membership highly desirable (Taipei Representative Office in the UK 2018).

But in focusing on current trade patterns, Taiwan's policy makers may be at risk of overlooking, or worse reinforcing, a trend in the structure of its trade which should be of greater concern than the dependence on China and which the *New Southbound Policy* on its own seems unlikely to address. This is the heavy, indeed growing, reliance on the ICT sector and even more, a sub-sector within it, to generate export growth. The statistics tell the story and make sobering reading. ICT products now account for over 44% of all Taiwan's exports; in the case of exports to China, over 60% are classified as 'electronic equipment.' Contrast this with South Korea, for whom ICT products comprise 27% of total exports. While this has suited Taiwan well over the years, such dependence on a single industry for economic vitality leaves the country heavily exposed to changes in technology, sentiment, or political attitudes.

Over the last two years the nature of these threats has become all too apparent as US President Donald Trump has ratcheted up pressure on China. The importance of Taiwanese companies in driving Chinese growth means they have already been caught in the crossfire: Taiwan's principal export market is China and its dominant export industry is electronics and ICT, both the target of President Trump's tariff increases. Although Taiwanese exports to China fell as the impact of the new American tariffs started to bite, the direct impact of the trade war on Taiwan is likely to be less than at one time feared. Its exports to the USA increased by just over 17% in 2019, offsetting the decline in its exports to China. The biggest beneficiary of the US-China trade war was Vietnam, to where some multinational companies and their sub-contractors, including some Taiwanese companies, hastened to re-locate production from China. It saw its exports to the USA surge as a result. Reflecting this, Vietnam's imports from Taiwan jumped by almost 20% between the third quarter of 2018 and that of 2019, further helping to absorb the drop in Taiwan's exports to China (Reilly 2020).

But Taiwanese businesses also face threats from China's 'Made in China 2025' indigenisation policy, under which the country seeks to reduce its reliance on imported components in key industries, including ICT, and from President Trump's attacks on this, for example his attempts to cut off supplies of semiconductors to Huawei. For good measure, Apple and the other ultimate customers for Taiwanese products are seeking to broaden their supply bases for business reasons, an approach that President Trump's policies have strengthened and the impact of the COVID-19 pandemic has further reinforced. In short, Taiwan has built much of its economic success on the key role its businesses have played in global supply chains. These supply chains are now under threat from several directions and Taiwan needs to respond (Hille 2020a).

To date, the principal domestic policy response of governments of both parties in Taiwan to this has been to try to identify 'new' industries and pour government money into them to try to generate momentum, so far with mixed results at best. In doing so, they have too often overlooked the barriers and impediments to trade diversification and new industry start-ups within the economy, often self-imposed through domestic regulations; or the way in which current trade agreements may unwittingly serve the interests of established industries at the expense of new ones. The World Bank's *Doing Business* report gives an excellent example of the problem and should be required reading for Taiwanese officials. In the overall assessment for 2020, Taiwan is ranked an impressive 15th out of 190 countries worldwide for ease of doing business generally, higher than all but four of the EU member states, albeit some way below Korea and Hong Kong (fifth and third respectively). But other Asian states have been rising up the rankings faster and in the latest report, Taiwan has been overtaken by Malaysia (12th). And for a country that depends on trade for its prosperity, Taiwan's 61st place for ease of cross-border trade should be a major concern. This places it behind not just Korea (36th) and Malaysia (49th) but countries such as Armenia, Belarus, and – surely most disconcerting of all – even China. For getting credit – so important for start-ups or companies seeking to diversify – Taiwan's ranking is even poorer – a lowly 104th, again, a lower ranking than that for China (World Bank 2020).

Successive *Doing Business* reports have noted improvements in the regulation of cross-border trade in recent years, principally the increase in electronic submission and clearance of export-related documents, but the cost of processing export documents remains high compared to some neighbouring countries. Ironically, some of the document processing arises from the growth of regional and bilateral free trade agreements and the need to produce certificates of origin for goods to be eligible to benefit from them. For SMEs, which form the bulk of Taiwan's business sector, the costs of processing these sometimes outweigh the benefits. The bureaucratic and regulatory costs associated with exporting are more than twice as high for a Taiwanese exporter as for a Korean counterpart for example, and almost one-third more than for a Japanese one. Given that so many Taiwanese businesses cut their margins to the bone to win business and depend on very high volumes of sales to turn a profit, improving this ranking by reducing the costs involved in exporting should be a key priority for policy makers.

Accession to the CPTPP would be a major step forward. It would reduce the amount of bureaucracy involved in exporting but, much more importantly, would require important structural adjustments to be made to the Taiwanese economy. The conditions for accession include a commitment to following common rules on regulations among members, greater transparency in the activity of state-owned enterprises and common standards for the treatment of pharmaceuticals, product labelling and testing, and more. While the Taiwanese government has committed to undertaking significant reforms along these lines as part of its preparations to apply to join the CPTPP, progress so far has been delayed, not least in convincing the electorate of the need for reform and the benefits it should bring. Given the major protests and demonstrations that accompanied efforts to pass the Cross-Strait Service Trade Agreement in 2014, the importance of such preparation cannot be understated.

With the *New Southbound Policy* and accession to the CPTPP as its priorities, the possibility of increasing trade and investment with the EU has not featured high on the Taiwanese government's list of priorities. And as officials increasingly grapple with the implications for Taiwan of President Trump's trade war with China, it seems likely that it has slipped even further down the order. But even without a nascent trade war to consider, there is little to suggest that concluding an agreement with the EU has been considered a priority by either side. In addition to the relative stagnation of bilateral trade, EU officials have shown no obvious enthusiasm to open negotiations with Taiwan. It was only pressure from the European Parliament that led to the Commission announcing its readiness in 2015 to 'explore launching negotiations' and since then Commission officials have repeatedly said that conclusion of an agreement with Taiwan must first await the satisfactory conclusion of one with China (Reilly 2017). But progress on this remains desultory and sluggish, with the 28 rounds of negotiations that have taken place between their launch in 2014 and April 2020 being characterised by what has been described as a continuing 'penny-wise pound-foolish' approach to market-opening measures on the part of China (Mitchell 2018).

Could the tariff increases and other Trump administration action against China offer an opportunity to Taiwan? The Taiwanese government certainly thinks so, as on 10 May 2019 President Tsai announced a series of policy measures to encourage Taiwanese businesses in China to relocate some of their production to Taiwan. The logical response of Taiwanese producers to higher tariffs should certainly be either to try to repatriate some of the final assembly in China back to Taiwan or to move it to a third country where it would be free from the higher tariffs. Shifting modest amounts of final assembly back to Taiwan should also be possible, especially as labour costs in Taiwan are competitive with those of the mainland and more of the final assembly operations are being mechanised (Reilly 2018).

But it will not happen overnight: Intel has calculated that moving a chip packaging plant out of China would cost between $650 million and $875 million. And most manufacturers are likely to prefer to avoid such a commitment. Nevertheless, as the US-China trade war has intensified, and the COVID-19 pandemic further highlighted the fragility of global supply chains, so companies are starting to rethink their investment strategies and plant locations. But it is far from axiomatic that they will move production to Taiwan. The Taiwanese labour market is probably too small to meet the large-scale needs of the big contract manufacturers, certainly without major accompanying structural adjustment in other sectors, while land use regulations and ownership patterns would also be obstacles. Research by the Japanese bank Nomura concluded that East Asia overall, not just China, would be worse off as a result of any trade war but that Malaysia stood to gain from increasing its exports of integrated circuits, while in the medium term Vietnam would be the major beneficiary of any relocation of plants from China, something borne out by the early trade statistics quoted above (Woodhouse 2018).

The attention given to the trade war with China risks diverting attention from broader shifts in US trade policy under President Trump, which also have the potential to cause significant damage to Taiwan's interests. Without the influence of the USA as a member for example, it is far from clear that the CPTPP members would be willing to stand up to likely Chinese lobbying against admitting Taiwan. And as President Trump also seems intent on moving the USA away from its historic leadership of championing multilateral free trade, its role in this regard is being taken over by the European Commission. But this, too, offers an opportunity to Taiwan. For, notwithstanding its focus on the USA as an ally and major trading partner, in trade policy terms the US attitude towards Taiwan has often been less than supportive, characterised by one expert as *an excuse to just do nothing until we get what we want on pork*, a reference to the insistence that Taiwan lifts its prohibition on the use of the additive ractopamine in pork (a prohibition it shares with the EU, which extends it to all meat), even though pork forms a miniscule percentage of US-Taiwan trade (Wang 2016). While European officials also seem lukewarm about any bilateral agreement with Taiwan, at present Europe does at least seem likely to offer more opportunities to Taiwan's potential growth industries of the future than either South East Asia or most of the broader CPTPP membership.

Taiwan therefore stands to gain twice over from adopting a more proactive approach towards an agreement with the EU: at the macro-policy level in support for a multilateral trading system and bilaterally in opening up new opportunities for exporters. Persuading both Taiwanese politicians and businesses that this is the case may not be straightforward, however. Although the relative stagnation in EU-Taiwan trade over the last two decades is most readily attributed to the growth of trade with China, part of the reason also lies in the underdeveloped nature of bilateral relations, which in turn reflects a mutual lack of interest, itself largely a consequence of past misunderstanding or disagreements.

From Taiwan's perspective, the EU offers neither the quiet but important political support it receives from Japan, nor the security guarantees provided by the USA, while EU policy towards China has often been seen as deeply suspect if not downright alarming, above all the ill-advised plan to lift the arms embargo on China in 2005.

The EU, however, has too often seen North East Asia generally, not just Taiwan, through the narrow prism of commercial opportunity and has lacked any strategic interest in or understanding of the region. It was significant that it was only after the near debacle of the plan to lift the arms embargo that any serious attempt was made to bring some coherence to its policy towards the region (Reilly 2017, ch.2). For good measure, the UK's departure from the EU's trading arrangements at the end of 2020 will create uncertainty over the future direction of both the EU's and UK's trade and diplomatic policies towards North East Asia. The Taiwanese would not be alone in wanting to wait for the dust to settle on Brexit before pursuing negotiations with either the EU or the UK.

The EU's relationship with Taiwan, especially in the 1990s, has been described as a 'functional' one, driven on the part of EU states by their desire to win big commercial contracts but rarely supported by any broader strategic or foreign policy foundation. Paradoxically, perhaps, the main beneficiary of this approach was Taiwan itself, which successfully used this desire and the competition it generated between European countries, to strengthen its external relations. By contrast, sustained commercial success by European companies was rarely achieved, not least because the companies concerned too often failed to build effective links within Taiwan (Mengin 2002). (Part of it too was almost certainly due to unrealistic expectations on the part of European politicians as to what their interventions could achieve.)

European interest was not only in exports but in trying to persuade Taiwanese companies to invest in their countries. Here too the pattern was similar. A flurry of investment by Taiwanese companies in Europe in the 1990s was usually in response to generous grants and other government incentives. But many of the projects barely outlasted the grants, creating resentment or irritation on the part of governments that only a little while earlier had been only too ready to disburse them without adequate prior scrutiny of the recipients and their long-term plans. Attempts by Taiwanese companies to gain market share or know-how through buying mature European ones have often been no more successful, as BenQ's ill-fated purchase of Siemens' mobile phone business in 2005 suggests. The company was declared bankrupt the following year, although some production was moved to Taiwan.

Although the European Commission describes the EU as *the major source of foreign direct investment in Taiwan*, nor can European investment in Taiwan be considered an unalloyed success. In terms of impact, if not value, the high point of such investment was at the turn of the millennium when Philips of the Netherlands was the largest foreign invested company in Taiwan, with seven plants employing over 12,000 staff and ranking second among Taiwan's manufacturing industries (Lin 2006). European investment successes since then have as often as not been counterbalanced by failures. The retail sector provides a good example – the success of companies such as Carrefour offset by the withdrawal from Taiwan of Tesco, Marks & Spencer, and others. Philips was subsequently involved in a long-drawn out legal battle over an attempt to force it to accept lower royalty payments from Taiwanese companies through compulsory licensing arrangements and while it was ultimately successful in fighting its case, the dispute did little to encourage European companies to consider investing in Taiwan.

Other high-profile conflicts and disputes from the first decade of this century include the award of major contracts for Taiwan's high-speed railway to a European consortium including Alstom and Siemens being overturned by the government in favour of Japanese companies, and a decision by China Airlines to buy Airbus planes fitted with Rolls-Royce engines also being overturned by the government, the contract going to Boeing and GE instead (Bedford and Hwang 2006, 34).[1] In each case, the decision was almost certainly political but for the EU, especially when seen against the broader background, they simply reinforced negative perceptions of the seemingly untrustworthy nature of Taiwan and its companies in business matters.

If Taiwan is to build its trade and investment links with Europe, work effectively with the European Commission to protect the multilateral trading system and persuade the EU to accelerate negotiations over a bilateral investment agreement, changing ingrained perceptions and suspicions going back two decades or more must therefore be a priority. Showing European companies that the country is more open and welcoming to business and investment than hitherto is an essential first step. Ironically for a country that remains so dependent for its success on export-led growth, the regulatory costs associated with *importing* products into Taiwan are lower than those for exporting from the country. But the time taken for imports to clear border and documentary checks is more than twice as long in Taiwan as in Hong Kong and more than *seven times* longer than it takes in Korea (World Bank 2020). The extra time involved raises costs for importers and deters them from approaching the Taiwanese market, which is perhaps the intention. But Taiwan needs the support of importers, current and potential, to lobby on its behalf in European capitals if its hopes of concluding an investment agreement are to bear fruit. So, reducing this time and the associated costs should be a priority.

Part of the reason for these obstacles lies in the continuing existence in Taiwan of its own unique technical standards and mandatory product testing requirements. These act as trade barriers, raising the price of imported goods for Taiwanese consumers and reducing competition. Removing, or at least reducing, these is a key demand of the EU if it is to start meaningful negotiations on a bilateral investment agreement. But the demand is not confined to the EU. Even before Donald Trump was elected president, the United States Trade Representative (USTR) had insisted that action by Taiwan to reduce trade barriers, especially in the area of agricultural exports, was a prerequisite even to discussing Taiwan's bid to join the then Trans-Pacific Partnership (TPP). Despite encouraging noises from Congress, notably the enactment in March 2020 of the TAIPEI Act, Taiwan would be unwise to assume US support for its own trade ambitions.[2]

With the USA having withdrawn from the TPP, some of the more ambitious or contentious proposals which were originally included at the behest of the USA have been dropped as the TPP has transformed into the CPTPP. But the latter remains an ambitious step forward in regional trade agreements and Taiwan will have to make significant adjustments to its economic structure and regulations if it is to join. Steps have already been taken with amendments to several key laws, including those covering trademarks, patents, and copyright protection approved by the Legislative Yuan since 2019. Implementation of these changes will also be an important positive step for EU negotiators.

Precedent suggests that Taiwanese officials may be inclined to see improved market access measures as a zero-sum game and resist agreeing further changes for as long as possible before climbing down, thereby hoping to show domestic interests that the concessions were forced upon the country by outsiders. But as the analysis of Taiwan's dependence on ICT exports has shown, internal restructuring of the Taiwanese economy should be a high priority for its government. To rejuvenate sluggish domestic growth, the government should be looking to liberalise the economy by easing regulations, reducing the influence of state-owned or quasi-state–owned enterprises and making access to credit easier for the SMEs that form the bulk of the domestic sector. The reforms that Taiwan will have to undertake if it is to accede to the CPTPP will be an important contributor to this. They will also be welcomed by European businesses, encouraging them to take more interest in the potential Taiwan has to offer and thereby increasing the attractiveness of an investment agreement with Europe.

An agreement with the EU should also lead to new opportunities for Taiwanese exporters. Products of the electronics sector currently feature strongly in Taiwan's exports to the EU, as they do in those to other markets. Under the WTO's Information Technology Agreement (ITA), they are also already free of tariffs in the EU. But they account for no more than 20% of Taiwan's total exports to the EU, compared to 60% in the case of China. Not only is the export mix to the EU more diversified than to other markets, in recent years it has also been growing faster – over 5% in 2016, a year when Taiwan's exports to Association of Southeast Asian Nations (ASEAN) member states fell. Even more importantly for the future prosperity of Taiwan, much of this growth is coming not from the traditional areas but new, albeit niche, areas where the value added is much higher.

A good if unlikely example is bicycles, EU imports of which are dominated by Taiwanese-owned companies. The lion's share of these may now come from large factories in China but in 2016 European imports of electric bikes from Taiwan jumped by 84% and Taiwan remains the import country of choice for premium quality bicycles for leisure and sporting use (Association of Cycle Traders 2017). An even less likely example is whisky. Taiwan has long been one of the biggest global markets for premium Scotch whisky but within the last decade it has also started producing its own high-quality whisky, which is being exported to Europe and elsewhere.

While tiny in relation to Taiwan's total exports, its nascent whisky industry also highlights the importance of adding value through building a brand, the very antithesis of Taiwan's traditional contract manufacturing model in which the brand value is added by the customer, Apple being only the most noteworthy example. In much the same way that first Japanese, then Korean, companies have built their success through producing high-quality goods to which their unique brand names can then be attached, so building greater brand recognition is essential to Taiwan's future prosperity and should be a core aspect of the government's industrial policy. Indeed, it goes further. Give the struggle Taiwan faces for international recognition, the promotion of distinct Taiwanese brands, or a specific Taiwan brand denoting quality, would help offset Chinese efforts to squeeze ever harder its diminishing international space. Encouraging greater competition and harmonising domestic standards with leading international ones would be an important first step towards this. It is against this background that Taiwan should be responding to the EU's offer to open negotiations for a comprehensive investment agreement. Based on past behaviour, the instinctive temptation of negotiators may be to seek benefits for the country's 'big players' in the ICT sector, while resisting efforts by the EU to improve market access to Taiwan for fear that this will be opposed by domestic interests. But this would be a mistake. The ICT sector already benefits from Taiwan's membership of the WTO's Information Technology Agreement (ITA) which makes 97% of world trade in ICT products tariff-free, while a reduction in or removal of some market access barriers will be a condition for CPTPP membership. And instead of trying to restrict these to the minimum, policy makers should seek to steal a march on China in its own protracted negotiations with the EU. The lesson from the 1990s was that European politicians responded to pressure from European business for help in winning big deals in Taiwan. If market access proposals make opportunities in Taiwan more attractive to European businesses, they are far more likely to press European politicians to support a bilateral investment agreement. Such pressure will carry far more weight domestically than any amount of lobbying by the Taiwanese government. And it will be essential if conclusion of an agreement is not to be held permanent hostage to progress, or the lack of it, in finalising one between the EU and China.

Taiwanese officials should also be consulting the country's new or potential exporters to Europe about the hurdles they face. Individually, Taiwan's bicycle manufacturers, whisky makers, orchid growers, tea producers, and service providers may be in niche areas but the opportunities for them in the large and prosperous EU market are far greater than in most of Asia. Why, though, did it take until late 2018 for a *Din Tai Fung* restaurant to open in Europe, for example, despite the chain's huge success in Asia and North America and the unmet demand?

A priority area for attention should surely be the myriad of sanitary and phytosanitary trade barriers (SPS). EU officials rail against Taiwanese restrictions in this area, notably product-labelling requirements, which seem more for bureaucratic convenience than genuine consumer protection. But EU measures can be similarly restrictive: as the UK negotiated its departure from the EU, the future of the border with Ireland became the most contentious issue and the handling of agri-food, sanitary, and phytosanitary issues featured prominently within this (Connelly 2018). Yet food and agricultural trade between the EU and Taiwan is more often complementary than competitive so these restrictions mainly serve to hamper trade, not to protect either consumers or producers. An encouraging step forward came in August 2018 when Taiwan opened its market to the import of British pork (having long been an importer of British breeding pigs). But Taiwan could do more. For example, it could learn from the EU by doing more to market, protect and promote its distinctive agricultural products. The spread of the systems of Protected Geographical Indication and Protected Designation of Origin within the EU has successfully protected the reputation and status of traditional regional produce, notably wines and cheeses. Taiwan could push for similar protection for its orchids, high mountain teas, or other agricultural produce and have them recognised in an agreement with the EU.

In conclusion, a bilateral investment agreement with the EU is an opportunity for Taiwan that it cannot afford not to pursue. But it should be seen not as an end in itself, or as simply another international agreement to support the legitimacy of Taiwan as a state, but as an essential component of a comprehensive approach to restructuring the Taiwanese economy, to ensure it is able to meet the challenges of the second quarter of the 21st century and sustain and enhance Taiwan's prosperity. In this it has much in common with accession to the CPTPP and officials should consider approaching the two objectives side by side. It is not a zero-sum game but an opportunity for Taiwan to shape the future of its economy and make it less beholden to the whims and threats of Chinese leaders. Reducing market access barriers at home will not just make Taiwan a more attractive destination for European exporters and investors but also increase choice and reduce prices for

Taiwanese consumers. Deregulation will make it easier for young entrepreneurial talent to develop the new businesses, in new areas, that Taiwan so badly needs, while increased trade and investment with Europe will reduce Taiwan's uncomfortable dependence on China. In turn, the experience of other countries, notably Japan and Korea but increasingly China too, is that a strong trading relationship with Europe is the foundation of deeper and more wide-ranging ties. There is no reason why this would not also be the case with Taiwan, notwithstanding the lack of formal diplomatic ties; the experience in the 1990s has already shown that increased trade will stimulate European political interest, thereby helping to underpin Taiwan's sovereignty in the face of Chinese pressure. Rebuilding this relationship is a sensible and important step for both sides.

Go west, Taiwan.

## Notes

1 This was in 2003–4 and not to be confused with China Airlines' later decision in 2008 to buy 14 Airbus A350s, also with Rolls-Royce engines.
2 The Taiwan Allies International Protection and Enhancement Initiative (TAIPEI) Act was passed by the US Congress in 2019 and enacted in March 2020. Its main provision calls on the US government to advocate, as appropriate, for Taiwan's membership in all international organisations in which statehood is not a requirement and in which the United States is also a participant; and for Taiwan to be granted observer status in other appropriate international organisations.

## References

Association of Cycle Traders. 2017. 'EU's E-Bike Imports Continue to Surge,' 23 August 2017, https://www.cycleassociation.uk/news/?id=2189, retrieved 1 March 2018.
Bedford, Olwen & Kwang-Kuo Hwang. 2006. *Taiwanese Identity and Democracy: The Social Psychology of Taiwan's 2004 Elections.* Basingstoke: Palgrave Macmillan.
Connelly, Tony. 2018. 'As Brexit Approaches, the Gulf between Britain and Ireland Widens,' Financial Times, 2 March 2018, https://www.ft.com/content/59d23dcc-1c96-11e8-a748-5da7d696ccab, retrieved 26 March 2018.
European Commission. 2020. 'European Commission Trade Policy: Taiwan,' http://ec.europa.eu/trade/policy/countries-and-regions/countries/taiwan/index_en.htm.
Hille, Kathrin. 2020a. 'Huawei Says New US Sanctions Put Its Survival at Stake,' Financial Times, 18 May 2020, https://www.ft.com/content/3c532149-94b2-4023-82e0-b51190dc2c46?desktop=true&segmentId=d8d3e364-5197-20eb-17cf-24378 41d178a#myft:notification:instant-email:content.
Hille, Kathrin. 2020b. 'US "Surgical" Attack on Huawei Will Reshape Tech Supply Chain,' Financial Times, 19 May 2020, https://www.ft.com/content/c614afc5-86f8-42b1-9b6c-90bffbd1be8b.
IMF. 2018. 'Direction of Trade Statistics,' http://data.imf.org/regular.aspx?key=61013712, retrieved 28 February 2018.
Lin, Chia-wu. 2006. Philips Semiconductors Kaohsiung (PSK), in Terence Tsai & Bor-Shiuan Cheng (eds.). *The Silicon Dragon: High-Tech Industry in Taiwan,* Cheltenham: Edward Elgar, 78–94.

Mengin, Françoise. 2002. 'A Functional Relationship: Political Extensions to Europe-Taiwan Economic Ties,' *China Quarterly* 169, 136–53.

Mitchell, Tom. 2018. 'Why China Should Agree a European Trade Deal,' Financial Times, 25 September 2018, https://www.ft.com/content/76b33a18-c0a1-11e8-95b1-d36dfef1b89a?desktop=true&segmentId=d8d3e364-5197-20eb-17cf-2437841d178a#myft:notification:instant-email:content, retrieved 26 November 2018.

MOFCOM. 2015. *Ministry of Commerce: Foreign Trade Statistics of the People's Republic of China.* Beijing: Ministry of Commerce People's Republic of China.

Rapoza, Kenneth. 2012. 'Apple Tops List of China's Top 10 Foreign Brands,' Forbes. com, 6 August 2012, https://www.forbes.com/sites/kenrapoza/2012/08/06/apple-tops-list-of-chinas-top-10-foreign-brands/#386e42565f63, retrieved 22 November 2018.

Reilly, Michael. 2017. *Towards an EU-Taiwan Investment Agreement, Prospects and Pitfalls.* Basingstoke: Palgrave Macmillan.

Reilly, Michael. 2018. *Whales Fight, Shrimps Get Hurt – What Trump's Trade War with China May Mean for Taiwan,* Global Taiwan Brief, Vol. 3, No. 16, http://globaltaiwan.org/2018/08/vol-3-issue-16/, retrieved 23 November 2018.

Reilly, Michael. 2020. 'Can Taiwan Decouple from the Chinese Economy?', Taiwan Insight, 17 February 2020, https://taiwaninsight.org/2020/02/17/can-taiwan-decouple-from-the-chinese-economy/, retrieved 19 May 2020.

TRO (Taipei Representative Office to the UK). 2018. London newsletter, February 2018, citing Bureau of Foreign Trade.

Wang, Robert S. 2016. 'Taiwan's Vibrant Democracy and Beleaguered Economy – Implications for U.S. Interests and Policies,' CSIS Washington, 1 August 2016, https://www.csis.org/analysis/taiwan%E2%80%99s-vibrant-democracy-and-beleaguered-economy, retrieved 26 November 2018.

Wang, Zhuoqiong. 2015. 'Nissin Snaps Ties with Instant Noodle Maker Jinmailang,' China Daily, 1 December 2015, http://www.chinadaily.com.cn/business/2015-12/01/content_22594062.htm, retrieved 22 November 2018

Woodhouse, Alice. 2018. *Malaysia Best Placed to Benefit from China-US Trade War: Nomura,* Financial Times, 20 November 2018, https://www.ft.com/content/2de5582a-ec75-11e8-89c8-d36339d835c0, retrieved 23 November 2018.

World Bank. 2020. 'Doing Business 2020,' https://www.doingbusiness.org/en/data, retrieved 18 May 2020.

Wu, Tsung-yu. 2006. 'Partner in the "Chip Gold Rush" Applied Materials Taiwan,' in Terence Tsai & Bor-Shiuan Cheng (eds.). *The Silicon Dragon: High-Tech Industry in Taiwan*, Cheltenham: Edward Elgar, 113–40.

# 9 Change and continuity in American policy towards Taiwan

*Harry Harding*

In 1962, the philosopher of science Thomas Kuhn published a book entitled *The Structure of Scientific Revolutions*. Now, around 45 years later, relatively few may remember Kuhn's name or even the title of his book. But many more will recognise the highly influential concepts presented in his work: the development of paradigms – essentially shared assumptions and conclusions – that guide scientific inquiry at any particular time, and then the paradigm shifts that constitute scientific revolutions. Like many great insights, Kuhn's idea is a very simple one: most scientific inquiry exists within an established paradigm, one that identifies key phenomena, and then the assumptions, variables, methodologies, and theories that enable scientists to explain those phenomena and even predict them. As new phenomena and data appear, scientists continue to work within those paradigms, on the assumption that by doing so, practicing what Kuhn called 'normal science,' they can provide the answers to new issues and explain the newly available data. At certain times, however, existing paradigms can no longer easily incorporate those new phenomena, despite the best efforts of scientists to do so. At that point, there may occur what Kuhn describes as a 'paradigm shift': the acceptance of a new paradigm that is able better to explain the new phenomena without losing the ability to understand the older phenomena that formed the foundations of the previous paradigm.

Practitioners of modern policy analysis – essentially applied microeconomists – believe that the study of policy issues and the development of effective solutions are also a kind of science; indeed at one time they used the term 'policy science' to describe their quest for better public policy. (In China more recently, there was also the term 'scientific development,' associated with the former leader Hu Jintao, that suggested that the policy issues associated with China's economic development could be addressed 'scientifically,' and indeed that they should therefore be assigned to skilled elites within the Chinese Communist Party, making pluralistic democracy unnecessary and even undesirable).

The concepts of established paradigms, normal science, paradigm shifts, and scientific revolutions can therefore be applied to policy, including

American policy towards Taiwan, as well as to the physical, natural, and behavioural sciences. Since the emergence of Taiwan as a political and economic entity separate from mainland China in the late 1940s, there has been a mixture of change and continuity in American policy towards the island. A small number of these changes – three in all – have represented paradigm shifts, in which the underlying interests, values, and assumptions shaping American policy towards Taiwan underwent a major transformation. Far more have been smaller changes, responses to more specific issues in the U.S.-Taiwan relationship that could be managed by an adjustment in American policy rather than through what might be called a 'policy revolution.' The three broad paradigms have included a short-lived policy that placed Taiwan outside the American defence perimeter in the Western Pacific, with the implication that the fall of Taiwan was inevitable, that the United States would not try to prevent it, and that that development could actually enable Washington to establish a normal relationship with the newly established People's Republic of China. The second, a reversal of the first, was the extension of a formal security commitment to Taiwan in the 1950s, as the direct result of the outbreak of the Korean War and as part of the global network of military alliances the United States was constructing to contain Communist expansion, itself the result of the policy paradigm that was guiding America's security policy during the Cold War. The third paradigm change was the normalisation of relations with China from 1972 to 1979, resulting in the derecognition of the Republic of China and a reduction, although not complete elimination, of the American security commitment to Taiwan.

Within these enduring policy frameworks, however, there were often variations in the details of American policy as Washington adjusted its approach to meet changing circumstances. Many of these variations reflected issues that emerged, albeit in modified forms, repeatedly over the course of the paradigm, representing persistent dilemmas that American policymakers needed to address and recurring choices that they needed to make. It is that pattern of big paradigmatic shifts followed by smaller adjustments that has produced the blend of change and continuity in American policy towards Taiwan. The main drivers producing that pattern have been changing American perceptions of mainland China's capabilities, ambitions, and domestic evolution, and its evaluations of Taiwan as an economic, political, and security partner. The question now is whether there may be another paradigm big shift as the United States decides how to respond further changes in these three drivers, particularly the growing imbalance of power in China's favour, the more negative American perceptions of the evolution of China's domestic and foreign policy, and the increasingly positive U.S. views of Taiwan as the first Chinese democracy in a world characterised by a growing ideological competition between Chinese (and Russian) authoritarian state capitalism and Western pluralistic democracies and market-oriented economies.

## 'Letting the dust settle'

As the Chinese Civil War reached its conclusion in 1949–50, U.S. Secretary of State Dean Acheson offered a definition of American policy towards the new Communist government, particularly in light of its intent to 'liberate' Taiwan after its victory on the mainland. In a speech to the National Press Club in January 1950, Acheson placed Taiwan outside the American defence perimeter in the Western Pacific. This followed the earlier announcement of a policy to 'let the dust settle' before the United States decided on its relationship with the new People's Republic of China. The two statements reflected the expectation that, without continued American military support, which the United States was reluctant to provide, Taiwan would also fall to the Communists. That would bring the Chinese Civil War to an end and, after the 'dust' of the conflict had 'settled,' the United States would see if it would be possible to establish diplomatic relations with Beijing as part of a restored relationship, probably correct but cool, with the 'new China.' This new paradigm policy also reflected the intense awareness of the Truman Administration that, with the Cold War intensifying in Europe, and with little American appetite to reverse the demobilisation of troops after the end of Second World War, there was a need to set priorities regarding the definition of America's global security commitments. As had been traditionally the case, in making that definition it would be Europe that would come first, and so the commitments in Asia would have to be limited to countries within what would later become known as the 'first island chain': Japan and the Philippines.

## Guaranteeing Taiwan's security

Rarely is a major foreign policy abandoned so quickly as was the policy of letting the dust settle, as occurred in June 1950 with the outbreak of the Korean War. The United States not only decided to help defend South Korea against the attack by North Korea, which was viewed as being undertaken in coordination with China and the Soviet Union as part of an effort to extend Communist influence in Asia. It also placed units of the 7th Fleet in the Taiwan Strait to prevent either the Nationalists or the Communists from spreading the war from the Korean Peninsula to Taiwan, thus limiting the American exposure to the risk of an escalating conflict. In the early months of the Eisenhower Administration in 1953, Washington clarified that the mission of the U.S. Navy was not even-handed, as it had originally been portrayed, but one-sided: to prevent a Chinese attack on Taiwan without providing a parallel security guarantee to Beijing. The resulting U.S. security commitment to Taiwan was then codified in the Mutual Defense Treaty of 1954–5, one of a series of American alliances established regionally and globally to contain the expansion of Communism. The continued recognition of the Republic of China, as not only as the government of

Taiwan but also as the rightful government of all China and the occupant of China's seat in the United Nations, were also parts of that new policy framework often described as 'containment and isolation' of the People's Republic of China.

To justify its support for one side in what both Taipei and Beijing regarded as an ongoing civil war, the United States argued that the legal status of Taiwan remained undetermined, in that it had been taken from Japan at the end of Second World War but not explicitly transferred to any other state. In so saying, the United States neither accepted nor rejected Beijing's claims to the island but was rationalising its insistence that the future of the island be determined peacefully and justifying the potential use of force to defend Taiwan against a Chinese attack.

Over time, however, American policy towards Taiwan underwent important changes within that broad Cold War framework. These involved two enduring issues and dilemmas inherent in the new American commitment to Taiwan's security that required frequent reconsideration: which territories controlled by the Nationalist government on Taiwan would the commitment cover, and what would be the American position with regard to the Nationalists' desire ultimately to recover the mainland by the use of force.

The Taiwan Strait crises of the 1950s led Washington to extend its security commitment beyond Taiwan and the Pescadores to some of the major offshore islands Taipei controlled, particularly Jinmen and Mazu, to the extent that Washington deemed them 'essential' to the defence of Taiwan. By making that broader commitment conditional, Washington was drawing a dotted, not a solid, line around the offshore islands. At the same time, concerned that Taiwan might take the opportunity to attack the mainland and draw the United States into another war with China, the Eisenhower Administration also demanded assurances from Taipei that it would not attack the mainland without Washington's consent, and that its goal of reunification would be pursued mainly by political, rather than military means. This was done by extracting a cleverly worded statement from Taipei that any military equipment provided by the United States would not be 'removed' from Nationalist-controlled territory without American approval – in other words, an attack on the mainland of any scale would require American consent. The 1953 change in American policy that redefined the role of the 7th Fleet as protecting Taiwan against a mainland attack, and not the other way around, had been unofficially described as 'unleashing Chiang Kai-shek.' Now, Washington was putting Chiang back on a tighter leash.

At the same time, recognising the risks of a military confrontation with China over the offshore islands or in the Taiwan Strait, the United States began limited overtures to Beijing. It began ambassadorial level negotiations with Beijing in Europe in the mid-1950s, in which it futilely sought a Chinese renunciation of force against Taiwan but also explored ways of resolving specific bilateral issues and even establishing symbolically significant unofficial relations with the mainland as tension-reduction mechanisms. However, under considerable domestic pressure to apply the broader Cold War paradigm consistently in both Asia and Europe, it continued to demand the exclusion of the Communist government from the United Nations. And while extending military and economic aid to Taiwan, it also pressed the Nationalist government to engage in political and economic reforms, including the creation of a stable local currency (the new Taiwan dollar), a thoroughgoing land reform, and then limited political liberalisation and the first steps towards democratisation.

## Derecognition of Taiwan and the 'one-China policy'

The Sino-Soviet dispute, the long and costly American war in Vietnam, and the threat that the rise of Soviet power in Asia posed to regional security together produced the third turning point in American policy towards Taiwan: U.S.-China rapprochement undertaken during the Nixon administration and the subsequent normalisation of diplomatic relations during the Carter years. China's preconditions for achieving normalisation required significant changes in American relations with towards Taiwan, leading to the second paradigm shift in U.S. policy towards the island. During the Kissinger and Nixon visits in 1971–2, the U.S. took important initial steps to meet Beijing's demands, providing assurances that it would not promote Taiwan's independence or allow the island to fall under Japanese influence. The United States also moved closer to recognising China's claims to Taiwan through ambiguous passages in the 1972 Shanghai Communique and the 1978 normalisation agreement that the United States 'acknowledged' the Chinese position that 'there is one China and Taiwan is part of China' and that the United States 'does not challenge' that position, in effect neither accepting nor refuting China's position on the status of Taiwan. Indeed, Washington occasionally reiterated its earlier position that the status of Taiwan remained to be determined, and consistently reiterated its interest in a peaceful future for the island. Similarly, the eventual American responses to the other Chinese terms for normalisation in 1978–9 were in each case also partial and qualified. The United States would terminate diplomatic relations with Taiwan but would maintain extensive 'unofficial' political ties through an exchange of nominally unofficial missions, as well as full commercial relations. The United States would terminate the Mutual Defense Treaty with Taiwan and withdraw its remaining military forces from the island, but would continue to sell defensive arms to Taiwan and, under terms that Congress added to the Taiwan Relations Act, would maintain the capacity to defend Taiwan and would regard the mainland's use of force or other forms of coercion against Taiwan to be a matter of 'grave concern.' Beijing insisted that these qualifications were unacceptable and that it reserved the right to challenge them later but did not allow the differences to prevent the normalisation of diplomatic and economic relations with the United States.

The terms of normalisation in 1978–9 established a new paradigm for the U.S.-Taiwan relationship that has endured for 40 years, down to the present. The United States would have diplomatic relations solely with Beijing but would maintain a robust unofficial relationship as well as normal commercial ties. It would end its formal security commitment to Taipei but would continue selling arms as a reflection of its interest in a peaceful future for Taiwan. This new paradigm came to be known as the American 'one-China policy,' a term carefully chosen to echo, but not duplicate, Beijing's 'one-China principle,' which included a more specific recognition that Taiwan was part of China and that the Communist government in Beijing was the sole legitimate government of China. But, once again, within these new parameters there were many variations and oscillations over time, as the United States responded to changing circumstances: the full democratisation of Taiwan, the emergence of a distinctive Taiwanese identity, the rise of independence sentiment on Taiwan, and a growing Chinese military capability to threaten or attack the island. In addition, directly elected Taiwanese presidents, beginning with Lee Teng-hui, wanted to symbolise the extent of the continuing U.S.-Taiwan relationship by visiting the United States and receiving high-level American visitors in return, and so pressed for modifications of American policy to meet those goals.

In response to these developments on Taiwan and the nervousness some of them produced in Beijing, the United States reinterpreted and clarified its one-China policy at various times after the adoption of the Taiwan Relations Act in 1979. It reiterated that it would not support a Taiwanese declaration of independence, placed quantitative and qualitative limits on its arms sales to Taiwan, and said it would oppose Taiwan's membership in international organisations whose membership was restricted to sovereign states, and refrain from adopting a 'two-China' (i.e., a dual recognition policy). From time to time, when Taiwanese presidents were regarded as 'trouble-makers' because of statements and actions that reflected the growing popular demand for independence or greater international space, the United States would repudiate them. To underscore that the residual American security commitment to Taiwan was conditional, the Clinton Administration enunciated the principle of 'strategic ambiguity,' indicating that the American response to a Chinese attack or other forms of coercion against Taiwan would depend on which side had provoked the conflict.

However, other modifications of American policy were more forthcoming to Taiwan. The United States eventually allowed limited official exchanges between the two countries, including visits to Taiwan by the heads of 'non-sensitive' U.S. cabinet agencies (i.e., departments other than State and Defense), and 'transit' stops by Taiwanese presidents in the United States en route to the shrinking number of countries that still maintained diplomatic relations with the Republic of China. But while it increased over time, American support for Taiwan was never absolute. Washington did not hesitate to express its differences with Taipei on some major bilateral issues, including Taiwan's security strategy, its defence budget, and its policies restricting imports of American food products. In particular, a frequent issue in the relationship was Taiwan's reluctance to spend more on its own defence, including purchasing weapons that Washington had offered to sell. The American perception was that Taipei planned simply to do the minimum for its own security, holding out just long enough for American naval and air forces to come to Taiwan's rescue. Understandably, this was deeply enmeshed in Taiwanese domestic politics. The Kuomintang, although historically more closely connected to the Taiwanese military, opposed military budget increases proposed by the Democratic Progressive Party when it was in office, on the grounds that those expenditures were necessary only because of the 'provocative-independence policy' that the DPP had adopted and that the KMT would obviate the need for such expenditures by achieving at least a limited accommodation with Beijing.

Just as Taiwanese leaders tested the limits of America's Taiwan policy, so did some American presidents. In their election campaigns or during their subsequent administrations, Ronald Reagan, George H.W. Bush, and George W. Bush all seemed to move the United States closer to Taiwan, whether by suggesting a recognition of the officiality of the non-diplomatic relations between the two countries (Reagan), offering to sell more advanced weapons to Taiwan (George H.W. Bush), or announcing their determination to 'do everything it takes to defend Taiwan' (George W. Bush). In each case, however, after strong Chinese objections or, in some cases, pressure from American analysts and political leaders committed to the 'one-China' policy paradigm, those initiatives were later reversed, either by the president who pursued them or by his successor. It was this pattern that produced the bilateral agreement limiting American arms sales to Taiwan signed by the Reagan Administration in 1982 (although a secret 'Reagan Codicil' declared that those limitations would depend on China's continued commitment to peaceful unification, reflecting another continuity in America's Taiwan policy dating back to the early ambassadorial talks in the mid-1950s: the persistent attempt to extract a renunciation of force against Taiwan by mainland China, an assurance that Beijing equally steadfastly refused to provide). Subsequently, the changing balance of military power in the Taiwan Strait in Beijing's favour has led to an increase in the quality and quantity of American arms sales to Taiwan, producing Chinese charges that the United States has violated the terms of the 1982 communique. There have also been periodic loosenings and tightenings of American restrictions on high-level official visits between the United States and Taiwan, and shortly after pledging that the United States would do 'everything it takes to defend' Taiwan. George W. Bush corrected his statement to read 'everything it takes to help Taiwan defend itself,' once again reflecting the enduring American concern that Taiwan would do the minimum in the event of a Chinese attack and would leave its defence almost entirely to the United States.

The election of Donald Trump seemed to herald a more fundamental disruption of the one-China policy framework and perhaps another paradigm shift. After his election but before his inauguration, Trump accepted a congratulatory telephone call from Taiwanese President Tsai Ing-wen, anathema to Beijing because of her refusal to reconfirm the ''92 Consensus' between Beijing and Taipei, an informal agreement interpreted as committing Taiwan to eventual unification although on as yet unspecified terms. This was the first direct contact between an American president and his Taiwanese counterpart since the Eisenhower Administration. The call completed, Trump went one step further by questioning America's continued adherence to the 'one-China policy' unless Beijing made concessions on issues of concern to Washington, particularly the chronic bilateral trade imbalance and the North Korean nuclear weapons programme. Like his predecessors, Trump later reversed course, saying that he would remain within the 'one China' framework, but nonetheless made further adjustments in American policy that favoured Taiwan, in some cases prodded by members of Congress sympathetic to the island. Congress passed, and the President signed, a Defense Authorization Act that urged further sales of advanced arms to China, a Taiwan Travel Act that encouraged the administration to exchange high-level military and civilian officials with Taiwan, and ultimately the ingeniously named and abbreviated Taiwan Allies International Protection and Enhancement Initiative (the 'TAIPEI Act'), which provided that Washington would advocate Taiwan's membership or participation in international organisations and encourage other nations to upgrade or establish unofficial ties with Taiwan, usually interpreted as also encouraging the small number of countries that had diplomatic relations with Taiwan (what Taiwan calls its 'diplomatic allies') to maintain that recognition despite political overtures and economic incentives from Beijing. President Tsai Ing-wen was then allowed to make transit stops in Los Angeles and Houston on trips to two of Taiwan's remaining 'diplomatic allies' in Central and South America (Paraguay and Belize) to visit government facilities in the United States (including the Ronald Reagan Library near Los Angeles and NASA's Johnson Space Center in Houston), and to meet in New York with the representatives of China's diplomatic allies to the United Nations. Hers thus became the highest profile visit of a Taiwanese president since Chen Shui-bian's trips to Los Angeles and New York in 2001. Shortly afterwards, in an unprecedented gesture of support for Taiwan, Washington recalled its top diplomatic representatives from the Dominican Republic, El Salvador, and Panama for consultations after those countries switched diplomatic recognition from Taipei to Beijing and threatened the reduction or termination of economic aid. When the United States established the new International Development Finance Corporation to promote private investment in infrastructure in emerging economies, partly in response to China's Belt and Road Initiative, there were indications that one target would be countries that were receiving offers of Chinese investment on the condition that they terminate their diplomatic relations with Taiwan. Although these actions reflected further modifications of U.S. policy in the direction of closer ties with Taipei, Washington still insisted that they did not constitute any departure from the one-China framework, a reassurance that Beijing never accepted, but did not actively challenge.

## The possibility of further change

The major changes and more limited adjustments in America's Taiwan policy over the 70 years since 1949 suggest the possibility of further changes in the future. As in the past, the changes might be relatively small gestures towards Taiwan, still described as adjustments within the one-China policy framework, or they could represent a more significant paradigm shift. In the past, as already noted, these changes have been driven by four main drivers: American perceptions of China's capabilities and ambitions, especially towards Taiwan; American evaluations of China's domestic political and economic evolution; U.S. appraisals of Taiwan's posture towards mainland China; and American judgements about Taiwan's domestic economy and political system. When China is seen as powerful and threatening, and Taiwan is seen as liberalising and non-provocative, Washington moves closer to Taiwan. When China is seen as more progressive in its domestic politics and foreign economic policy and peaceful and responsible in its foreign policy, but Taiwan is regarded as too aggressive in its pursuit of independence or recognition of its international status, the United States has distanced itself from Taipei.

Going forward, either marginal or fundamental policy change could move in one of three directions: Taiwan could be sacrificed as the United States seeks to preserve a cooperative relationship with China, it could move closer to Taiwan in order to protect it from the growing security threats from a rising China. As of now, the second of these possibilities is more likely than the first, but either is possible depending on the evolution of the broader relations between the U.S. and Taiwan's relationship with the mainland.

As China becomes stronger militarily, and as the Chinese economy nears the point where it will pass America's, at least in terms of aggregate GDP, maintaining a cooperative relationship with China could be seen in Washington as more important than ever, both to avoid the costs and risks of military confrontation, and to foster collaboration on critical regional and global issues such as climate change, terrorism, North Korea's nuclear weapons programme, and pandemics such as SARS or COVID-19. To reduce those risks and to promote that more cooperative relationship, some American analysts have suggested that the United States make a fundamental shift of policy away from Taiwan, reducing its security commitment to the island as part of a 'grand bargain' with a rising China. This might involve a reduction in arms sales, a diminution in the level and frequency of visits by American officials, or even a statement that the United States prefers or foresees the peaceful unification of Taiwan with the rest of China, or even the repeal of the Taiwan Relations Act. Several Chinese accommodations have been suggested in exchange, particularly accepting the preeminent American role in the Asia-Pacific Region, and even globally.

So far, these voices are thus far in the minority, especially given the tensions with China over such sensitive issues as human rights, trade, investment, Being's territorial claims in the South China Sea, and most recently its policies towards Xinjiang and its more blatant intervention in Hong Kong in the name of national security. In addition, such a grand bargain would be difficult to negotiate, and perhaps even more difficult to enforce.

The other possibility would be even closer ties with Taiwan. Some conceivable steps would arguably stay within the framework of the 'one-China policy,' such as increasing arms sales and official contacts, allowing the president of Taiwan more opportunities to make 'unofficial' visits to the United States, perhaps for 'vacations' (reminiscent of the 'vacation diplomacy' conducted by Taiwan with some Southeast Asian countries in earlier decades), or to give speeches at American universities (similar to Lee Teng-hui's controversial visit to Cornell in 1995). The United States might also reduce its level of financial support to international organisations, such as the International Civil Aviation Organization and the World Health Assembly, that have bowed to pressure from Beijing and denied Taiwan the observer status that it had previously enjoyed. In fact, the Trump Administration did just that in the midst of the COVID-19 pandemic, both because of its belief that the organisation had uncritically accepted China's lack of transparency around the disease, and because it had allegedly ignored warnings from Taiwan health specialists that the disease was more serious and more easily transmitted than Beijing had acknowledged.

As we have already seen, a more fundamental policy shift was suggested by Donald Trump shortly after his telephone call with Tsai Ing-wen: that the United States might abandon its 'one-China' paradigm altogether in the absence of major concessions by Beijing on issues of great importance to Washington, presumably including trade and investment, North Korea, and other major security issues. But it is unclear which policy would replace it or the name the new paradigm be given. Would the United States then state a preference for Taiwan's independence, re-establish diplomatic relations with Taiwan, or support full Taiwanese membership even in international organisations that have previously required members to be sovereign states? Certainly such a step would remove a fundamental underpinning of the U.S.-China relationship and move the two countries closer to a confrontation, including increasing the probability of China's use of military force against Taiwan. These factors are powerful constraints against Washington adopting so drastic a shift in that direction.

Accordingly, neither of these two possible paradigm shifts has sufficient support to be probable. The increasingly negative views of China among the American public, rising tensions between the United States and China, the growing pressure China is placing on Taiwan and Hong Kong, and the difficulties in negotiating a 'Grand Bargain' that would provide enough benefits to justify a fundamental American accommodation of Chinese interests regarding Taiwan make such an accommodation unlikely under present conditions. At the same time, a shift away from the 'one-China policy' would produce not only a furious reaction from Beijing, but also significant reservations from some in Taiwan, where a desire simply to maintain the status quo is far stronger than the willingness to accept the costs and risks intendant upon more fundamental changes in American policy.

There is also a possibility of smaller adjustments in another direction that is thus far unprecedented but no longer inconceivable, The United States could pressure Taiwan not to move too close to the mainland by seeking a political accommodation or by expanding its trade and investments there. It could, in effect, force Taiwan to choose sides between Washington and Beijing, rather than flirting with a hedge strategy of trying to maintain good relations with both. At the time of writing, this is a possibility much feared by Taiwan's high-tech companies, which are already under pressure from America to limit their trade and investments in sensitive technologies where China has great ambitions and Taiwan has both comparative advantages and economic incentives to participate, but instead to shift at least some of their production facilities and export markets to the United States or American allies.

The most important driver in the relationship between the United States and Taiwan will be the evolving U.S.-China relationship. The growing power and ambitions of China could give greater weight to the proponents of change, both from those who want a closer relationship with democratic and friendly Taiwan to counterbalance China and to demonstrate that a society that is culturally Chinese can develop consolidated and effective democratic institutions, and from those who believe that America needs to accommodate an increasingly powerful China and that concessions on Taiwan are the best way to do so.

The history of the relationship suggests that paradigmatic shifts of this magnitude are rare, while adjustments within the framework that is in place in any given period are more likely. But with tensions between China and the U.S. mounting, the balance of power between them shifting, and the anticipation of a new Cold War between them growing, the possibility of a fundamental change in U.S. policy in either of these directions is greater than it has been in decades.

# 10 China's marginalisation of Taiwan

*Richard C. Bush*

Around the time of the School of Oriental and African Studies (SOAS) workshop in May 2018, several events illustrated the ways in which China has worked to isolate Taiwan from its own region and the world. Some of these tactics – getting the Dominican Republic to switch diplomatic relations to Beijing and denying Taiwan participation at the World Health Assembly (WHA) – were neither new nor unexpected, but they were still tough to bear. Others were unprecedented, such as China's effort to get international airlines to 'rectify names' in reference to Taiwan. These actions were only the latest episodes in a sustained campaign to limit and reduce Taiwan's role in the international system.

At the outset, this chapter explores the shifting geographic concentration of Taiwan's economic activity. It then focuses on the ways the government of the People's Republic of China (PRC) has sought to benefit from Taiwan economically but marginalise it politically. My conclusion is that Taiwan's political marginalisation stems not from anything idiosyncratic about Taiwan, but from the circumstances of its political history. The government and armed forces of the Republic of China (ROC) fled to the island of Taiwan after their defeat at the hands of the armies of the Chinese Communist Party on the Chinese mainland in 1949. The new government of the People's Republic of China (PRC), declared by Mao Zedong on 1 October of that year, would have liked to seize Taiwan and destroy the ROC right away but had to abandon those plans once the Korean War broke out. Instead, the PRC government tried to enhance its own legitimacy by shifting to political warfare and, from then on, driving the ROC from the international system. The ROC survived on Taiwan longer than most expected, in part because it was able to maintain its economic and political freedom of action. But Beijing's campaign continues – on economic as well as political fronts.

## Context

Several contextual factors are worth considering. First of all, we should distinguish between the position and actions of the Taiwan government on the one hand, and the situation and behaviour of the private sector on the other.

To be sure, the ROC government has played a *dirigiste* role in some sectors of the economy, and one hears complaints to this day about over-regulation by bureaucrats. Still, the private sector is dominant and, in some ways, it has greater flexibility than the government. For example, on the question of whether Taiwan will be allowed to participate in the Regional Comprehensive Economic Partnership (RCEP), Taiwan companies that are manufacturing at home would prefer that Taiwan be able to join the RCEP so that they will enjoy the benefits without disruption. But if China successfully induces other governments to refuse entry to Taiwan (as it likely will), then the affected companies have the option of moving their operations inside the boundaries of the new grouping. But the consequences are less favourable for some Taiwan workers, who will lose job opportunities, and the government, which will suffer the embarrassment of being excluded yet again from another regional economic club.

Second, Taiwan has had a limited number of trading partners throughout its history. Comparative advantage and markets did not always define who those trading partners were. Often, domestic and foreign policy dictated the environment for trade. In the later years of the Qing dynasty, key exports were sugar, camphor (an ingredient in celluloid and explosives), tea, and, decreasingly, rice. Sugar and rice went to China and tea to the United States. Opium was the leading import. Markets determined trade. But that pattern changed once Taiwan became a Japanese colony in 1895. The same commodities remained Taiwan's leading exports, but Tokyo dictated that sugar, camphor, and rice ship to the home country. Only tea still went to Europe and America (Gardella 1999; Lamley 1999).

At the end of Second World War, when Japanese rule over Taiwan ended and the officials of the ROC assumed control, it was expected that the island's relatively advanced economy would contribute to China's national reconstruction project. Yet, political developments made what might have been a simple transfer from one regime to another far more complicated, with profound economic consequences. China erupted into civil war in late 1946 and the result, by the end of 1949, was two rival regimes – the ROC on Taiwan and the PRC on the mainland. Taiwan's economic integration with the Mainland did not occur and all business interactions ceased between the two. Rhetorically at least, Taiwan became the base for Chiang Kai-shek's illusory mission of recovering the Mainland. For a while, that military mission distorted the island's economy by consuming a significant share of the government budget, funds that were not available to stimulate economic growth.

Taiwan also became a link in the U.S.-forged chain of containment against the PRC. The Eisenhower administration did not support Chiang's military goal and the import-substitution policy that went with it. Instead, Washington proposed a more focused emphasis on export-led development, which helped stimulate Taiwan's 'economic miracle.' As a result, Taiwan was not only tied to the United States by virtue of a military defence treaty; it also became more economically linked to both Japan and the United States and remained so until the 1980s. Together, these two markets accounted for between 50% and 60% of Taiwan's exports and imports.

As an aside, it is worth noting that debate persists over whether the ROC state or Taiwanese private companies were more responsible for Taiwan's economic growth. On the one hand, Taiwan is held up as an example of the East Asian developmental state, where governments play a key role in designating the most likely sectors for future economic growth, allocating capital accordingly, and ensuring adequate public infrastructure and human capital (Wade 1990). On the other hand, some have argued that although the government created infrastructure and human capital – and although it sometimes picked what turned out to be a growth industry (semi-conductors being the best example) – true credit goes to private entrepreneurs who identified and exploited product niches fostered by consumer demand in advanced economies like the United States. These entrepreneurs created networks of small and medium-sized companies that showed great skill in nimbly abandoning the manufacture of products and components that were no longer profitable and moving on to new enterprises, always staying one step ahead of the competition (Hsing 1998; Hamilton & Kao 2018).

Returning to the historical context for Taiwan's economic development, it was in the 1980s that an economic logic once again determined Taiwan's place in the regional and global economies. Taiwan companies came to play a key role in the PRC's emergence as the world's factory and as major employers of Mainland Chinese labour. Some Taiwan companies provided goods for the Chinese market. Others used the Mainland for final assembly of goods produced by complex, global supply chains (e.g., toys, shoes, bicycles, iPhones, and iPads). Networks of Taiwan companies moved across the Strait. As interdependence has grown since the early 1990s, China has become Taiwan's largest market for exports and its largest destination for direct investment (Lee & Chu 2016). In Taiwan's trade statistics, China (including Hong Kong) receives 40% of total exports and is the source of 20% of imports (also number one) (Bureau of Foreign Trade 2020). Of course, much of this activity reflects Taiwan's position as a key, intermediate link in global supply chains, which are, by definition, global. Still, China has become central to Taiwan's prosperity, even as Japan and the United States have remained significant trading partners. Nowadays, those two countries combined with China account for around 60% of Taiwan's exports and close to 50% of its imports.

Deeper economic integration across the Taiwan Strait was a boon to both economies, boosting China's economic growth and sustaining Taiwan's prosperity so that it avoided the middle-income trap. None of this would have happened, of course, if the political leadership in Beijing and Taipei did not see value in removing their respective barriers to business interaction. Even when Taiwan leaders sought to place limits on Taiwan investment on the Mainland, as Lee Teng-hui and Chen Shui-bian did, Taiwan companies found ways around these barriers.

Ironically, however, it was during this time of greater economic cooperation – from the early 1990s to the present day – that cross-Strait contention over Taiwan's role in the international system intensified. Sentiment in Taiwan favoured an elevated position, which Beijing resisted.

## Taiwan's International marginalisation and the U.S. role

As we know, the PRC's campaign to drive the ROC from the international system began with the founding of the regime. At every stage, moreover, the United States took actions that it thought were appropriate to defend the ROC's position, thus putting Taiwan at the centre of a U.S.-China relationship that was already hostile because of the Cold War. Under pressure from conservative, pro-KMT forces in Congress and the media, successive administrations worked to protect Taipei. There were also times when, despite those voices, the U.S. government sacrificed Taiwan's interests, particularly in the Nixon and Carter administrations.

The first stage of this campaign concerned diplomatic relations with third countries and the United Nations system. Early on, Beijing won diplomatic recognition from the countries of the Soviet bloc and Western Europe and established relations with most of the newly independent states once decolonisation began in the late 1950s. In turn, that trend improved the PRC's chances in the UN, where U.S. diplomats had worked tirelessly to keep the PRC out and the ROC in. Doing so had been relatively easy in the 1950s, when the membership of the organisation was small and U.S. influence was relatively large, but the task became more complicated with decolonisation. In the early 1960s, partly in response to growing PRC strength, the Kennedy and Johnson administrations devised a clever scheme to bring about a two-China solution for the UN, but Chiang Kai-shek rejected the proposal until it was too late. The PRC assumed the China seat in the UN in October 1971 and gradually in other organisations in the UN system thereafter. (The United States also tried, with declining success, to discourage friendly countries that had diplomatic relations with Taipei from recognising Beijing.)

Attention then turned to the institutions of the Bretton Woods system, the pillars of the international economy. The PRC entered the World Bank and the International Monetary Fund in 1980. Soon after, Beijing set its sights on the Asian Development Bank (ADB), which, like the World Bank, was a potential source of funds to underwrite the PRC's economic development. With Taiwan's expulsion from the ADB looming, its friends in the U.S. Congress threatened to terminate appropriations for the U.S. contribution to the institution. The Reagan administration was able to broker an arrangement whereby the PRC joined and Taiwan stayed. This required the creation of a new term for Taiwan that avoided the sovereignty issue and did so in a balanced way. The compromise was 'Taipei, China.'

In 1990, Australia and the United States collaborated in creating the Asia-Pacific Economic Cooperation forum (APEC) in order to head off an effort by Malaysia's Prime Minister Mahathir to establish an Asia-only regional economic forum. The George H.W. Bush administration worked to include Taiwan and was able to do so because the PRC was not yet a member. The term used to refer to Taiwan in the Olympics – 'Chinese Taipei' – was adopted.

The World Trade Organization (WTO) proved more complicated because accession usually requires the prospective member to complete extensive market-access agreements with any of its trading partners that sought them. Taiwan and the PRC would be no exception. Taiwan understood that, as with APEC, its best chance to join the WTO was at the same time as the PRC; if the latter was able to enter first, it would block Taiwan's entry or impose unacceptable terms. It also understood that the hurdles to membership were much higher than for APEC.

The Clinton administration exploited this situation, deciding in late 1997 to accelerate its negotiations with Taipei on the U.S.-Taiwan bilateral accession agreement, which would frame Taiwan's negotiations with any other trading partner that sought a bilateral agreement. The Clinton administration made this decision because Taiwan was a good candidate for WTO membership and enjoyed congressional support. But its strategy also carried the Machiavellian motive of leveraging Taipei's and Beijing's desire for membership to get each to negotiate seriously on market access. In effect, Washington pressured the PRC by threatening to bring about Taiwan's prior entry while also signalling to Taipei that if it were laggard, Beijing would enter first. The tactic worked on both sides of the Strait, and they entered the WTO at virtually the same time in early 2002. This time, the nomenclature for Taiwan was the 'Separate Customs Territory of Taiwan-Penghu-Jinmen-Mazu.'

## Taiwan's democracy and international space

Taiwan's democratisation introduced a new and very public layer to Taiwan's struggle against marginalisation. Political forces, particularly within the opposition Democratic Party (DPP), argued that it was not enough to stay in the Asian Development Bank or enter APEC and the WTO, all of which were special cases in one way or another. Instead, the DPP argued, Taiwan should seek to re-enter those international organisations which it had left when the PRC claimed China's seat. The key targets were the World Health Organization (WHO), promoted by many Taiwan doctors, and the United Nations itself. Securing this type of international participation became a matter of general dignity and affirmation that Taiwan, as a developed society, had valuable experience and resources that could be deployed to help solve global problems. This objective has enjoyed broad public support, something that no political party on the island can ignore.

Just as Taiwan looked to the United States to help keep its place in international organisations when the PRC was knocking at the door, so too has it sought American help in securing re-entry to the WHO, the UN, and other bodies. For its own part, the Clinton administration refined U.S. policy on Taiwan's participation in international organisations through the Taiwan Policy Review of 1994. It stated that the United States would support Taiwan's membership in those institutions for which statehood was not required as a prerequisite. In those organisations where membership was not possible, Washington would support Taiwan's 'voice being heard.' Subsequent administrations would speak of facilitating Taiwan's 'meaningful participation' as an objective.

This formulation reflected both policy principles and hard reality. As to the former, there is the U.S. one-China policy as Washington continues to define it (Bush 2017). That is, by stating in the normalisation communique of December 1978 that the United States 'recognized the government of the People's Republic of China as the sole, legal government of China,' it was effectively saying that it was the U.S. position that the PRC should occupy China's seat in international governmental organisations. For better or for worse, supporting Taiwan's membership in those institutions as the government of China or as a second government of China would violate that commitment. (Washington has never contemplated the idea that Taiwan is its own separate state and, by extension, deserves a seat as a member in these organisations.)

The hard reality is that most of the organisations that Taiwan would like to enter or re-enter operate by consensus, and China exploits that norm to get its way. Although Washington favours Taiwan's 'meaningful participation' in these institutions as a matter of formal policy, it does not have the power to require or induce member states to support its position, a reality reinforced by China's increasing economic and political influence around the world. Moreover, the United States is restrained from investing substantial political capital on Taiwan's behalf because it faces issues regarding the work of these bodies on which it needs the PRC's cooperation. Beijing, having already reduced Taiwan's participation in these organisations to a low level, is not about to cede those gains. Taiwan, of course, lacks the resources to compete with Beijing on a country-by-country basis. The best it has been able to do, again with U.S. help, is to occasionally persuade some European countries and Japan to speak out on its behalf.

### Lessons learned

In brief, there are grim lessons to be learned from Taiwan's efforts to preserve and expand its international presence. For those international organisations where China is already a member and Taiwan is not, China has an absolute veto over Taiwan's entry and is prepared to use it.

The same is true of multilateral trade groupings, be they existing or proposed. Again, these usually operate by consensus, so China can overrule any proposal that Taiwan be included. For example, Taiwan would like to be a member of – or at least play a role in – the RCEP. But the PRC has figured prominently in the creation and design of the grouping, and it can force other prospective members to choose between Taiwan and a successful negotiation. The same was true of the Association of Southeast Asian Nations (ASEAN) Regional Forum and the East Asia Summit. Even, theoretically, for groupings where the PRC might be excluded, it would likely have sufficient influence with at least a few of the members to ensure, based on the consensus principle, that Taiwan be excluded.

The same is true of bilateral economic arrangements that Taiwan might pursue, such as free trade agreements (FTAs). Most of the countries that might be its targets would weigh the potential value of any such agreement against the potential long-term cost to its relationship with the PRC.

There are four exceptions to these rules.

The first is when China decides that letting up on Taiwan is in its own interests. That happened during the Ma Ying-jeou administration. Beijing facilitated Taiwan's presence at major meetings of the WHA and the International Civil Aviation Organization (ICAO) and it gave the green light to Singapore and New Zealand to conclude bilateral FTAs. It did so, in each case, for political reasons: indeed, I understand that China was more eager for the two FTAs than were Singapore and New Zealand themselves. China's goal was to signal to Taiwan that it would be able to play a greater external role both politically and economically if it went through Beijing and not around it and, more broadly, if it accommodated Beijing's desire to define Taiwan's relationship to China in ways that Beijing preferred. But even when dealing with President Ma, China's willingness to let Taiwan have more international space was both limited and grudging.

The second exception, as already noted, occurs in multilateral groupings where China is not a member but the United States is. In these scenarios, Washington plays a strong leadership role on Taiwan's behalf to circumvent China's indirect pressure on other members. That was true in the ADB, the APEC, and the WTO. Unhappily for Taiwan, there are not many such organisations left.

The third exception – related to bilateral arrangements like FTAs – is where the country concerned is willing to stand up to Chinese pressure. Japan demonstrated that kind of resolve in concluding a bilateral investment treaty with Taiwan in 2011 and a fisheries agreement in 2013. In principle, the United States has that kind of courage but it will not deploy it until Taiwan makes some concessions on market barriers, a subject that will be discussed more below.

The fourth exception (to date, only a theoretical one) concerns groupings where China is not a member *and* where membership is open to members of another grouping of which Taiwan is already a part. For instance, the Trans-Pacific Partnership (TPP) was open to all members of APEC. So is the Comprehensive and Progressive Agreement for Trans-Pacific Partnership.

Even here, the PRC can try to exploit the consensus principle to get one or more members to veto Taiwan's entry.

## Explaining China's behaviour

Why is Beijing so determined to block Taiwan's participation in international organisations and inclusion in trade liberalisation arrangements? Two factors are at play. First, it takes a zero-sum approach to the matter, fearing that Taiwan's goal is one of three outcomes to which the PRC is opposed: two Chinas; one China, one Taiwan; or Taiwan independence. It does not accept at face value Taiwan's assertions that it has a legitimate contribution to make to international organisations or the right to its own role in promoting trade liberalisation. China was more lenient during the Ma administration only because Taipei conducted quiet, advance consultations with Beijing *and* because it believed that Ma would be willing to enter into political talks sometime during his tenure. Second, the PRC's Ministry of Foreign Affairs (MFA) has pursued the exclusion of Taiwan from the international system as one of its core missions since 1949. This is a way that the MFA can demonstrate its patriotism.

The PRC's effort to drive the ROC and Taiwan from the international system was not an end in itself but one important means of achieving its fundamental goal of national unification. A Taiwan with little or no international presence was a Taiwan that was more likely to capitulate to Beijing's approach to resolving the cross-Strait dispute, or so the logic went. The PRC allowed Taiwan limited international space during the Ma administration as a deliberate way of exerting leverage over Taipei to undertake political talks that would improve prospects for the PRC to achieve its ultimate objective of unification. Since at least the early 1990s, however, Taiwan's democratic politics have assured that this exclusionist approach would be counterproductive. In the early 1990s, the DPP gained political capital by proposing that Taiwan seek to join – or re-join – the UN and that it seek to be an observer in the WHO. Recently, more aggressive efforts by the PRC to peel away Taiwan's diplomatic allies and otherwise limit its international role have only hurt Beijing's image with broad segments of the public and kept those who favour unification to a relatively low number.

A rolling poll that the Election Studies Center of National Chengchi University has conducted on behalf of the Mainland Affairs Council found that the share of those surveyed who want unification immediately or at some time in the future is consistently around 10%. The Taiwan Security Survey has sought to measure Taiwan views of China relative to the United States and Japan. Respondents were asked to rank each country – first, second, or third – and were also permitted to list two countries tie for either first or second place. In the 2015 survey, China was in first place for only 12.24% of those surveyed, below both the United States and Japan, which were 24.25% and 37.21% respectively. Another 9.24% believed China was tied for first with another country. But 55.58% of respondents ranked China in third place, far more than either Japan or America. That is, the share who put China in third place was close to three times those who said it was in first place or tied for first (21.48%) (Niou 2016). Another 6.12% put China second, while 16.81% thought it was tied for second.

One might think that the PRC government would understand that it could score points with the Taiwan public and win their hearts and minds by being flexible towards Taiwan's desire for participation in international organisations and in trade arrangements. But that does not seem to be the case. A couple of years ago, several American colleagues and I met with fairly senior Chinese officials, and we emphasised the need to accommodate Taiwan's desires for international participation. The answer we heard was that China understood one way it could 'win the hearts and minds' of the Taiwanese people was by providing benefits. But, they said, it could also secure Taiwan's acquiescence by displaying and exercising power, even if playing a power game makes Taiwanese people unhappy. Sooner or later, it was said, they would accommodate to reality.

## Economic marginalisation

Those are the general parameters of the relatively weak position in which Taiwan finds itself. But the ground beneath it continues to shift. All Asian countries have sought to deepen their economic ties with China, whatever the nature of those ties. As a result, China has become the centre of a truly regional economy. It is the hub and its neighbours are the spokes. The United States is still important, particularly as a final market, but China has become the main regional player. As business activities became more integrated, pressures have intensified for trade and investment facilitation on a regional basis. For some time, there has been a noodle bowl of FTAs and other preferential arrangements. But Taiwan was excluded from trade-facilitation integration in the region as a member economy, even though it was becoming more integrated in terms of business.

Hence, the creation of the ROK-PRC FTA stokes fears that Taiwan firms will not be able to compete with their Korean peers in the Chinese market. The proposed Regional Comprehensive Economic Partnership, whose main objective is to rationalise the string of ASEAN+1 FTAs, has great potential, depending on the quality of the liberalisation effort. RCEP negotiations have proven difficult and slow-moving, but one study estimates that trade liberalisation among RCEP economies could yield annual income gains of approximately $500 billion dollars by the year 2025. It is not in the interest of Taiwan to be outside of this bloc, but when the Ma administration expressed interest in the RCEP, Beijing told Taipei that it needed to finish the Economic Cooperation Framework Agreement (ECFA) first. And we know where ECFA is now. And, of course, the United States is totally outside of the RCEP and so is unable to help Taiwan as it did in the case of the WTO.

Even though Taiwan is excluded from many of the 'clubs' it would like to join, Taiwan companies are not necessarily constrained by inter-governmental arrangements. Indeed, when Taiwan is excluded from re-gional trade and investment groupings, companies can sometimes move their operations behind the walls of the group to gain the relevant prefer-ences. If ASEAN creates an FTA, Taiwan companies can move operations to ASEAN countries even more than they already have. That may benefit the companies and their stockholders, but it is not necessarily good for em-ployment opportunities in Taiwan and the country's international position.

China is not the only reason for Taiwan's marginalisation. U.S. govern-ment policy does not help. Although some in the Trump administration – and in previous administrations – have regarded Taiwan as a strategic asset, the U.S. Trade Representative (USTR) is given a free hand to pursue a tough negotiation strategy towards Taiwan. USTR takes the view that on market access for beef and pork, Taiwan has both maintained barriers to U.S. ex-ports for a long time and reneged on commitments to remove some of those barriers. So, in USTR's view, until Taiwan carries out its commitments, the United States will not begin negotiations on initiatives that would be good for Taiwan and for U.S. business, such as a bilateral investment agreement. Which raises a question: if Taiwan is indeed a strategic asset for America, should Washington treat it more leniently on trade?

It is difficult for any Taiwan president to make concessions on market access for beef and pork in order to induce Washington to *start* negotia-tions on an issue like investment. Pork farmers are an important political bloc and many consumers worry about food safety. The Taiwan government probably has ideas about how to resolve these issues *in the course of* ne-gotiations, but that is unacceptable for USTR. Consequently, U.S.-Taiwan economic relations remain suboptimal in their result.

Officials at USTR might have their own way of framing the issue of Tai-wan's marginalisation. They might ask: to what extent is Taiwan perpetuat-ing its own marginalisation? Are Taiwan's own policies preventing it from escaping excessive dependence on China by diversifying its external eco-nomic profile? Both the KMT and DPP would like to promote trade and investment diversification and reduce dependence on China. But they have disagreed about how to do it.

A central goal of Ma Ying-jeou's presidency was to normalise, liberalise, and institutionalise cross-Strait economic relations. To bring that about, he was willing to say flat out that he accepted the 1992 consensus – with his own interpretation, of course. At least rhetorically, he also understood the need for increasing Taiwan's economic relations with its other major trading partners and the need to remove barriers in order to do so.

The DPP has been reserved about interdependence with China. In 2013 and 2014, the party mounted procedural and substantive opposition to the Ma administration's Service Trade Agreement. Both as a candidate and as president, Tsai Ing-wen has not willing to accept the 1992 consensus in the explicit way that China demanded. But she did not reject Beijing's formula for normal relations. In her inaugural address, she addressed it ambiguously. But that was not good enough for China, which, I believe, simply did not wish to coexist with her government and legitimise the DPP in the process. Squeezing Taiwan in cross-Strait relations in this way and marginalising it in the international economy signals to Taiwan that it is trapped and has no choice but to base its economic future on integration with China and, ultimately, to accept unification. Tsai remained restrained until early 2019 when, in response to a major speech by Xi Jinping on Taiwan policy, she began to conflate the 1992 consensus and one country, two systems.

Of course, Taiwan companies have more options than the government does, and they are likely to exercise this flexibility. But Taiwan voters will have their own view of how the Mainland is trying to achieve its goals, and young voters are particularly important. At least some politically conscious young people worry about Taiwan's shrinking presence in the international space. And although others have responded positively to Beijing's new policy of providing incentives to Taiwanese to study and work in China, these economic benefits will probably not buy the political loyalty of those who accept them.

The Trans-Pacific Partnership presented the best opportunity for Taiwan to reverse this process of politically motivated marginalisation by the PRC and help integrate it economically with the East Asian region. Also, joining TPP would have forced on Taiwan the domestic structural adjustment that it needed anyway. Of course, the usual impediments would have been at play. Even though TPP was open to all APEC members and therefore to so-called Chinese Taipei, China would have pressured some of the original 'TPP Twelve' to block Taiwan from joining in a second round.

Still, the process by which Taiwan became a member of the WTO, as described above, served as a model for how Taiwan could join TPP in a second round. Taiwan's path to membership was quite narrow, but there was still a path. In my own analysis, the only scenario in which Taiwan would have a chance at joining TPP would be if China decided that it was in its own interests to join. That would give the United States and Japan leverage to facilitate entry for Taiwan, as the United States did for the WTO. Likewise, China seeing TPP membership as attractive – as it did for WTO membership – would serve as a lever to carry out domestic economic reform. But this scenario for Taiwan and TPP was only relevant before Donald Trump pulled the United States out of the group. As long as it stands outside of the TPP process, the United States cannot exert leverage on Taiwan's behalf. It remains to be seen if the Comprehensive and Progressive Agreement for TPP will be sufficiently robust to interest China and if Japan will have the ability and desire to counter Beijing's efforts to deny Taiwan entry. Regrettably, this is another way in which U.S. policy has contributed, unwittingly, to Taiwan's marginalisation.

Make no mistake: the significant economic liberalisation that arrangements like the TPP require are really hard for the countries concerned. It disrupts the status quo. Corporations, small and medium-sized enterprises, white and blue-collar workers, and farmers must make significant adjustments.

For Taiwan, in particular, anxiety that the opening of the domestic market will lead to further and deeper integration with China is real. The Sunflower Movement was only a symptom of a larger phenomenon, one that any Taiwan administration will have to address. The Ma administration did propose internal reforms that were needed to improve Taiwan's competitiveness, which is one way to address the economic side of the anxiety. The concern that economic interdependence is a slippery slope to political subordination also needs to be addressed. This slope exists, but it need not be slippery as long as Taiwan has a good sense of its interests in political and security matters.

Those in Taiwan who wish to slow down economic interdependence with China face their own challenges. First, they must consider the possibility that economic interdependence with China will continue whatever the bias of government policy, because Taiwan businesses can simply circumvent Taipei's restrictions to the China market. Second, because those who fear excessive interdependence with China want to pursue a better balance in Taiwan's relations with China and with other markets, they must contend with China's ability to impose obstacles to Taiwan's liberalisation via diplomacy with other countries. Finally, and most profoundly, they must recognise the consequences to Taiwan's economy of *not* being able to liberalise with others: that is, the further marginalisation and isolation of Taiwan from the regional and global economies. This is a slippery slope of another kind.

To sum up, Taiwan faces severe challenges going forward. One is to preserve the access to the international community that it has. But with the election of Tsai Ing-wen, Beijing chose to use its global political clout to chip away at that status quo, stealing away diplomatic allies, pressing its preferences regarding nomenclature on countries and companies, and again blocking Taiwan's limited participation in international organisations like the WHA. This PRC behaviour was part of a shift in its larger policy on Taiwan, from one of persuasion to that of intimidation (Bush 2019). Yet this shift is more about means than ends. As this chapter makes clear, China for decades has sought to marginalise Taiwan in the international community, in part to build its own dominant position and in part to box in the island in the hope that sooner or later it will capitulate and accept unification on China's terms. A second challenge, one that most affects a party like the KMT that seeks to protect Taiwan's interests by accommodating China, is how to avoid PRC pressure to begin political talks. The experience of the Ma administration demonstrated that this element of Beijing's agenda is growing in salience. The third is to remove the obstacles to improved relations with friendly countries like the United States and Taiwan, as a way of extricating itself from the isolation that Beijing continues impose. And the fourth is building broader public support for pursuing all three of those objectives at once.

Amid the challenges there are opportunities. One is to create paths to international participation that do not confront the PRC where it is strong. For example, the Ma and Tsai administrations, in league with the United States, created the Joint Cooperation Training Framework to engage developing countries on issues where Taiwan over its post-war history learned positive lessons from which they can benefit. The second is to engage in self-help on issues where Taiwan's access to international cooperation is limited. The best example concerns COVID-19, on which Taiwan is restricted by PRC interference from drawing on the resource available at the World Health Organization, just as it was during the SARS epidemic of 2003. In the wake of SARS, however, Taiwan's health authorities learned from their mistake and aggressively strengthened their capacity to respond to future pandemics. That learning and capacity-building stood Taiwan in good stead during COVID-19. Not only did it keep the number of cases and deaths to a low level. It also earned the praise of the international community, praise that the PRC could not block.

Beijing faces its own challenges. Its approach to Taiwan's participation in the life of the East Asian region and the international community has become short-sighted. For Beijing to secure Taiwan's voluntary consent towards unification, it needs the agreement not just of Taiwan's leaders but of the public at large. Indeed, unification would require a very broad consensus that doing so is in the island's long-term interests. But the Taiwan public has long sought dignity in the international community, so efforts by China to deny that dignity through a policy of political marginalisation only fosters anti-unification sentiment. Moreover, for China to exclude Taiwan from the East Asian and global economies is, in my mind, particularly myopic. If I am correct that the only way Taiwan can achieve long-term prosperity is to carry out multi-directional economic liberalisation, then China's efforts to block that liberalisation will leave Taiwan people worse off economically. That is an outcome that will undermine China's unification goals much more than the denial of dignity. In that case, the policy of marginalisation becomes self-defeating.

## References

Bureau of Foreign Trade (ROC). 2020. 'Republic of China Import and Export Trade Statistics,' https://cus93.trade.gov.tw/FSCE040F/FSCE040F.

Bush, Richard C. 2017. 'A One-China Policy Primer,' East Asia Policy Paper #10, Brookings Institution, March 2017, https://www.brookings.edu/research/a-one-china-policy-primer/.

Bush, Richard C. 2019. 'From Persuasion to Intimidation: China's Approach to Taiwan and Taiwan's Response,' Brookings Institution, November 2019, www.

brookings.edu/research/from-persuasion-to-coercion-beijings-approach-to-taiwan-and-taiwans-response/.

Gardella, Robert. 1999. 'From Treaty Ports to Provincial Status, 1860–1894.' In *Taiwan: A New History*, Murray Rubenstein (ed.). Armonk, NY: M. E. Sharpe, pp. 163–200.

Hamilton, Gary G. and Cheng-Shu Kao. 2018. *Making Money: How Taiwanese Industrialists Embraced the Global Economy*. Stanford, CA: Stanford University Press.

Hsing, You-tien. 1998. *Making Capitalism in China: The Taiwan Connection*. New York: Oxford University Press.

Lamley, Harry J. 1999. 'Taiwan Under Japanese Rule, 1895–1945: The Vicissitudes of Colonialism.' In *Taiwan: A New History*, Murray Rubenstein (ed.). Armonk, NY: M. E. Sharpe, pp. 201–60.

Lee, Pei-shan and Chu Yun-han. 2016. 'Cross-Strait Economic Integration (1992–2015).' In *Routledge Handbook on Contemporary Taiwan*, Gunter Schubert (ed.). New York: Routledge, pp. 410–25.

Niou, Emerson M. S. 2016. 'Taiwan Public Opinion on National Security Issues,' Talk delivered at Center for Strategic and International Studies, February 5, 2016, https://sites.duke.edu/pass/publications/.

Wade, Robert. 1990. *Governing the Market: Economic Theory and the Role of Government in East Asian Industrialization*. Princeton, NJ: Princeton University Press.

# 11 Walking towards China or towards the world? Taiwan's international space under Ma Ying-jeou and Tsai Ing-wen

*Mariah Thornton*

The concept of international space has long been invoked by Taiwanese politicians since the 1990s to describe the island's level of involvement in the global community, including participation in IGOs, engagement with other international institutions and multilateral regimes, as well as formal diplomatic and unofficial relations with other states (DeLisle 2016: 550). Since it first appeared in political discourse during Lee Teng-hui's presidency, the concept of international space has shifted with successive administrations to suit changing foreign policy objectives. During Nationalist Party (KMT) President Ma Ying-jeou's tenure from 2008 to 2016, international space was largely defined in terms of Taiwan's economic integration with China and positive cross-Strait relations. However, Democratic Progressive Party (DPP) President Tsai Ing-wen has sought to lessen Taiwan's dependence on China as well as broaden the scope of international space with a greater emphasis on public diplomacy and soft power. These contrasting approaches to international space have given rise to questions over which strategy better serves Taiwan's global interests and engagement over the long term.

At the Fourth Cross-Strait Economic Forum in June 2017, Ma argued 'the 1992 Consensus does not undermine Taiwan's sovereignty; in fact, only under the Consensus will both sides of the Strait have a diplomatic ceasefire and Taiwan will have international space.'[1] Throughout his presidency and since departing from office, Ma has consistently emphasised that maintaining positive relations with China is key to Taiwan's economic and diplomatic success. In November 2018, on the third anniversary of the historic meeting between Ma and Chinese leader Xi Jinping, Ma pointed out that Taiwan's deteriorating relationship with China under the DPP had damaged Taiwan's international space by negatively impacting Taiwanese people's livelihood economy and political diplomacy.[2] Ma's approach to expand international space has been hailed by many as the best strategy for maximising Taiwan's economic and diplomatic returns (Chen 2013: 23).

However, President Tsai has pursued a strategy to decouple Taiwan's international space from China by strengthening relations with other countries, including expanding non-economic and cultural links. Under this policy, trade and non-trade areas have been treated with relatively equal importance. In 2011, Tsai aptly summarised the contrasting approaches of the KMT and her party in a debate with Ma over the Economic Coopera- tion Framework Agreement (ECFA): 'The DPP walks towards the world and walks towards China *with the world* while the KMT walks towards China and walks towards the *world with China*' (Taiwan Public Television Service Foundation 2011, Tsai in Liu 2016: 15).

Since Tsai's ascension in 2016, Taiwan's international space has come un- der acute pressure as China accelerates efforts to isolate the island interna- tionally. Over the past four years, Taiwan has endured the loss of five formal diplomatic allies to China and exclusion from key international governmen- tal organisations (IGOs) in which it had previously enjoyed observer status, including the World Health Assembly (WHA) and the International Civil Aviation Organisation (ICAO). China also continues its campaign to pres- sure private sector organisations, ranging from major airlines like British Airways to prominent institutions, such as the London School of Econom- ics and Political Science, to designate Taiwan as part of China.

However, events in the run-up to President Tsai's landslide re-election in January 2020 played a significant role in bolstering public support for her strategy to expand international space with minimal dependence on China. The Chinese government's violent and heavy-handed approach to pro- democracy protestors in Hong Kong gave rise to an increasingly negative perception of China in Taiwan. The president's New Year's address empha- sising the failure of 'one country, two systems' in Hong Kong and the need to ensure Taiwan's sovereignty is stronger and more sustainable seemed to resonate with public opinion as her approval ratings soared.[3] The recent recall of Tsai's main opponent in the 2019 elections, former KMT candidate and Kaohsiung mayor Han Kuo-yu, also appears to indicate a decisive shift of public opinion against the KMT's more China-oriented policies.

Taiwan's campaign of humanitarian assistance during the global outbreak of novel coronavirus (COVID-19) has also highlighted the advantages of a soft power approach to international space. Taiwan's early response to the outbreak, the effectiveness of its healthcare system, as well as its donations of face masks and personal protective equipment (PPE) to countries hard hit by the virus have garnered widespread praise from the international me- dia, raising Taiwan's global visibility. Amidst the outbreak, Taiwan has also received growing international support for its re-admission into the World Health Organization (WHO) as an observer member. These developments raise questions over how the concept of international space should be de- fined and understood, as well as how progress in international space is to be measured (Huang 2018).

This chapter will first explore the origins and development of the term 'international space' in Taiwan, and how the Ma and Tsai administrations have added new dimensions to the concept. Second, it will assess the effec- tiveness of these strategies across a range of sectors, including economic integration, IGO membership and participation, formal diplomatic allies, unofficial ties, international law and the South China Sea as well as relevant domestic reforms.

Overall, while Ma's strategy of prioritising positive relations and economic engagement with China initially yielded positive results for Taiwan's international space, it ultimately failed to deliver meaningful and lasting progress. However, while at a first glance Taiwan's international space seems to have deteriorated under the current administration, Tsai's strategy of diversifying Taiwan's international relations by decoupling from China and enhancing non-economic ties may in fact result in more meaningful progress for the island's international space over the long term. In addition, in facing an increasingly authoritarian China under the rule of Xi Jinping, Tsai's soft power-oriented strategy has proved more effective in demonstrating the attractiveness and legitimacy of Taiwan's democratic system to the international community in contrast to its regional neighbour.

## Origins and development of 'international space' in Taiwan

The term 'international space' appeared in Taiwanese political discourse in the early 1990s, and became commonplace under President Lee Teng-hui.[4] In September 1992, the term was used in a Taiwan Mainland Affairs Council report about direct flights between the two sides, which cited China pressuring Taiwan's space in international society as one of the main challenges.[5] Later in a speech on 28 January 2000, China's then Vice Premier also articulated international space to include 'economic, cultural and social activities for Taiwan' (Vice Premier Qian Qichen 2000 in Sheng 2001: 127). This demonstrates a broad understanding of Taiwan's international space as the conditions of its engagement with the international community.

However, the concept has also been moulded in accordance with the foreign policy objectives of each new government. When Chen Shui-bian took office in May 2000, his administration began pursuing a diplomatic strategy that emphasised Taiwan's democratic values and commitment to democracy as a means of facilitating peace and co-operation with other countries (Rawnsley 2003: 6; Geldenhuys 2009: 224). During Chen's tenure, progress in international space could therefore be interpreted as effectiveness in communicating Taiwan's democratic values as a means of expressing its separate, democratic statehood. Through their different strategies for international space, Ma and Tsai have also added new dimensions to the concept, such as Ma's emphasis on economic integration and positive relations with China in contrast to Tsai's focus on soft power and decoupling from China.

As Huang rightly points out, when it comes to this abstract concept, quantitative methods are not so useful in assessing whether Taiwan has 'more' or 'less' international space (Huang 2018). However, while international space has been measured according to the policy orientation of Taiwan's government, domestic support for foreign policy programmes aimed at international participation, endorsement of the international community, cross-Strait, and Sino-US relations, this means of evaluation remains limited. In assessing strategies to expand Taiwan's international space, short- and long-term impact as well as soft power elements must also be taken into account. While Ma's strategy yielded certain diplomatic and economic returns in the short term, overall, it did not result in significant progress for Taiwan's international relations for the long term. However, though Tsai's strategy has not achieved the same significant diplomatic and economic benefits from China, it may in fact prove more effective in strengthening the island's international role for the long term.

## International economic engagement

One of the defining themes of Ma's approach to international space was to increase Taiwan's global economic engagement through free trade agreements (FTAs) and participation in economic IGOs. In certain respects, this strategy did result in meaningful progress for Taiwan's international space. For example, Taiwan was able to secure its entrance into the World Trade Organisation (WTO)'s Agreement on Government Procurement (GPA) in 2009 (Winkler 2014: 248). By entering the GPA as a separate entity from China, Taiwan was free to negotiate with existing contracting parties to open government procurement markets on a plurilateral basis. This was a significant achievement in terms of Taiwan's international space as such action put it on equal footing with other GPA participants and allowed it to operate more independently within the WTO (Winkler 2014: 248–9).

The signing of the ECFA with China in 2010 also strengthened Taiwan's ability to negotiate international economic agreements with other countries on its own terms (Winkler 2014: 249). Much like Taiwan's accession to the GPA, ECFA '[offered] a framework through which China is expected no longer to object to [Taiwan's] negotiations of FTAs with third parties' (Van-Grasstek 2013: 488). The signing of ECFA also paved the way for more FTAs with other nations, culminating in the New Zealand-Taiwan Economic Co-operation Agreement and the Singapore Taiwan Economic Agreement. These achievements under Ma helped put Taiwan on a more equal footing with other regional economic powers.

While this strategy resulted in important diplomatic and economic gains for Taiwan, it also exposed pre-existing limitations imposed by China on the island's international space. This is evident in the fact that Taiwan remained by and large excluded from multilateral economic frameworks of the Asia-Pacific region under Ma, a trend which continued under Tsai. For example, although the Ma expressed an interest in joining the Trans-Pacific Partnership (TPP) and the Regional Comprehensive Economic Partnership (RCEP), Taiwan has remained excluded from negotiations (Liu 2016: 11).

Taiwan has also been excluded from China's key policy for regional economic integration, the Belt Road Initiative (BRI), with Asian Infrastructure Investment Bank President Jin Liqun firmly rejecting any notion of Taiwan's participation in 2016 (Liu 2016: 13). Furthermore, even though ECFA arguably led to the signing of more FTAs with New Zealand and Singapore, Taiwan has still been shut out from the multilateral FTA negotiations and exchanges among three of its crucial trading partners in the Asian region: China, South Korea, and Japan (Liu 2016: 5). This yet again indicates that despite warmer cross-Strait relations under Ma, there remained significant limitations on Taiwan's ability to expand its international role through economic integration in the Asian region.

In addition, ECFA yielded significant gains mainly for the duration of Ma's tenure. Within a few years, it became clear the initial economic gains of the agreement were on a short-term basis. For example, the benefits of ECFA's 'early harvest list,' which included reduced tariffs on 539 items compared to the 267 items of the previous administration, were exhausted within the first few years of its signing. Although these export items jumped by 35% the year ECFA was inked, they declined in each successive year since. In addition, according to Taiwan customs statistics, exports dropped from US\$84.7 billion in 2014 to US\$73.4 billion in 2015, while imports fell from US\$49.25 billion to US\$45.26 billion in the same period, indicating a slump in cross-Strait trade towards the end of Ma's second term.[6] Therefore, while ECFA initially yielded certain economic returns for Taiwan, these were largely limited to the duration of Ma's time in office.

Despite thornier relations with China under Tsai, cross-Strait trade has not decreased since the change of administration. In fact, according to trade statistics from Taiwan's Mainland Affairs Council, in the first 11 months of 2017 cross-Strait trade was valued at \$125.6 billion, up 17.6% from the same period in the previous year. Taiwan's exports to China during the 11-month period grew even more year on year, indicating a 20.4% rise of \$80.1 billion.[7] Although figures indicated a slight decline from 2015 to 2016, cross-Strait trade has by and large remained consistent across the Ma and Tsai administrations.

Overall, this suggests the gains of Ma's strategy resulted in limited progress for Taiwan's international space. While closer relations with China may have initially heighted hopes for Taiwan's greater economic integration in the region, Ma encountered strict limitations in this respect. As such, Ma's strategy, rather than leading to a long-term expansion of Taiwan's international space, exposed pre-existing barriers imposed by China, barriers that have remained in place under the current administration.

### The New Southbound Policy: balancing economic and non-economic links

Facing stagnating cross-Strait relations and wishing to decrease Taiwan's reliance on China, Tsai has pushed to increase links, both economic and non-economic, with other Asian nations under the New Southbound Policy (NSP). The NSP's economic goals are similar to those of the previous administration, and significant progress has been made under Tsai. According to the Ministry of Finance, Taiwan's exports to NSP countries rose 13.4% year on year to US$67.4 billion in 2017, the highest rate in six years and the third highest total on record.[8] In December 2017, Taiwan signed an updated bilateral investment agreement with the Philippines and an updated bilateral investment protection treaty with India the following year.[9] Exports to Malaysia increased 32.7% from 2016, and those to Laos surged 74.5% on the year. Among the top ten NSP countries that received Taiwanese exports, seven were Association of Southeast Asian Nations (ASEAN) countries.[10] Overall, Taiwan exports to 18 southbound countries grew their fastest in five years, up 13.5% in the first half of 2017.[11] This reflects Tsai's commitment to the goal 'to bid farewell to our past overreliance on a single market.'[12]

Compared to her predecessor, Tsai's version of the Southbound Policy has also focused more on strengthening cultural and institutional links with Southeast Asian countries. In November 2018, the Executive Yuan approved a draft of the New Economic Immigration Law, which aimed to increase the recruitment of skilled professionals by making permanent residency in Taiwan more attainable for mid-level technical personnel and foreign students.[13] The NSP Promotion Plan also included expansion of education ties through scholarships and 'conducting talent exchange' among students, young scholars, and industry professionals from ASEAN countries.[14] The NSP Office has also overseen the easing of visa regulations for students from these regions wishing to pursue education and work in Taiwan. According to statistics from Taiwan's Ministry of Education, 28,000 ASEAN students took part in tertiary education in 2016 and this figure rose to 38,000 the following year.

In addition to deepening educational links, the NSP has made progress in terms of increasing tourism between Taiwan and ASEAN countries. Of the 2.3 million tourists from NSP countries in 2017, 2.14 million were from the ASEAN region. In 2016, the number of tourists travelling from ASEAN countries to Taiwan increased 16%, and up more than 29% in 2017, likely due to Taiwan's easing of visa regulations for travellers from Brunei and Thailand under the NSP. The number of tourists from the Philippines and Vietnam also saw significant increases for this reason.[15]

The Tsai administration is also boosting institutional links and increasing non-economic engagement with Asian nations through the Yushan Forum. The forum seeks to provide a platform for leaders in the region to exchange ideas and facilitate greater cooperation in the areas of society, culture, technology, and youth engagement, in many ways paralleling Singapore's Shangri-La Dialogue and India's Raisina Dialogue.[16] The forum signifies Tsai's emphasis on building soft power among other countries in the region beyond China.

On the one hand, the NSP has made headway in terms of Taiwan's economic integration in the Asian region, as trade and bilateral-investment agreements with NSP countries have risen significantly. On the other hand, although many of the benefits to Taiwan's soft power under the NSP are not as easily quantified or measured, Tsai's strategy has contributed to the expansion of international space in a meaningful way. By focusing on non-trade areas, the Tsai administration is building significant and long-standing links across the fields of education, tourism, and culture. Increased visitations from NSP countries through tourism and education have also served to reinforce an image of Taiwan as a multicultural and progressive nation.[17] Moreover, although no FTAs have been secured under the Tsai administration thus far, perhaps deepening ties with regional allies in non-economic areas under the NSP may lay the foundations for long-term trade and investment for the future.

## IGO membership and participation

Taiwan's international space has more commonly been understood and measured in terms of its membership in IGOs. Warmer cross-Strait relations helped Taiwan secure participation in the WHA and facilitate its inclusion in the WHO's International Health Regulations (IHR). Previously, Taiwan had been rejected in 2002 after applying for observer status in the WHA as a 'health entity.' Only in 2004 after the outbreak of SARS and pressure from Japan and the USA was Taiwan able to enter the WHA as an observing health entity, but this was subject to a Memorandum of Understanding between the WHA and China in which Taiwan's participation could be blocked at any point. By contrast, following from Ma's strategy of close cooperation with China, Taiwan was granted observer status in the WHA under the title 'Chinese Taipei,' included in the WHO's IHR, and was allowed to send representatives as guests to the WHA (Winkler 2014: 250–2). Taiwan was also offered the status of 'guest of the ICAO Council president.' In addition to its inclusion as an observer in WHA and ICAO, Taiwan was able to participate in eight IGOs as a full member.

On the surface, Taiwan's successful participation in these IGOs might suggest that Ma's overall strategy for international space yielded the greatest diplomatic benefits. However, much like Ma's achievements in the economic sphere, these victories in Taiwan's international participation were dependent upon China's continued support and approval which dissipated after his departure from office. First, Taiwan's observer status in the WHA remained subject to annual review (Winkler 2014: 256). On 6 May 2016, Taiwan received an invitation to participate in the WHA subject to three conditions: Taiwan's participation would be under the title 'Chinese Taipei,' the basis for attendance would be the UN Resolution 2758 and that Taiwan's participation must be in accordance with the One-China Principle. Taiwan responded by sending Minister of Health designate Lin Tzou-yien as its representative at the WHA and stating that the government does not accept the conditions posed by the WHO Secretariat on Taiwan's participation.[18] However, Taiwan's invitation to the WHA has not been renewed since 2016.

China's limitations on Taiwan's international activity have manifested themselves not only in the WHA and WHO but in other UN specialised agencies. For example, following Taiwan's inclusion in the WHA in 2008, the Ma administration attempted to replicate the success of this model in other UN specialised bodies (Winkler 2014: 247). However, Ma's application of the WHA/WHO model also produced mixed results. For instance, this model could not be successfully applied to the United Nations Framework Convention on Climate Change (UNFCCC) or the International Maritime Organisation (IMO), two organisations from which Taiwan has remained continually excluded (Winkler 2012).

Moreover, since the DPP assumed power in 2016, China has further restricted Taiwan's access to the UN specialised bodies it had participated in under the previous administration. Even in the few successful cases where Taiwan was able to secure participation as an observer under Ma's leadership, Taiwan's international space overall remained severely restricted and subject to China's approval.

The global outbreak of coronavirus in early 2020 led to mounting international pressure on China and the WHO to allow Taiwan's participation, resulting in the body's decision to grant Taiwanese experts access to the WHO's online forum on COVID-19 in mid-February.[19] This was due in part to Taiwan's successful response to the virus, which has seen around 440 confirmed cases and only six deaths as of early May, despite its proximity and higher people-to-people exchanges with China. In addition, Taiwan's acts of humanitarian assistance through donations of personal protective equipment (PPE), ventilators, and other medical supplies have helped increase international support for the country's WHO participation as well as boost its image as a proactive member of the international community. Several key global figures and politicians have publicly expressed thanks to Taiwan, including President of the EU Commission Ursula von der Leyen, UK Foreign Minister Dominic Raab, Deputy Speaker of the House of Commons Nigel Evans MP, and others.

Underpinning these humanitarian efforts, several Taiwanese government officials have played an important role in voicing Taiwan's contributions to the fight against COVID-19 and highlighting its unfair exclusion from the WHO in the international press. Vice President Chen Chien-jen, Foreign Minister Joseph Wu, and Health and Welfare Minister Chen Shih-cheng have authored articles or participated in interviews with *The Times, The Telegraph, The New York Times, Sky News*, all of which promote Taiwan as a model for other countries in tackling the pandemic.[20] While Taiwan remains barred from the WHO, its campaign for meaningful participation has undoubtedly gained greater attention and support from countries around the world, thereby increasing the island's international visibility and strengthening its case for separate statehood from China.

### Formal diplomatic allies: China's 'diplomatic ceasefire' with Ma and dollar diplomacy against Tsai

Taiwan's international space has been commonly evaluated in terms of the number of formal diplomatic ties it holds with other countries. The greater the number of diplomatic allies, the stronger the case is for recognition of Taiwan's international statehood and the more beneficial it is for Taiwan's international space. Conversely, the less diplomatic allies Taiwan holds, the weaker its claim to international statehood, and more harmful it is to its international space.

When Ma came to power, he announced a 'diplomatic truce,' signalling that Taiwan would abandon competing with China for formal diplomatic partners and stop making its bid for UN membership (Zhe 2012).[21] With warmer cross-Strait relations under Ma, Beijing by and large upheld this 'diplomatic truce' for the whole of Ma's tenure except for the loss of Gambia in 2013, which left Taiwan with 23 allies by the end of his presidency.

However, since the election of Tsai's DPP government in 2016, China has resumed its efforts to court Taiwan's remaining diplomatic allies. As a result, since the change of administration, Taiwan has lost five allies to China at an alarming rate, leaving Taiwan with only 15 formal diplomatic allies. The resumption of China's diplomatic war against Taiwan has certainly given rise to doubts over the Tsai administration's strategy for increasing the island's international space.

At a first glance, Ma's strategy to pacify China through acceptance of the 1992 Consensus and his policy of instituting a diplomatic truce proved successful preventing the dwindling of Taiwan's formal diplomatic allies. However, the dramatic loss of diplomatic allies since the change of administration reveals this strategy for international space, while successful under a China-friendly government, did not translate into meaningful and enduring success for Taiwan's international space unless such an administration were maintained in Taiwan. This strategy could therefore only ever serve as a temporary delay to China's diplomatic war against Taiwan. The rapid decrease of Taiwan's diplomatic allies since the transfer of power to a more China-wary administration therefore proves that Ma's strategy for international space was highly risky as it was always contingent upon China's continued approval and support.

Despite the Tsai administration's initial attempts to reassure China of its more moderate position, and its willingness to negotiate, China has been unwilling to be flexible until the government agrees to the 1992 Consensus. In June 2016, a spokesperson for China's Taiwan Affairs Office announced that cross-Strait communication was suspended as Taiwan has not accepted the Consensus.[22] As such, China's resumption of diplomatic war has severely damaged Taiwan's international space.

However, though formal diplomatic allies are a significant aspect of international space, the concept remains multi-dimensional. Therefore, although Taiwan's international space decreased following the loss of several diplomatic allies under Tsai, Taiwan's international role has improved in other areas that are not quantifiable or easily measured. China's relentless poaching of diplomatic allies under Tsai has forced her administration to think more creatively about expanding Taiwan's international engagement and involvement.

## Unofficial ties and parliamentary diplomacy

Tsai's soft power-oriented approach to international space is also evident in her administration's emphasis on parliamentary diplomacy. Citing the establishment of the Taiwan Foundation for Democracy (TFD) under President Chen Shui-Bian in 2002, Geldenhuys argues that Taiwan promoted democratic values as means of expressing its statehood (Geldenhuys 2009: 224). Under Ma, the TFD began hosting an 'East Asia Democracy Forum' annually in 2014 to bring together civil society representatives from across East Asia in the spirit of promoting the spread of democratic principles in the region.[23] Ma also argued that warmer cross-Strait relations meant Taiwan's democratic politics would have a considerable impact on mainland China.[24] Under Tsai, Taiwan has continued democracy-based diplomacy efforts, especially in the area of unofficial inter-parliamentary exchanges with democratic allies.

In a speech on 14 November 2018, Taiwan Foreign Minister Joseph Wu stated the importance of parliamentary diplomacy in contributing directly to the expansion of the island's international space. Since the ascension of Legislative Yuan President Su Jia-chyuan in February 2016, Taiwan's parliament has received 751 delegations from 106 countries and territories. As of August 2018, the number of parliamentary friendship groups has increased from 48 to 71. Legislative Yuan President Su Jia-chyuan has also remarked on parliamentary diplomacy helping to deepen Taiwan's ties with Europe, Japan, and the USA.[25] Increased exchanges with parliamentarians from like-minded countries has meaningfully demonstrated Taiwan's place alongside other democracies across the world, and is yet another means by which Taiwan increases awareness of and expresses its statehood. This is consistent with Tsai's predecessor, who met with several parliamentary delegations and parliamentary friendship groups over the course of his presidency. However, there appears to be an increased focus on and significant expansion of parliamentary diplomacy under Tsai.

This is evident in Taiwan's developing ties with Europe in recent years. For example, Legislative Yuan President Su led a Taiwan delegation to the UK in 2018, the first time an acting President of the Legislative Yuan made an official visit to Britain. In the year 2018 alone, three UK parliamentary delegations have visited Taiwan, demonstrating the UK's desire to strengthen unofficial ties with Taiwan.[26] Increasing inter-parliamentary exchanges between Taiwan and Europe also signifies development in Taiwan's unofficial relations, and the success of these exchanges in reinforcing Taiwan's democratic values and statehood has contributed to enhancing its international space.

Parliamentary diplomacy has also featured prominently in the Taiwan-US relationship. Since US President Donald Trump came to power, there have been frequent visits of senior officials to Taiwan under the Taiwan-US Global Cooperation and Training Framework Agreement (GCTF).[27] The US's passing of the 'Taiwan Travel Act' on 13 January 2017, which received broad bipartisan support, also indicated the US's strong desire to preserve and even enhance unofficial ties with greater exchanges between Taiwan and US officials at all levels.[28]

Inter-parliamentary exchanges have also played a prominent role in Taiwan's building non-economic links with NSP countries. On 18 April 2017, the Taiwan-Philippines Congressional Association (TPCA) was inaugurated with the aim of increasing bilateral collaboration and exchanges between the two nations' law-making bodies and provides a formal channel for both Taiwanese and Philippine law makers to communicate. According to Taiwan's Ministry of Foreign Affairs, Taiwan's legislators currently maintain over 50 organisations that fulfil a similar purpose.[29] Enhancing bilateral parliamentary ties has also been an important part of Taiwan-India relations under Tsai. For example, in February 2017, DPP Legislator Kuan Bi-ling led a parliamentary delegation's visit to India.[30] The year prior, the Taiwan-India Parliamentary Friendship Association was founded to forge closer ties between India and Taiwanese lawmakers as well as strengthen overall bilateral collaboration.[31]

## International law and the South China Sea

The South China Sea is yet another area which reflects Ma and Tsai's contrasting approaches to international space. Hickey and DeLisle have argued that the Ma and Tsai administrations' policies on the South China Sea are fairly consistent, with only small changes when Tsai came to power in 2016 (DeLisle 2016: 562; Hickey 2018: 65). However, while the adjustments under Tsai have been minor, they also demonstrate her more soft-power–oriented approach to Taiwan's international space in contrast to Ma's more China-friendly and economically focused strategy. Much like economic integration, the South China Sea has been another area which reveals China's 'red lines' for Taiwan's international space.

Ma's South China Sea Peace Initiative (SCSPI) and East China Sea Peace Initiative (ECSPI) emphasised the economic benefits of sharing resources, such as fish, oil, and gas, by shelving sovereignty disputes with China. Ma adopted this position to avoid expressing a position on Taiwan's international statehood as well as remain in alignment with China on the issue, even perhaps signalling Taipei's willingness to cooperate with China and other South China Sea disputant states in 'seeking joint development of resources.' To a certain extent, this policy improved Taiwan's international space by helping secure a place for Taiwan as 'a near-peer participant in regional disputes.' For example, the Ma administration claims the SCSPI and ECSPI directly contributed to the fisheries agreement between Taiwan and Japan in 2013 and a fishing-related law enforcement accord with the Philippines in 2015. This in turn enhanced Taiwan's international status by allowing it to be an equal party in pacts that are usually among sovereign states (DeLisle 2016: 559–62).

However, Taiwan's involvement in the South China Sea disputes during Ma's tenure also exposed pre-existing barriers maintained by China on Taiwan's international space, one of which was clearly the island's territorial sovereignty. For example, despite Ma's attempts to position Taiwan in co-operation with the PRC under the SCSPI and ECSPI, and despite the fact that Taiwan and China shared the same historical claims to territories in the region dating back to the early Republic of China, Taiwan remained excluded from participating in the process of international dispute settlement. When the Philippines submitted its case to the PCA in 2013 challenging both Taiwan and China's historical claims in the Spratlys, Taiwan was only able to submit an *amicus curiae* briefing on 23 March 2016, as it was not deemed a party subject to the case due to its international status. Similarly, Taiwan has also been excluded from ASEAN negotiations over developing a Code of Conduct for the South China Sea, despite the fact it holds substantial stakes in the region. This yet again shows that Ma's strategy of prioritising cross-Strait relations did not necessarily yield significant gains for international space as Taiwan remained largely excluded from international dispute settlement mechanisms as well as multilateral negotiations over developing a Code of Conduct in the region.

Though the basis for Taiwan's claims to territories in the South China Sea remained largely consistent between the Ma and Tsai administrations, the few changes enacted under Tsai also reflect her more soft-power–oriented strategy to expand international space. Ma's policy on the South China Sea advocated working with international conservation groups to develop the Taiwan-controlled island of Itu Aba (also known as 'Taiping Island') into a peace park. Similarly, Tsai's policy also involved cooperating with international organisations to develop a base on the island for providing humanitarian aid and supplies. In addition to developing the territory in this way, Tsai went further by calling on Taiwan's Ministry of Science and Technology to invite international scholars to come to Taiping Island to conduct scientific research on climate change, earthquakes, meteorology, and other such fields (Hickey 2018: 67–73).

Tsai's administration has also implemented shifts in its legal position on the South China Sea that may help to further harmonise Taiwan's position with that of the United Nations Convention on the Law of the Sea (UNCLOS). For example, the Tsai administration has eliminated references to historic claims in its legislative process and executive regulations, and has also adjusted the phrasing of its official statements on the South China Sea by using the more ambiguous term of 'South China Sea Islands' instead of referring to each territory as the Ma administration had done. These changes may keep the door open to future adjustments to Taiwan's claims. More importantly, they demonstrate that Taiwan's position on the South China Sea remains in adherence with UNCLOS and international law. In addition, the basis of the Tsai administration's objection to the PCA ruling did not challenge the legitimacy of the arbitration panel. The president instead issued a statement noting the arbitrators had rendered their award in the case brought by the Philippines under UNCLOS, signalling her government's recognition of the panel's legality.[32] Although China and Taiwan both objected to the PCA's ruling, the contrast between China's refusal to recognise the ruling and Taiwan's decision to respect the legal outcome reinforced Taiwan's image as a responsible and law-abiding actor.

These shifts in Tsai's South China Sea policy therefore demonstrate Taiwan's commitment to respecting and upholding international law as a dedicated member of the international community, a move which remains consistent with her broader soft-power–oriented strategy for improving Taiwan's international space. In addition, the contrast between Taiwan's adherence and respect for international law and China's bypassing international law indirectly strengthens Taiwan's soft power and image within the international community.

## Boosting soft power at home: domestic reforms under Tsai

According to Nye, one key component of soft power is a nation's political values and whether it lives up to those principles at home and abroad (Nye 2008: 96). Therefore, although not explicitly linked with her policies on international space, certain domestic reforms have contributed to Tsai's soft power strategy overseas by marking Taiwan out as an alternative and attractive model of political development in the region. Ironically, Beijing's harsh approach towards Taiwan under the Tsai administration, coupled with its increasingly authoritarian rule at home, has contributed to the success of this approach by highlighting a clear contrast between democratic Taiwan and authoritarian China. As such, Tsai's reforms at home may also contribute to the long-term progress of Taiwan's international space.

As Chen and Fell point out, the legalisation of same-sex marriage in Taiwan is a good example of how Tsai's domestic reforms are reinforcing the country's foreign policy strategy. Although there are still some significant limitations on same-sex marriage in terms of adoption rights as well as couples in which one partner is a national of a country where same-sex marriage is illegal, the passing of the law demonstrates Taiwan's government has taken a meaningful step in realising progressive values shared by other democratic countries.

The legalisation of same-sex marriage also received significant media attention around the world, with several international news outlets including the *BBC* and *Telegraph* referring to Taiwan as the first country in Asia to legalise gay marriage. In addition, famous TV personality Ellen DeGeneres also acknowledged Taiwan as the first Asian country to allow same-sex marriage in a tweet on 24 May 2019. Widespread international attention to the legalisation of same-sex marriage in Taiwan on traditional and social media outlets is testament Taiwan's strengthening soft power abroad. This in turn has helped to raise awareness of Taiwan's identity as a separate nation from China, where same-sex marriage remains illegal, as well as reinforced its image as a progressive and democratic nation in Asia.

Furthermore, several of Tsai's proposed legal reforms to Taiwan's judicial system demonstrate her attempts to set the country up as a model for democratic development in Asia. In July 2017, the sixth general meeting of the Preparatory Committee convened to focus more in depth on civic participation in trials, with Committee Deputy Executive Secretary Lin Feng-jeng stating that the Judicial Yuan was drafting a trial system to introduce 'citizen judges.'[33] Furthermore, in an address at the International Conference of the Constitutional Court in October 2018, Tsai discussed reforms underway at Taiwan's Constitutional Court which would empower the body to review the constitutionality of rulings made by general courts and the Supreme Court. The proposed reforms, which are set to take force two years after the promulgation of the relevant bill, are based on the duties of Germany's Federal Constitutional Court. Although these proposals have yet to be fully implemented, they reflect Taiwan's commitment to bringing its legal system more in line with that of other modern, liberal democratic countries around the world.

In addition to these reforms, Taiwan's Ministry of Justice has been working closely with several legal experts and scholars from around the world since 2015 to amend the Law of Extradition. The Ministry of Justice has also completed a draft of the 'International Mutual legal Assistance in Criminal Matters Law' as the legal basis of mutual legal assistance in criminal matters between Taiwan and the other nations. The retention of the death penalty, however, remains at variance with international trends. During the second Human Rights Consultations between the European Union (EU) and Taiwan, Europe called upon Taiwanese authorities to apply and maintain a de facto moratorium on the death penalty in Taiwan and expressed regret over the resumption of executions in Taiwan in 2018.[34] However, overall, Taiwan is taking meaningful action to bring its legal system more in line with international standards.

As Taiwan is seeking to strengthen rule of law at home, China has been expanding the Chinese Communist Party's grip on power through *rule by law*. This is evident in Hong Kong, where 'one country, two systems' is in theory meant to preserve its separate legal system under the Basic Law. However, the National People's Congress has undermined this system in drafting new national security legislation which completely bypassed Hong Kong's Legislative Council. The new law criminalises acts of secession, subversion, terrorism, or those that Beijing would consider foreign interference in Hong Kong.[35] Leading up to Hong Kong's national security law, the Hong Kong National Party was banned in August, with authorities citing a colonial-era law, Hong Kong's Societies Ordinance, which supposedly empowered the government to ban groups 'in the interests of national security, public order or the protection of the rights and freedoms of others,' including Hong Kong pro-independence groups.[36] In addition to Hong Kong, Beijing's mass internment of Uighur Muslims in Xinjiang has drawn widespread criticism from the international community.

In contrast to China, domestic reforms to bring Taiwan's judicial system more in line with international standards are serving the country's long-term goal of boosting soft power abroad by strengthening Taiwan's democracy-based diplomacy. Moreover, strengthening rule of law may also prove a more effective strategy in increasing the prospects of foreign investment and trade for the future, as Taiwan will be able to provide a more secure environment for international businesses to thrive. Perhaps in this way, Taiwan's international space may improve in not just soft but also hard power terms.

## Conclusion

Although many may view Ma Ying-jeou's tenure as a time when Taiwan's international space reached its peak, I would argue the diplomatic and economic gains obtained under Ma did not signify meaningful progress for Taiwan's international space. Many of Ma's achievements in international space were temporary and contingent upon China's continued support. As it was always a possibility that Taiwan's democratic process would elect a leader less palatable to China than Ma, this strategy proved short-sighted and risky. Therefore, rather than expanding international space, Ma's strategy in fact exposed the pre-existing limitations placed by China on Taiwan's international involvement and engagement.

Throughout Ma's tenure, Taiwan remained excluded from multilateral frameworks for economic integration in the Asian region. Ma's emphasis on cooperation with the PRC also did not prove beneficial in allowing Taiwan's inclusion in legal disputes over territorial sovereignty in which it was directly involved, revealing China's inflexible barriers on Taiwan's international space. Moreover, the rapid restriction of Taiwan's international space by China since the change of administration is further testament to the limitations of Ma's strategy. Since Tsai's ascension in 2016, Taiwan has been blocked from several IGOs in which it had previously enjoyed participation. Ma's approach to international space demonstrates that if the conditions for Taiwan's international development are entrusted to China, developments in international space will continue to be limited and temporary.

On the other hand however, Tsai sought to lessen Taiwan's dependence on China in this respect by pursuing a strategy to develop Taiwan's international role in other areas. Her administration's focus on deepening non-economic links alongside trade relations has helped build substantial rapport among other Asian neighbouring countries. As Tsai has sought to navigate Taiwan through a more turbulent period in cross-Strait relations, her administration has also become increasingly adept at reinforcing Taiwan's image as a sovereign democratic state abroad in contrast to China. Parliamentary exchanges with like-minded countries have also boosted Taiwan's democracy-based diplomacy by consistently highlighting Taiwan's shared democratic and progressive values. Tsai's more soft-power–oriented approach has also manifested itself in her treatment of the South China Sea issue. While Tsai has expanded upon the soft-power elements of Ma's South China Sea Policy, the subtle changes in phrasing territorial claims made by her administration also demonstrate that Tsai is signalling Taiwan's adherence to international law and UNCLOS. This soft-power–oriented foreign policy strategy abroad has been reinforced by key domestic reforms within Taiwan, including the legalisation of same-sex marriages as well as legal reform.

The more Taiwan strives to improve its democratic and legal system in line with other liberal democratic countries around the world, the more common ground it will have with other likeminded allies to strengthen co-operation for the future. This strategy may improve the quality of Taiwan's official and unofficial relations for the long term as well as increase awareness of Taiwan's status as a sovereign democratic state separate to China. Therefore, Tsai's strategy for international space may prove more effective for the future.

## Notes

1 Hsieh, Li-hui 謝莉慧, "Ma Ying-jeou: 'Only under the 1992 Consensus will Taiwan have International Space'" 馬英九: 有九二共識 台灣才有國際空間, *New Talk*新聞, 26 June 2017, https://newtalk.tw/news/view/2017-06-26/90346, accessed 5 May 2019.
2 Hsu, Cheng-hsuan 徐政璿,"Ma Ying-jeou: Shopkeepers tell me 'Nowadays it seems we're closed 5 days a week'" 馬英九: 商家告訴我「現在幾乎週休五日」, *ET Today*, 7 November 2018, https://www.ettoday.net/news/20181107/1299904.htm#ixzz5mVM5OP5Z, accessed 5 May 2019.
3 Sui, Cindy, "Taiwan election: How Tsai stayed one step ahead", *BBC*, 10 January 2020, https://www.bbc.co.uk/news/world-asia-51029280, accessed 2 February 2020.
4 Yu, Hsin-tien, 俞新天 "Reflections on expanding Taiwan's International Space" 對擴大台灣國際空間的思考, *China Review News Agency*中國評論新聞網, 18 March 2009, http://hk.crntt.com/doc/1009/0/1/9/100901906.html?coluid=9&kindid=4291&docid=100901906&mdate=0318082703, accessed 3 March 2019.
5 Hsieh, Hsiao-ch'ing, 謝曉慶 "On the concept and features of Taiwan's 'International Space' Issue" 試論台灣 "國際空間" 問題的概念與特徵, *China Review News Agency* 中國評論新聞網, 21 December 2011, http://hk.crntt.com/

188    *Mariah Thornton*

doc/1019/4/8/5/101948510.html?coluid=63&kindid=0&docid=101948510&
mdate=1221162729, accessed 26 October 2019.

6  Lubin, Matthew, "China-Taiwan trade slips 0.7% in 2016: MAC", *Taiwan News*,
   20 March 2017, https://www.taiwannews.com.tw/en/news/3121080, accessed
   4 May 2019.

7  Tiezzi, Shannon "A cross-strait chill? You wouldn't know it from Taiwan's economic data", *The Diplomat,* 16 February 2018, https://thediplomat.com/2018/
   02/a-cross-strait-chill-you-wouldnt-know-it-from-taiwans-economic-data/,
   accessed 6 May 2019.

8  "New Southbound Policy powers Taiwan 2017 exports", *Taiwan Today*,
   22 January 2018, https://taiwantoday.tw/news.php?unit=2,6,10,15,18&post=
   128298, accessed 28 October 2019.

9  Brown, Kerry and Sageman, Chloe, "Taiwan's geopolitical challenges and domestic choices", *Chatham House*, 12 April 2019, https://www.chathamhouse.
   org/publication/taiwan-s-geopolitical-challenges-and-domestic-choices-state-
   ambiguity, p. 10, accessed 15 April 2020.

10 Marston, Hunter and Bush, Richard, "Taiwan's engagement with Southeast Asia
   is making progress under the New Southbound Policy", *Brookings Institute,* 30 July
   2018, https://www.brookings.edu/opinions/taiwans-engagement-with-southeast-
   asia-is-making-progress-under-the-new-southbound-policy/#footnote-11,   accessed 26 October 2019.

11 Yu, Jessica Macy, "Taiwan seeks to build soft power with retooled southbound
   policy", *Reuters*, 13 October 2017, https://www.reuters.com/article/us-taiwan-
   policy-southbound/taiwan-seeks-to-build-soft-power-with-retooled-south
   bound-policy-idUSKBN1CI0P1, accessed 6 May 2019.

12 Marston and Bush, 2018.

13 "New Economic Immigration Bill", National Development Council, 2019,
   https://www.ndc.gov.tw/en/Content_List.aspx?n=999F9864EFDB5F6F&upn=
   6CE244D6E7DAF831, accessed 8 January 2020.

14 "'New Southbound Policy' Promotion Plan launched", Executive Yuan, Republic
   of China (Taiwan), 5 September 2016, https://english.ey.gov.tw/News_Content2.
   aspx?n=8262ED7A25916ABF&sms=DD07AA2ECD4290A6&s=64BB71A
   3D16A49CB, 20 October 2019.

15 Marston and Bush, 2018.

16 Yang, Alan and Chiang, Jeremy, "Taiwan is retaking the initiative with its
   New Southbound Policy", *The Diplomat*, 23 October 2018, https://thediplomat.
   com/2018/10/taiwan-is-retaking-the-initiative-with-its-new-southbound-policy/,
   accessed 20 October 2019.

17 Parameswaran, Prashanth, "Assessing Taiwan's New Southbound Policy",
   *The Diplomat*, 23 April 2019, https://thediplomat.com/2019/04/assessing-
   taiwans-new-southbound-policy/, accessed 2 May 2019.

18 Van der Wees, Gerrit, "Taiwan and the World Health Assembly", *The Diplomat*,
   10 May 2016, https://thediplomat.com/2016/05/taiwan-and-the-world-health-
   assembly/, accessed 3 May 2019.

19 Tang, Pei-chun and Chiang, Yi-ching, "Taiwanese experts to participate online
   in WHO global forum", *Focus Taiwan*, 9 February 2020, https://focustaiwan.tw/
   politics/202002090007, accessed 4 June 2020.

20 Chen Shih-chung, "China can't be allowed to block Taiwan from WHO", *The
   Times*, 29 April 2020, https://www.thetimes.co.uk/article/china-cant-be-allowed-
   to-block-taiwan-from-who-p57hbj6xx, accessed 6 May 2020.

21 Zhe, Sun, "Ma Ying-jeou's Second Term and Taiwan's International Participation", *Brookings Institute*, 8 May 2012, https://www.brookings.edu/opinions/

ma-ying-jeous-second-term-and-taiwans-international-participation/, accessed 7 June 2020.

22 Hernández, Javier, "China suspends diplomatic contact with Taiwan", *New York Times*, 25 June 2016, https://www.nytimes.com/2016/06/26/world/asia/china-suspends-diplomatic-contact-with-taiwan.html, accessed 26 October 2019.

23 "The Founding Assembly of East Asia Democracy Forum (EADF)", Taiwan Foundation for Democracy, 13 September 2014, http://www.tfd.org.tw/opencms/english/events/data/Event0460.html, accessed 20 October 2019.

24 "President Ma attends Taiwan Foundation for Democracy ceremony to open new headquarters and mark 10th anniversary", Office of the President Republic of China (Taiwan), 16 June 2013, https://english.president.gov.tw/NEWS/4180, accessed 20 October 2019.

25 "MOFA Minister Wu, Legislative Yuan President Su laud role of parliamentary diplomacy," *Taiwan Today*, 15 November 2018, https://taiwantoday.tw/news.php?unit=2,6,10,15,18&post=145457, accessed 6 November 2019.

26 "President Tsai affirms strength of Taiwan-UK relations", *Taiwan Today*, 6 September 2018, https://taiwantoday.tw/news.php?unit=2,6,10,15,18&post=144817, accessed 20 October 2019.

27 "Taiwan thanks US for signing Taiwan Travel Act into law", *Taiwan Today*, 19 March 2018, https://taiwantoday.tw/news.php?unit=2,6,10,15,18&post=131179, accessed 20 October 2019.

28 H.R. 535—Taiwan Travel Act, Congress.gov, https://www.congress.gov/bill/115th-congress/house-bill/535/text, accessed 20 October 2019.

29 "Inter-parliamentary group to enhance ties with Philippines", *Taiwan Today*, 19 April 2017, https://taiwantoday.tw/news.php?unit=2,6,10,15,18&post=114082, accessed 7 November 2019.

30 "China lodges protests with India over visit by Taiwan legislators", *Reuters*, 15 February 2017, https://www.reuters.com/article/us-china-taiwan-india-idUSKBN15U134, accessed 9 November 2019.

31 Ghosh, Rudroneel, "Taiwanese parliamentary delegation visits India", *Times of India*, 14 February 2017, https://timesofindia.indiatimes.com/blogs/talkingturkey/taiwanese-parliamentary-delegation-visits-india/, accessed 7 November 2019.

32 Lin, Ting-hui, "Taiwan's Policy Evolution after the South China Sea Arbitration", *Maritime Awareness Project*, 22 March 2018, http://maritimeawarenessproject.org/2018/03/22/taiwans-policy-evolution-after-the-south-china-sea-arbitration/, accessed 8 November 2019.

33 Chin, Jonathan, "Tsai highlights targets for judicial reform", *Taipei Times*, 11 July 2017, http://www.taipeitimes.com/News/front/archives/2017/07/11/2003674315, accessed 20 October 2019.

34 Kaznowski, Adam, "Taiwan and the European Union hold 2nd Human Rights Consultations", European Union External Action Department, 14 May 2019, https://eeas.europa.eu/headquarters/headquarters-homepage/62602/taiwan-and-european-union-hold-2nd-human-rights-consultations_en, accessed 21 October 2019.

35 Tsoi, Grace and Lam, Cho Wai, "Hong Kong security law: What is it and is it worrying?", *BBC,* 29 May 2020, https://www.bbc.co.uk/news/world-asia-china-52765838, accessed 1 June 2020.

36 "Hong Kong pro-independence party formally outlawed in first such move since handover", *Reuters*, 24 September 2018, https://www.reuters.com/article/us-hongkong-politics/hong-kong-pro-independence-party-formally-outlawed-in-first-such-move-since-handover-idUSKCN1M409S, accessed 21 October 2019.

## Bibliography

Brown, Kerry and Sageman, Chloe, "Taiwan's Geopolitical Challenges an Domestic Choices", Chatham House, 12 April 2019, p. 10, https://www.chathamhouse.org/publication/taiwan-s-geopolitical-challenges-and-domestic-choices-state-ambiguity, accessed 15 April 2020.

Chen, Dean P. "The Strategic Implications of Ma Ying-Jeou's 'One ROC, Two Areas' Policy on Cross-Strait Relations", *American Journal of Chinese Studies*, Vol. 20, No. 1, (2013), pp. 23–41.

Chen Shih-chung, "China Can't Be Allowed to Block Taiwan from WHO", *The Times*, 29 April 2020, https://www.thetimes.co.uk/article/china-cant-be-allowed-to-block-taiwan-from-who-p57hbj6xx, accessed 6 May 2020.

"China Lodges Protests with India over Visit by Taiwan Legislators", *Reuters*, 15 February 2017, https://www.reuters.com/article/us-china-taiwan-india-idUSKBN15U134, accessed 9 November 2019.

Chin, Jonathan, "Tsai Highlights Targets for Judicial Reform", *Taipei Times*, 11 July 2017, http://www.taipeitimes.com/News/front/archives/2017/07/11/2003674315, accessed 20 October 2019.

DeLisle, Jacques, "Taiwan's Quest for International Space: Ma's Legacy, Tsai's Options, China's Choices, and U.S. Policy", Foreign Policy Research Institute, 18 August 2016.

Geldenhuys, Deon, *Contested States in World Politics*, Springer, 2009.

Ghosh, Rudroneel, "Taiwanese Parliamentary Delegation Visits India", *Times of India*, 14 February 2017, https://timesofindia.indiatimes.com/blogs/talkingturkey/taiwanese-parliamentary-delegation-visits-india/, accessed 7 November 2019.

Hernández, Javier, "China Suspends Diplomatic Contact with Taiwan", *New York Times*, 25 June 2016, https://www.nytimes.com/2016/06/26/world/asia/china-suspends-diplomatic-contact-with-taiwan.html, accessed 26 October 2019.

Hickey, Dennis, "Continuity and Change: Ma Ying-Jeou, Tsai Ing-Wen and the Dispute in the South China Sea", *Journal of Territorial and Maritime Studies*, Vol. 5, No. 1, Winter/Spring 2018, pp. 64–82.

"Hong Kong Pro-Independence Party Formally Outlawed in First Such Move since Handover", *Reuters*, 24 September 2018, https://www.reuters.com/article/us-hongkong-politics/hong-kong-pro-independence-party-formally-outlawed-in-first-such-move-since-handover-idUSKCN1M409S, accessed 21 October 2019.

H.R. 535—Taiwan Travel Act, Congress.gov, https://www.congress.gov/bill/115th-congress/house-bill/535/text, accessed 20 October 2019.

Hsieh, Hsiao-ching, 謝曉慶 "On the Concept and Features of Taiwan's 'International Space' Issue" 試論台灣"國際空間"問題的概念與特徵, *China Review News Agency* 中國評論新聞網, 21 December 2011, http://hk.crntt.com/doc/1019/4/8/5/101948510.html?coluid=63&kindid=0&docid=101948510&mdate=1221162729, accessed 26 October 2019.

Hsieh, Li-hui 謝莉慧, "Ma Ying-jeou: 'Only under the 1992 Consensus Will Taiwan Have International Space' 馬英九: 有九二共識 台灣才有國際空間, *New Talk*新聞, 26 June 2017, https://newtalk.tw/news/view/2017-06-26/90346, accessed 5 May 2019.

Hsu, Cheng-hsuan 徐政璿, "Ma Ying-jeou: Shopkeepers Tell Me 'Nowadays It Seems We're Closed 5 Days a Week'" 馬英九: 商家告訴我「現在幾乎週休五日」, *ET Today*, 7 November 2018, https://www.ettoday.net/news/20181107/1299904.htm#ixzz5mVM5OP5Z, accessed 5 May 2019.

Huang, Kwei-bo, "More International Space for Taiwan or Less?" in Beckershoff, André and Schubert, Gunter, *Assessing the Presidency of Ma Ying-Jiu in Taiwan*, Routledge, 2018, pp. 249–275.

"Inter-Parliamentary Group to Enhance Ties with Philippines", *Taiwan Today*, 19 April 2017, https://taiwantoday.tw/news.php?unit=2,6,10,15,18&post=114082, accessed 7 November 2019.

Kaznowski, Adam, "Taiwan and the European Union Hold 2nd Human Rights Consultations", European Union External Action Department, 14 May 2019, https://eeas.europa.eu/headquarters/headquarters-homepage/62602/taiwan-and-european-union-hold-2nd-human-rights-consultations_en, accessed 21 October 2019.

Lin, Ting-hui, "Taiwan's Policy Evolution after the South China Sea Arbitration", Maritime Awareness Project, 22 March 2018, http://maritimeawarenessproject.org/2018/03/22/taiwans-policy-evolution-after-the-south-china-sea-arbitration/, accessed 8 November 2019.

Liu, Tony Tai-ting, "Walking a Tight Rope: Taiwan's Search for Integration Amidst Strait Politics", Presented at the International Studies Association Asia-Pacific (ISA-AP) Regional Conference, City University of Hong Kong, Hong Kong, China, June 2016.

Lubin, Matthew, "China-Taiwan Trade Slips 0.7% in 2016: MAC", Taiwan News, 20 March 2017, https://www.taiwannews.com.tw/en/news/3121080, accessed 4 May 2019.

Marston, Hunter and Bush, Richard, "Taiwan's Engagement with Southeast Asia Is Making Progress under the New Southbound Policy", Brookings Institute, 30 July 2018, https://www.brookings.edu/opinions/taiwans-engagement-with-southeast-asia-is-making-progress-under-the-new-southbound-policy/#footnote-11, acessed 26 October 2019.

"MOFA Minister Wu, Legislative Yuan President Su Laud Role of Parliamentary Diplomacy," Taiwan Today, 15 November 2018, https://taiwantoday.tw/news.php?unit=2,6,10,15,18&post=145457, accessed 6 November 2019.

"New Economic Immigration Bill", National Development Council, 2019, https://www.ndc.gov.tw/en/Content_List.aspx?n=999F9864EFDB5F6F&upn=6CE244D6E7DAF831, accessed 8 January 2020.

"New Southbound Policy Powers Taiwan 2017 Exports", *Taiwan Today*, 22 January 2018, https://taiwantoday.tw/news.php?unit=2,6,10,15,18&post=128298, accessed 28 October 2019.

"'New Southbound Policy' Promotion Plan Launched", Executive Yuan, Republic of China (Taiwan), 5 September 2016, https://english.ey.gov.tw/News_Content2.aspx?n=8262ED7A25916ABF&sms=DD07AA2ECD4290A6&s=64BB71A3D16A49CB, 20 October 2019.

Nye, Joseph Jr, "Public Diplomacy and Soft Power", The Annals of the American Academy of Political and Social Science, Vol. 616, Public Diplomacy in a Changing World (March 2008), pp. 94–109.

Parameswaran, Prashanth, "Assessing Taiwan's New Southbound Policy", *The Diplomat*, 23 April 2019, https://thediplomat.com/2019/04/assessing-taiwans-new-southbound-policy/, accessed 2 May 2019.

"President Ma Attends Taiwan Foundation for Democracy Ceremony to Open New Headquarters and Mark 10th Anniversary", Office of the President Republic of China (Taiwan), 16 June 2013, https://english.president.gov.tw/NEWS/4180, accessed 20 October 2019.

"President Tsai Affirms Strength of Taiwan-UK Relations", *Taiwan Today*, 6 September 2018, https://taiwantoday.tw/news.php?unit=2,6,10,15,18&post=144817, accessed 20 October 2019.

Rawnsley, Gary, "Selling Democracy: Diplomacy, Propaganda and Democratisation in Taiwan", *China Perspectives*, 47, May to June 2003, p. 6, http://journals.openedition.org/chinaperspectives/361.

Sheng, Li-jun, "Chen Shui-bian and Cross-Strait Relations", *Contemporary Southeast Asia*, Vol. 23, No. 1, (April 2001), pp. 128–42.

Sui, Cindy, "Taiwan Election: How Tsai Stayed One Step Ahead", *BBC*, 10 January 2020, https://www.bbc.co.uk/news/world-asia-51029280, accessed 2 February 2020.

"Taiwan Thanks US for Signing Taiwan Travel Act into Law", *Taiwan Today*, 19 March 2018, https://taiwantoday.tw/news.php?unit=2,6,10,15,18&post=131179, accessed 20 October 2019.

Tang, Pei-chun and Chiang, Yi-ching, "Taiwanese Experts to Participate Online in WHO Global Forum", *Focus Taiwan*, 9 February 2020, https://focustaiwan.tw/politics/202002090007, accessed 4 June 2020.

"The Founding Assembly of East Asia Democracy Forum (EADF)", Taiwan Foundation for Democracy, 13 September 2014, http://www.tfd.org.tw/opencms/english/events/data/Event0460.html, accessed 20 October 2019.

Tiezzi, Shannon, "A Cross-Strait Chill? You Wouldn't Know It from Taiwan's Economic Data", *The Diplomat*, 16 February 2018, https://thediplomat.com/2018/02/a-cross-strait-chill-you-wouldnt-know-it-from-taiwans-economic-data/, accessed 6 May 2019.

Tsai Ing-wen, Taiwan Public Television Service Foundation, 2011, in Liu, Tony Tai-ting, "Walking a Tight Rope: Taiwan's Search for Integration Amidst Strait Politics," Presented at the International Studies Association Asia-Pacific (ISA-AP) Regional Conference, City University of Hong Kong, Hong Kong, China, June 2016.

Tsoi, Grace and Lam, Cho Wai, "Hong Kong Security Law: What Is It and Is It Worrying?", *BBC*, 29 May 2020, https://www.bbc.co.uk/news/world-asia-china-52765838, accessed 1 June 2020.

Van der Wees, Gerrit, "Taiwan and the World Health Assembly", *The Diplomat*, 10 May 2016, https://thediplomat.com/2016/05/taiwan-and-the-world-health-assembly/, accessed 3 May 2019.

VanGrasstek, Craig, *The History and Future of the World Trade Organization*. Geneva, Switzerland: World Trade Organization, 2013.

Vice Premier Qian Qichen's Speech on 28 January 2000 in Sheng, Li-Jun, "Chen Shuibian and Cross-Strait Relations", *Contemporary Southeast Asia*, Vol. 23, No. 1, (April 2001), pp. 127, 128–42.

Winkler, Sigrid, "Taiwan in International Organisations: New Road Ahead or Dead-End?" in Cabestan, Jean-Pierre, *Political Changes in Taiwan under Ma Ying-Jeou: Partisan Conflict, Policy Choices, External Constraints and Security Challenges*, Routledge, 2014, pp. 247–264.

Winkler, Sigrid, "Taiwan's UN Dilemma: To Be or Not to Be", Brookings, 20 June 2012, https://www.brookings.edu/opinions/taiwans-un-dilemma-to-be-or-not-to-be/, accessed 22 December 2020.

Yang, Alan and Chiang, Jeremy, "Taiwan Is Retaking the Initiative with Its New Southbound Policy", *The Diplomat*, 23 October 2018, https://thediplomat.

com/2018/10/taiwan-is-retaking-the-initiative-with-its-new-southbound-policy/, accessed 20 October 2019.

Yu, Hsin-tien, 俞新天 "Reflections on Expanding Taiwan's International Space" 對擴大台灣國際空間的思考, *China Review News Agency* 中國評論新聞網, 18 March 2009, http://hk.crntt.com/doc/1009/0/1/9/100901906.html?coluid=9&kindid=4291&docid=100901906&mdate=0318082703, accessed 3 March 2019.

Yu, Jessica Macy, "Taiwan Seeks to Build Soft Power with Retooled Southbound Policy", *Reuters*, 13 October 2017, https://www.reuters.com/article/us-taiwan-policy-southbound/taiwan-seeks-to-build-soft-power-with-retooled-southbound-policy-idUSKBN1CI0P1, accessed 6 May 2019.

Zhe, Sun, "Ma Ying-jeou's Second Term and Taiwan's International Participation", Brookings Institute, 8 May 2012, https://www.brookings.edu/opinions/ma-ying-jeous-second-term-and-taiwans-international-participation/, accessed 7 June 2020.

# 12 Tongzhi Diplomacy and the queer case of Taiwan

*Chen Nai-chia and Dafydd Fell*

## Introduction

For decades China has been seeking to squeeze Taiwan's international space. This had led Taiwan to lose most of its formal diplomatic allies and to be excluded from most international government organisations. Since Tsai Ing-wen was elected president in 2016, China has adopted new policies and strategies to accelerate Taiwan's international isolation. Therefore Taiwan struggles to maintain its visibility in international politics under the threat of being swallowed up by a rising China. Despite this challenging international environment, Taiwan is known for its economic and political miracles. After the lifting of martial law in 1987 Taiwan went through a gradual democratisation process that culminated in the first direct presidential election in 1996. It has since gained the reputation as one of the most democratic and liberal states in Asia. For instance, it is now widely viewed as a beacon of Lesbian, Gay, Bisexual, and Transgender (LGBT) rights. Taiwan has hosted the largest annual LGBT Pride in East Asia for almost two decades. Furthermore, in May 2019, Taiwan's parliament, the Legislative Yuan, legalised same-sex marriage. This historical moment not only signals the progress of human rights in this contested island state, Taiwan's marriage equality movement was widely praised all over the world. However, the politics of LGBT rights in East Asia, including the case of Taiwan, has often not received the academic attention it deserves.

In May 2018, Ma Ying-jeou, the former President of Taiwan, told the press that when he was the Mayor of Taipei in 2004, he visited Berlin and successfully met the City Mayor Klaus Wowereit, who is openly gay. Ma recalled how he introduced the first Pride in Taipei to Wowereit and claimed that it was a successful example of 'Tongzhi Diplomacy' (Liu, 2018). Although Ma did not elaborate on what he meant by Tongzhi Diplomacy, based on his remarks, we can surmise it to be diplomacy related to 'gay people' and 'gay rights.' Ma's claim raises the questions which will be further discussed in this chapter: what is 'Tongzhi Diplomacy'? What are the differences between Tongzhi Diplomacy and traditional foreign policies? Could 'Tongzhi Diplomacy' become a new approach for Taiwan to expand its international space?

We argue that, compared to the existing LGBT rights foreign policy in the West, Taiwan does not have a sophisticated Tongzhi Diplomacy or LGBT rights foreign policy agenda. Instead of a top-down style of foreign policy, it should be understood as the product of both government and non-governmental forces. More precisely, as a 'queer state,' Taiwan is using a 'queer way' to do 'queer diplomacy.' We term it a 'queer state,' as Taiwan's statehood and status in international law are contested; by a 'queer way,' we mean that Taiwan's approaches are different from the formal diplomatic approaches; and 'queer diplomacy' refers to the very different goals of Taiwan's LGBT-related diplomacy. In other words, Taiwan does not seek to influence other countries' LGBT-related policies, but instead it tries to use the LGBT issue to enhance its reputation in the world as a liberal democracy with a sovereign status. By promoting LGBT rights, Taiwan has cultivated an image of being 'the beacon of human rights in Asia,' while its Tongzhi Diplomacy has allowed it to broaden its international space, an arena where Taiwan had long been excluded.

In the literature on LGBT rights diplomacy, the most well-known case concerns US foreign policy during the Obama era. In 2011, Secretary of State Hillary Clinton gave a speech at the UN in which she argued 'gay rights are human rights.' The US not only promoted LGBT rights on multilateral platforms but also introduced a series of LGBT rights-based foreign policies. The Obama administration initiated the Global Equality Fund to support LGBT rights activism overseas and the US also sought to influence fund-receiving countries through foreign development aid. For instance, the infamous case of Uganda's anti-gay bill caused the USA to threaten to cut off aid. Obama also used bilateral engagements to promote 'homosexual decriminalisation' when visiting Senegal and Kenya. However, some argued this was counterproductive (Encarnación, 2016).

This empirical study of foreign policies will start by defining the key terms, then the evolution of LGBT rights in Taiwan and Tongzhi Diplomacy will be reviewed. Next a comparison will be made between two events to highlight the different level of attention received by Taiwan's traditional diplomacy and its LGBT rights diplomacy. These are the failed participation in the World Health Assembly (WHA) and the Ruling by the Constitutional Court that favoured same-sex marriage, both events took place in the same week of May 2017. The comparison shows that although Taiwan's government invested heavily in its public diplomacy campaign to join the WHA, when it comes to media exposure to make Taiwan visible, the Court Ruling proved to be far more effective. Then we will consider how Taiwan's civil society led LGBT diplomacy evolved by examining the case of Taiwan Tongzhi Hotline Association (Hotline). Hotline received funds from the government-funded legal foundation, Taiwan Foundation for Democracy (TFD), and has established the connections to participate in international LGBT rights initiatives and institutions. By examining the case of Hotline, we show that Tongzhi Diplomacy is different from the existing patterns of the West, in that it is 'queer' as it does not seek to impose a human rights agenda on other countries. We treat Hotline as a case study of Taiwan's attempts to expand its international space. We conclude that there are two key factors that explain why Taiwan has taken a different path in its international LGBT rights politics. First, Taiwan's ambiguous status as a 'queer state' seems to make Tongzhi Diplomacy possible in the international realm. Second, that non-state actors are taking the lead to expand this international space is the key to the development of such diplomacy. If this LGBT diplomacy had been a largely state-led project, it would have struggled to have an impact. The queer case of Taiwan also challenges the discipline of international relations which often takes the 'state' for granted, and the assumption that 'states are states' and 'states are homogeneous.' Both assumptions fail to explain how Taiwan as a 'queer state' is using 'queer ways' to act in international politics. Apart from these implications, Tongzhi Diplomacy faces both domestic and international challenges. This again reveals the complexity of Tongzhi Diplomacy, which should not be simply reduced to transnational LGBT rights activism or LGBT rights diplomacy.

## Terminology

The definition of tongzhi is contested. In this chapter, tongzhi is an umbrella term that stands for the gender and sexual minorities, including people who are not heterosexual nor cisgender. 'Tongzhi' was said to be first used in Hong Kong for the first 'Lesbian and Gay Film Festival,' and it is usually understood as the translation for homosexual. Chou argues that tongzhi is an 'indigenous representation,' which 'connotes an entire range of alternative sexual practices and sensitivities in a way that "lesbian," "gay," or "bisexual" does not' (Chou, 2000).

'Queer' in this chapter has two meanings. First, it serves as an adjective that stands for 'unusual, unconventional, unorthodox and peculiar.' The other queer is a noun which refers to an identity that incorporates the whole LGBT community, 'queer' implies the idea of gender or sex nonconforming. We will term 'LGBT rights' to describe Taiwan's gender and sexual rights movement, since Hotline uses 'Taiwan Tongzhi (LGBT) Hotline Association' as its official English name, instead of using LGBTQ or LGBTQIA.

When discussing the peculiar case – Taiwan is a 'queer state' using a 'queer way' to do 'queer diplomacy,' the term 'queer' plays with the dual meaning to portray the complexity of Tongzhi Diplomacy. It is important to note that in Taiwan's context, queer as an identity does not have exactly the same meaning as in the West. The connotation of 'queer' in Taiwan is not as radical as in the West, and queer is usually the synonym of LGBT due to the different historical background in the rights movement. To put it another way, 'tensions between queer and "lesbian and gay" in English speaking societies does not equate to the relationship between Taiwan's version of "ku'er" and "tongzhi"' (Lim, 2008).

What's more, terms such as queer, lesbian/gay, or LGBT were all introduced to Taiwan at different occasions. As Chi Da-wei suggests, 'searching for the specific definition of tongzhi and ku 'er, falls into the myth of authenticity and genuineness' (Chi, 2015). This chapter is not going to investigate the discrepancy and tension between the terms, nor does it try to make tongzhi and Tongzhi Diplomacy an alternative for queer/LGBT and LGBT rights diplomacy. But we would like to use the fluidity and flexibility of these phrases, to draw a picture of the possible Tongzhi Diplomacy narrative in Taiwan, instead of building a fixed structure of Tongzhi Diplomacy. Thus tongzhi, queer, and LGBT are used interchangeably. We view the contested boundaries of what these terms represent as an advantage, because in the queer case of Taiwan, ambiguity is the fuel for diplomacy.

## The history of Taiwanese LGBT rights and Tongzhi Diplomacy

### *1987–99: struggles at the beginning of democratisation*

The birth of Taiwan's LGBT rights movements was only possible in the aftermath of the lifting of martial law in 1987 and the subsequent gradual political liberalisation and removal of freedom of expression restrictions. Initially there was not an organised LGBT rights movement but a noticeable sign of change was the growing representation of LGBT issues in the mainstream visual culture, particularly in Taiwan's cinema. Instead LGBT rights activism was initially under the umbrella of the feminist movement. It started to bloom in universities and was led by scholars and intellectuals (Chou, 2000; Chu, 2003; Damm, 2011; Lin, 2013). The first tongzhi organisation, a lesbian group called 'Wo Men Zhi Jian,' was founded in 1990. Meanwhile, the leading women's organisation the 'Awakening Foundation' had published articles about homosexualities in their magazine, and the two organisations cooperated on women's issue in the 1990s (Lin, 2013). The Awakening Foundation was involved in the HIV/AIDS movements as well. However, unlike in the West, Taiwan's HIV/AIDS-related self-help groups did not work well with other tongzhi groups. Damn argues that HIV/AIDS topics were usually marginalised from the tongzhi discourse in order to avoid undermining public support for the normalisation of tongzhi issues (Damm, 2011).

Although the social order regulations had been loosened, tongzhi gathering places and related businesses were often raided by the police. The most infamous cases were the 'Chang-De Street Incident' in 1997, and the 'AG Gym Incident' in 1998. The police took obscene photos deliberately and then arrested the gays for 'conducting illegal transactional sex.' It was taken for granted the Tongzhi were criminal before the trial, and they were portrayed as perverts in the media (Ho, 2010; Gofyy, 2016a). In another notorious incident in 1998 a reporter used a hidden camera to film a lesbian bar and then exposed it on TV. The peeping clips not only violated the privacy of the LGBT community but also stigmatised tongzhi lifestyles and tongzhi-oriented businesses (Ho, 2010). These incidents revealed not only the public curiosity about tongzhi but also a unique dilemma for tongzhi activism. In other words, many were reluctant to openly come out and so they were hesitant to do press conferences or march on the streets to make themselves visible (Chu, 2003).

### 2000s: a strategically positive time for Tongzhi?

In 2000 Taiwan experienced its first change of ruling parties when the DPP's Chen Shui-bian won the presidential election. Some scholars claim that this marks the start of a new era for the LGBT rights movement, as the DPP itself was born out of the democratic movement and thus it has strong connections with many social movements (Fan & Wu, 2016). Chen's presidency (2000–8) gave LGBT rights a political opportunity, and the focus of the movement shifted from making tongzhi visible to the 'sexual citizenship' of legal rights (Chu, 2003). The dynamics of party politics and civic activism meant there was both progress and setbacks in the area of LGBT rights, and this period has left a legacy on the subsequent development of LGBT rights in Taiwan.

When Chen established the Presidential Office Human Rights Consultative Committee in October 2000, he promised to turn Taiwan into 'a nation founded upon the principles of human rights' (Lin, 2000). With the commitment of complying with international norms, the committee was given the task of improving Taiwan's human rights policies and pushing for participation in international human rights initiatives (Office of The President Republic of China (Taiwan), 2007). The committee launched a project to draft a 'Human Rights Basic Law,' including legalising the family rights of same-sex couples and their adoption rights. Furthermore, the draft stated that 'governments worldwide are now protecting rights of homosexuals, thus this clause is dedicated to giving legal protection [to tongzhi]' (Ministry of Justice, 2001). But the drafting procedure was never completed, and Damm argues that this was due to the DPP's concern that it could damage its election prospects (Damm, 2011). Ho claims the government created this publicity stunt to gain international media attention but then let down the LGBT rights groups (Ho, 2010). In Liu's analysis, Chen was using same-sex marriage 'to solidify the pro-independence, anti-PRC stance and to rally American support, while carefully keeping it from realization to avoid alienating the conservative and religious electoral bases' (Liu, 2015).

This period featured a fascinating case of competition between Chen's central government and Ma's Taipei city government over who had the most 'tongzhi-friendly image.' This added another layer to the LGBT rights discourse. Taipei city government hosted the very first 'Taipei LGBT Civil Rights Movement Festival' on 2 September 2000. American activists, Michael Bronski and Nan Hunter, were invited to Taipei for the events. On 4 September,

Chen received Bronski, Hunter, and Taiwanese activists in the Presidential Office. Chen commented that homosexuality is neither a crime nor a disease, then Chen had a photo with them and a rainbow flag. However, the Presidential Office did not issue any press release about the meeting until it had been criticised by the activists (Gofyy, 2016b). Damm believes that Chen and Ma's promises on LGBT rights 'tended to be directed towards the outside world' (Damm, 2011). Similarly, Liu argues that 'the rhetoric of tolerance, liberalism and progress' is designed to win American sympathy and support, and to alienate China in order to serve Chen's pro-independence agenda' (Liu, 2015, p. 158). Although the tongzhi-friendly gestures did not result in substantive legal breakthroughs, the political competition between Chen and Ma did suggest an optimistic future for LGBT rights.

The environment for LGBT activism was still complex. According to the 'Taiwan Human Rights Report,' Hotline intended to register at the Ministry of the Interior in November 1999, but was refused because 'It is not proper to advocate gay relationships; the formation of a gay community centre and the provision of gay peer counselling and assistance could possibly have ill effect' (Taiwan Association for Human Rights, 2000). However, Hotline successfully registered in June 2000 and became the first nationwide tongzhi organisation. It is difficult to say whether this was related to the DPP's Chen coming to power. Meanwhile in KMT-run Taipei, the first Pride march took place in Taipei in 2003, and since then the scale of the rally has grown from less than 1,000 participants to almost than 200,000 in 2019.

However, the tongzhi movement faced a mixed picture on the legal front and at times, it was clear that the bureaucracy still discriminated against tongzhi. For instance, there was the lawsuit against Gin Gin Bookstore and censorship against a lesbian radio programme (Chen & Wang, 2010).[1] From the legislative viewpoint, some important achievements were made that were consistent with Chen's manifesto: the 'Gender Equality Education Act' was passed in 2004 after the tragedy of 'Rose Boy' Ye Yong-zhi who had died after being bullied in school due to gender nonconformity in 2000; and the 'Act of Gender Equality in Employment' was introduced in 2002 and amended in 2008 to cover different sexualities.

### The 2010s: globalised Tongzhi

In 2008 Chen was replaced by Ma as president and the competition between them came to an end. Although Ma had cultivated a tongzhi-friendly image in his mayoral term, Damm suggests that there was 'Nothing new under Ma Ying-jeou' during his presidency (Damm, 2011). The new trend of activism would be the globalisation of the marriage equality campaign, especially after DPP was re-elected as the ruling party in 2016.

In 2006, a DPP legislator introduced a 'Same-sex Marriage Act' to parliament but it was blocked due to opposition from both major parties and was not reviewed. The Taiwan Alliance to Promote Civil Partnership Rights

TAPCPR (伴侶盟), the first major organisation advocating for same-sex marriage, was established in 2012. It issued a draft amendment to the Civil Code for legalising same-sex marriage, civil partnerships, and multiple-person families. The bill was introduced to parliament by DPP legislators in 2013, and public hearings were held and provoked heated public debates. However, the bill did not make it to a vote in parliament in Ma's presidency.

The next campaign kicked off in October 2016. Besides TAPCPR, another major force was led by Hotline, in cooperation with the Awakening Foundation and other gender/sexuality groups. Hotline was funded by the Open Society Foundations with US$20,000 in 2017 to support its marriage equality campaign (Taiwan Tongzhi Hotline Association, 2017b; Open Society Foundations, 2017). Furthermore, members of Hotline participated in the Human Rights Campaign's Global Innovative Advocacy Summits in 2016 and 2017 to exchange experiences with activists worldwide (Human Rights Campaign, 2017). The way Hotline reached out for international resources symbolises the globalisation of domestic activism and it also implies that the marriage equality campaign possesses a layer of international dynamics.

## The great potential of Tongzhi Diplomacy – case study of WHA incident and the historical ruling in May 2017

Although the campaign for same-sex marriage legislation faced much domestic resistance, it has unintentionally made Taiwan visible and celebrated throughout the world, suggesting the great potential of Tongzhi Diplomacy. Fan Chi-fei, a Taiwanese journalist stationed in the USA for two decades, found that the number of Google results about Taiwan's failed participation in the WHA in Geneva was far less than the historical ruling of the Constitutional Court on same-sex marriage, which happened in the same week. Fan argues that apparently the world paid more attention to same-sex marriage than Taiwan's exclusion from the WHA (Fan, 2017). Fan's insight inspired the first author to investigate the two incidents (Chen, 2018).

Since President Tsai came into office, Taiwan has faced greater challenges in participating in world affairs due to the pressure from China. The government initiated a series of campaigns to advocate for Taiwan's participation in the WHA. Besides emphasising the danger of isolating Taiwan, the government published videos on social media to introduce Taiwan's excellence in medicine. Several Taiwanese Representatives abroad wrote articles in newspapers to raise awareness of Taiwan's WHA bid. In addition to regular diplomatic channels to gain support from other countries, the government also sought to raise awareness through social media platforms such as Twitter to highlight the absence of Taiwan in the WHA. Subsequently, Taiwan failed to obtain observer status in the WHA due to China's opposition. The Minister of Health and Welfare hosted an international press conference in Geneva to express Taiwan's disappointment about the outcome. Two days later, the long-anticipated ruling by the Constitutional Court on same-sex marriage was released. Unusually, the Court released a bilingual notice to the press and public explaining that it had ruled in favour of same-sex marriage. However, in contrast to the WHA incident, both MOFA and the Taiwan embassies remained silent on the Court's ruling.

An examination using Google Trends, during the week of 21–27 May of 2017, showed the hit count for searches using 'same-sex marriage'-related keywords was at least 50 times more than for those using 'WHA'-related phrases, with a strong correlation between 'Taiwan' and 'same-sex marriage' (Chen, 2018). It is surprising that although the ruling on same-sex marriage was simply a domestic issue, it attracted far more attention worldwide than the frustration of Taiwan's diplomatic setback. This comparison implies that, although the government of Taiwan invested heavily in the WHA bid through a wide variety of different channels, when it comes to the visibility of Taiwan, the ruling on same-sex marriage was more effective. Furthermore, the articles about the ruling in English news outlets portrayed Taiwan as an independent polity that upholds human rights and liberal democracy. Unlike many news reports on Taiwan, these stories were not centred on Taiwan's relations with China, which implies that Taiwan is not yet overshadowed by China in the field of LGBT rights (Chen, 2018). This phenomenon is not suggesting that the WHA bid is less important than the ruling, or that traditional diplomatic channels are not effective, but through the comparison, the potential strength of LGBT rights issues in expanding Taiwan's international space should be taken more seriously from the perspective of international relations.

Critiques of the marriage equality campaign arose from scholars who were mainly in the fields of cultural studies and queer studies. Hong contends that Hotline receiving support from American sources symbolises that Taiwanese activism was echoing American imperialism (Hong, 2016). Ho states that gender equality has become a branding material for Taiwan to distinguish itself from the 'rich but less civilised' China (Ho, 2017). In contrast Liu Wen claims that Hong's accusation overlooks the historical background of the local LGBT movement. Moreover, Liu asserts that the critiques constructed a 'queer China' as if 'China is not complicit with neoliberalism and Western neo-imperialism' (Liu, 2016). This chapter would like to focus on the practice of Tongzhi Diplomacy via empirical cases; thus, we will leave these theoretical debates for future studies.

## Case study: Hotline's international engagement and Tongzhi Diplomacy

### Hotline and TFD

In Geldenhuys' 'Contested States in World Politics,' he argues that President Chen conducted 'democracy-based diplomacy' in order to 'persuade the community of democracies that Taiwan deserved to enter their ranks'

(Geldenhuys, 2009). In the Foreign Policy Report of 2006, MOFA clearly stated that 'Democracy, human rights, humanitarianism, mutual interest and peace' were the core values of Taiwan's national policy; furthermore, 'through democracy and human rights, we can appeal for Taiwan's sovereignty to be strengthened' (Ministry of Foreign Affairs, Republic of China (Taiwan), 2006). Geldenhuys takes the establishment of the TFD as an example of how the Chen administration manoeuvred 'promoting democracy' to consolidate its legitimacy and the statehood of Taiwan. TFD was founded in 2003, initiated and funded by MOFA. The Chairperson of TFD is the Speaker of the parliament, and the Vice Chairperson is the Foreign Minister. Geldenhuys indicates that although the TFD is a non-governmental organisation, it plays a key role in expanding channels and links for Taiwan to participate in international affairs. Through its promotion of democracy, the TFD supports 'semi-official partnerships' with other democracies and democratic activists in authoritarian states (Geldenhuys, 2009).

Besides strengthening ties with other democracies, TFD supports three major categories of events: (1) funding political parties which have seats in parliament to conduct human rights and democracy-related events; (2) international grants for civil society organisations, think tanks, and academic institutions overseas to promote democracy and human rights; (3) domestic grants for civil society organisations, think tanks, and academic institutions to consolidate democracy and human rights through conferences, publications, and other initiatives. This chapter will examine the queerness of Tongzhi Diplomacy by looking at how Hotline used its TFD grants. Hotline has been applying for TFD grants since 2014 and was awarded funding with NT$80,000 for the project 'Participating in International Conference on LGBT Human Rights' in 2014, NT$ 500,000 for the 'Look Beyond Taiwan, Go See the World International Exchange and Collaboration Programme of Gender and Human Rights' in 2017, and NT$ 400,000 for the 'Attract Worldwide Attention on Taiwan' in 2018. The reasons why Hotline was not granted TFD funding in 2015 and 2016 could be: (1) Hotline hosted the ILGA-Asia's 2015 annual conference in Taipei; (2) the key person of Hotline who's in charge of external affairs, Jennifer Lu, was running for the legislative election in January 2016; hence, as an NGO with about ten staff, Hotline might not have been able to engage in international LGBT rights projects those two years.

As stated in the 2017 'Report of the Taiwan Foundation for Democracy Grant,' the grant was used on three projects: the 61st session of the Commission on the Status of Women (CSW) at UN Headquarters in New York, an institutional visit to Hong Kong, and participation in the ILGA-Asia's biennial conference in Cambodia. Hotline stated that due to the progress of the marriage equality campaign in 2016, they started to evaluate how to make Taiwanese experiences visible and available to the world via more efficient international cooperation, and how Hotline could align with organisations from different regions to enhance tongzhi rights (Taiwan Tongzhi Hotline Association, 2017a).

A case worthy of attention is attending CSW. Since Taiwan is not a member of the UN, it is impossible for government officials to participate in any events hosted by UN organs, but Hotline was able to take part due to being an NGO. Hotline took the opportunity to meet with the activists from abroad to learn about their experiences in doing international lobby work. According to the report, Hotline states that Taiwan's 'different status' in the international realm forced Taiwan to proactively make itself seen. The report continued, 'Taiwan developed its own methods to do international engagements,' and Taiwanese activists were unfamiliar with transnational activism and ways to put pressure on Taiwan government through international mechanisms due to the long exclusion from international institutions (Taiwan Tongzhi Hotline Association, 2017a). Fan and Wu argue that Taiwan had limited knowledge of the UN's 'gender mainstreaming' policies, so in order to catch up with the 'global trend,' the government proactively adopted 'gender mainstreaming' during the Chen presidency. They believe that the gap gave feminist activists leverage (Fan & Wu, 2016), but in the case of LGBT rights, what Hotline describes is a different facet of human rights.

Hotline did participate in CSW in 2013 and 2015 but was not supported by TFD. According to MOFA's website, in the section of 'Participation in International Organizations,' it notes that Taiwan has sent NGOs to attend CSW annually and that these have been supported by MOFA (MOFA, 2015). Therefore it is highly likely that Hotline was supported by MOFA in previous years, and this indirect and discursive route perfectly demonstrates Taiwan's queer nature.

The visit to Hong Kong symbolises another form of international connection that Hotline built up. The report notes that Hong Kong is a society that is close to Taiwan, both geographically and culturally, and on this occasion Hotline brought 15 team members to Hong Kong to work closely with their civil society organisations (Taiwan Tongzhi Hotline Association, 2017a). According to the report, Hotline visited Amnesty International's East Asia Regional Office (EARO), where one of the EARO team members suggested that 'the same-sex marriage movement in Taiwan is not only limited to Taiwan but is an Asian international movement, which shows that same-sex marriage is not a Western issue' (Taiwan Tongzhi Hotline Association, 2017a). This programme to Hong Kong echoes TFD's core goal of democracy promotion and Hotline's efforts to create connections between both civil societies correspond with this TFD objective. In the case of Hotline's participation in the ILGA-Asia's biennial conference, it sent three representatives and all of them were panellists on different subjects. Interestingly, the Swedish Embassy was one of the sponsors of the 2017 ILGA-Asia regional conference; while when Hotline hosted ILGA-Asia regional conference in

2015, neither TFD nor Sweden sponsored, instead only the European Union, supported both events.

### Hotline's diversified connections

The TFD 2014 grant was used to participate in WorldPride 2014 Toronto, but compared to the 2017 programmes, this programme mainly served as resources for Hotline's services rather than for its international activities. However, Jennifer Lu was invited by IGLHRC, now known as OutRight Action International (OutRight), to join the '2014 Advocacy Week' to push the UN to adopt LGBT friendly policies. OutRight is the only LGBT organisation that has a permanent presence to advocate at the UN Headquarters in New York and holds a special consultative status in the UN (OutRight, 2017). Lu wrote 'Tongzhi Diplomacy – International Advocacy on Human Rights Day' for a newsletter published by the 'Foundation of Women's Rights Promotion and Development (FWRPD)' to share her experiences. FWRPD was established by the Executive Yuan in 1997 to advance women's rights in Taiwan, and it shares a similar character with TFD as a 'non-governmental' organisation. In the article, Lu explained how her participation in CSW in 2013 had given her the connections that had enabled her to be invited by OutRight (Lu, 2015). Lu gives a thorough introduction about what she did during that week, including visiting UN WOMEN, United Nations Development Programme (UNDP), and diplomats from 25 countries. Another highlight of the article is the forum hosted by the EU during the Advocacy Week, in which Lu was invited to introduce Taiwan's LGBT movements. At first, the forum was due to take place in UN Headquarters, but due to Chinese pressure, Lu had to be switched to the EU office (Lu, 2015). Lu states that Taiwan's 'special status' always makes participation in international affairs difficult, even when attending CSW events as NGO representatives could be an issue. Although Taiwan's non-governmental forces have built up some connections in international society, 'whenever it comes to entering the UN, holding a Taiwanese passport makes you feel helpless.' Moreover, she suggests that LGBT issues could be an entry point for Taiwan to seize more opportunities in participating in global affairs, but she kept wondering whether the government should take the lead (Lu, 2015). Since then Lu has continued to participate in the Advocacy Week event and she shared on her Facebook during the 2017 event this remark, 'I shared the intertwined situation of being a Taiwanese, I wish to be recognized by the world, and being a tongzhi, I wish to be recognized by the mainstream society' (Lu, 2017).

Another case is the workshop 'LGBTQ Movement And Conservative Power In East Asia,' hosted by Hotline and sponsored by the EU in July 2017, the workshop invited 50 LGBT activists from Japan, Korea, and Taiwan to exchange their knowledge and experiences. According to the press release, the director of the EU office in Taiwan, Ms Majorenko, commented that the 'EU valued highly on human rights issues, it is our pleasure to support LGBT rights and contributing to regional cooperation' (Hotline, 2017). Therefore apart from the government and INGO, Hotline was supported by a foreign governmental organisation to coordinate with other LGBT rights activists in the region. This not only demonstrates the EU's LGBT rights diplomacy but also implies the importance of Taiwan in LGBT rights politics in East Asia.

### Taiwan as a 'queer state'

Taiwan, or the Republic of China, could be the 'queerest' country on earth. The Republic of China (Taiwan) was replaced by the People's Republic of China (China) in 1971 at the UN, from then on, the number of countries that hold diplomatic relationships with Taiwan dropped from 65 in 1971, to 15 in 2020. Taiwan has no representation in most of the UN-affiliated governmental organisations, but Taiwan is a member of WTO under the name of 'Separate Customs Territory of Taiwan, Penghu, Kinmen and Matsu.' Whether Taiwan is qualified as a state has been long debated among academics, as this is not the main issue in this chapter, Geldenhuys' argument will be the root of the following analysis. Geldenhuys indicates that Taiwan's statehood is a political issue 'rather than a legal dispute,' and no matter how qualified Taiwan's statehood is under international law, 'the vast majority of states have decided collectively that it was not entitled to separate statehood – for reasons that have more to do with China's might than with Taiwan's rights' (Geldenhuys, 2009). To some extent it is similar to the situation of queer people in most of the societies – 'they are but they are not' qualified citizens, they exist but they do not enjoy all the normal rights as citizens.

Taiwan as a 'queer state' could be understood perfectly with reference to its semi-official diplomatic relationships with other countries. Due to the 'One-China Principle,' most of the countries operate non-governmental organisations in Taiwan to act as embassies. The EU's 'European Economic and Trade Office' (EETO) in Taiwan functions as the 'Delegation of the European Union.' In the Factfile 2017 published by EETO, it is highlighted that 'Taiwan has one of the friendliest environments towards LGBTI people and has a lot to offer in terms of experience and best practices to others in the region.' Interestingly in its Chinese version, the EETO states 'Taiwan is one of the most LGBTI-friendly countries' (台灣是對 LGBTI 最友善的國家之一) (EETO, 2017). Is this just a 'miswriting,' or does it imply that Taiwan is a de facto independent state?

Furthermore, Taiwan is not represented in the UN due to the sovereignty disputes with China; thus, in most of the UN documents, Taiwan does not exist, or if mentioned, it is 'a province of China.' We can see this in a UNDP document 'Leave no one behind: Advancing social, economic, cultural and political inclusion of LGBTI people in Asia and the Pacific – Summary,' which provides an overview of LGBT communities in the region. The project was sponsored by the UNDP, the Embassy of Sweden in Bangkok, and the US Agency for International Development. Interestingly, Taiwan was mentioned once in the document in the section of 'Selected milestones towards LGBTI inclusion in Asia and the Pacific.' It stated that 'Taiwan (Province of China) enacts laws against discrimination based on sexual orientation in employment (2002) and education (2004), and debates proposals for marriage equality for same-sex couples (2014),' but in the next line, Hong Kong is simply 'Hong Kong,' not 'Hong Kong, Special Administrative Region of China' (UNDP, 2015: 6).

### Taiwan using 'queer way'

As described previously, Taiwan could not send official delegations to CSW, neither could Taiwanese officials contribute to UN-related conventions, but in the case of LGBT rights, there were some breakthroughs. Unlike the USA using government-to-government engagements or multilateral platforms, Taiwan is making indirect efforts which the government, Hotline, INGO, and foreign governmental organisations are all involved in.

In the first case of Hotline and TFD grants, we saw how an NGO was using indirect government resources to achieve certain diplomatic goals. The TFD hoped to support the Chen administrations' aim of promoting democracy and human rights in order to strengthen Taiwan's statehood through more participation in global affairs. Therefore Hotline's initiatives are aligned with these goals and thus it received grants to do international engagements. The way Hotline used the grants benefited not only the organisation itself but their appearance in CSW was significant for Taiwan's foreign relations. The case shows just how complicated it is for Taiwan to simply attend multinational platforms even as an NGO. What Taiwan's government was unable to do, had been carried out by Hotline.

The case in which Lu was invited by OutRight to join an advocacy programme represents a different route of participation for Taiwan, which was made possible through the connections among non-governmental actors. Again, Lu as a Hotline member joined the global LGBT rights initiatives to influence the global human rights regime, while this could not have happened if Lu had been a Taiwanese government official. Moreover, Lu's experience of the venue-change issue perfectly illustrates the complexity and ambiguity of what Tongzhi Diplomacy stands for in Taiwan's context.

As Taiwan does not have the same mechanisms and tools as other countries, it could not promote LGBT rights abroad through official mechanisms; Taiwan could not participate in CSW and other UN multilateral conferences, but Hotline could attend with the support from the government; last but not least, Lu was invited by an INGO to take part in advocacy programmes to contribute to the global LGBT rights regime, and Lu as an LGBT rights activist represents Taiwan in global human rights initiatives where the Taiwanese government is not eligible to do so. These interesting and obscure dynamics are the 'queer approaches' which indicate that due to the queer status of Taiwan non-state actors took the role as representatives of Taiwan on various international occasions.

### Taiwan's 'queer diplomacy'

The TFD grants and Lu's appearance at the UN were aimed at maintaining or expanding Taiwan's presence as a state rather than influencing other countries' policies on LGBT rights. The government of Taiwan did not seek to enhance LGBT rights in its diplomatic allies; in fact, among these countries, six of them had criminalised same-sex relationships. Instead of advocating the decriminalisation of LGBT people overseas, the existing approaches in Taiwan have not been sophisticated; they were neither initiated by MOFA, nor were they executed through official mechanisms. Since Taiwan is a 'queer state,' its foreign policy agenda is shaped by its contested status. MOFA explains that it is dedicated to 'implementing policies that enhance Taiwan's prosperity and promoting foreign relations that strengthen the international status of the ROC' (MOFA, 2016). Therefore compared to maintaining the formal diplomatic ties with its remaining allies, decriminalising same-sex relationships overseas is not a major concern for the Taiwan government.

Taiwan is sharing its LGBT rights experiences with others, especially East Asian neighbours such as Hong Kong, Japan, and Korea, while also receiving support from the West. In an article about Hotline's participation in ILGA-Asia's regional conference in 2017, Lin indicates that 'Taiwan, a UN outcast, is unable to tap into important funding nor participate in or conduct studies through organizations like the UNDP,' but he suggests that Taiwan's isolation enabled the local LGBT movements to develop their own strategies with local knowledge and resources (Lin, 2017). This is why Taiwan's progress has really surprised the world, since it was not officially covered by global LGBT rights initiatives. This unique experience could provide an alternative for global LGBT rights politics, as Taiwan's development experience was not simply transplanted from, or supported by the West.

As discussed earlier, some scholars criticised Chen's regime for using tongzhi as a tool to sustain Taiwan's international status. However, when looking at the cases in this research, it is very difficult to conclude that the current government is intentionally 'using' LGBT rights to promote Taiwan for international inclusion. The Tsai government hesitated to amend the Civil Code for the same-sex marriage, taking three years to achieve its pledge. It has neither consistently supported the activists in global platforms nor did the government support LGBT rights initiatives abroad. Clearly, the government does not have a sophisticated Tongzhi Diplomacy. The actual content of its Tongzhi Diplomacy is also questionable since so far there is no similarity between Western LGBT rights diplomacy models and Taiwan's international LGBT rights engagements. Taiwan's version of Tongzhi Diplomacy relies heavily on activism and non-state actors instead of state-initiated policies. Even under the Tsai administration there is a degree of continuity from the Chen era, or what Geldenhuys called 'democracy-based diplomacy.' In other words, Taiwan still frames its adoption of LGBT rights as part of its international human rights diplomacy in order to seek the recognition and support from Western democracies.

### Recent challenges and opportunities for Tongzhi diplomacy

In the aftermath of Tsai's election in 2016 Tongzhi Diplomacy has faced both challenges and opportunities. Gary Rawnsley has argued that Taiwan's public diplomacy frequently is undermined by what he terms a 'disabling environment' of both domestic and international constraints (Rawnsley, 2017, 989). One of the reasons that Taiwan's governments have been cautious about open advocacy for LGBT rights in its public diplomacy has been the fear of domestic criticism, particularly from the conservative counter-movement. This movement though has been able to build a broad anti-LGBT alliance well beyond its Christian Church base. It also has an international dimension. Cole has shown the close ties between American Evangelical groups and Taiwan's anti-LGBT movements (Cole, 2017). Their mobilisation was able to see anti-same-sex marriage and anti-gender-equality education national referendums pass in late 2018 and this temporarily undermined Taiwan's reputation as an Asian model of LGBT rights (Fell, 2018). However, Tsai's government did eventually pass same-sex marriage legislation in May 2019 and this would provide a similar level of positive international media coverage to that seen in the 2017 Court Ruling. Opposition to legalisation in parliament mainly came from the largest opposition party, the KMT, and some of its legislators promised they would repeal the law once they came back to power in 2020. Unsurprisingly the conservative counter-movement strongly backed the KMT's presidential candidate Han Kuo-yu in 2020.

Tsai Ing-wen's re-election and the DPP's retained parliamentary majority in January 2020 means it is likely the government will continue to support Tongzhi Diplomacy. Since legalisation, Tsai has made frequent statements on the issue to international audiences. For instance, in October 2019 at the 40th Congress of the International Federation for Human Rights, Tsai stated, 'this year, Taiwan became the first country in Asia to legalize same-sex marriage. I have to tell you that it was not an easy process to go through, but finally, we made it' (Office of the President, 2019). Similarly MOFA has been more active in incorporating LGBT rights into their agenda. One such case was the EU-Taiwan LGBTI Human Rights Conference in October 2019, which was co-organised by the Cabinet-level Gender Equality Committee, the Ministry of Foreign Affairs, and the European Economic and Trade Office (MOFA, 2019). This was held the same week as the 2019 Taipei Pride, and was a very big step forward for Tongzhi Diplomacy. However, it remains to be seen whether this conference will become a regular collaborative event or just a one off. Taiwanese diplomats abroad are now also trumpeting Taiwan's LGBT rights to international audiences far more since May 2019. Each year MOFA representatives give a briefing to students at our university on the advantages of studying and working (youth mobility visa) in Taiwan. Alongside Taiwan's democratic system, convenient public transport, scenery and fine cuisine, being the first Asian country to legalise same-sex marriage first appeared on their PowerPoint presentations in 2019. This represents a marked change from the very cautious approach that Taiwanese diplomats had taken towards the issue under Ma and in the first two years of Tsai's presidency.

Externally, it is impossible to discuss Taiwan's foreign policy without reference to the China factor. This challenge could be seen during the 2018 Gay Games in Paris. At first, Taiwan's team was going to compete under the name of 'Taiwan,' but later it was changed to 'Chinese Taipei' in accordance with the Olympic protocol on the official website. It was reported that this change was the result of Chinese pressure. According to the news, the organisers of the Gay Games said they were reminded not to display the name 'Taiwan' and the ROC national flag. But after objections were raised by Taiwan, Taiwan's athletes competed under the name of 'Taipei' and could freely demonstrate flags and signs during the opening ceremony. The organisers also separated the China and Taiwan teams in different processions (Maxon, 2018). This incident signals the uncertainties of Taiwan's international participation in LGBT-related events. No matter 'how progressive' Taiwan is on LGBT rights, the fundamental issue remains the 'queer state.' Another potential challenge arises from China's tongzhi policy. Some scholars argue that the success of marriage equality in Taiwan depends on the government's determination to gain recognition from the international society through human rights in contrast with China. However, it is possible that China will eventually improve its LGBT rights since China does not have strong Christian opponents of same-sex marriage due to its political system. Perhaps the comparison on human rights between China and Taiwan would continue, but 'who' is doing the comparison and whether Tongzhi Diplomacy is utilised in this comparison remains to be seen.

## Conclusion

Since Tongzhi Diplomacy as a term has been used in different contexts without being critically examined, this chapter has contributed to developing an understanding of Tongzhi Diplomacy in the context of the unique status of Taiwan in international politics. Taiwan is incapable of conducting a multilateral approach, not simply because Taiwan is not powerful enough, but because Taiwan is not even entitled to participate in the international governmental institutions. Through the case of TFD funding and Hotline's participation in international and regional LGBT rights initiatives, Tongzhi Diplomacy seems to have been employed by non-government actors due to

Taiwan being a 'queer state.' In the case of Taiwan, MOFA did not incorporate LGBT rights into their policy agenda, Taiwan did not seek to promote LGBT rights with its formal diplomatic allies. In fact, LGBT rights act as a channel for non-governmental actors to represent Taiwan in international institutions where the government has been blocked from attending. While the international engagements are supported by the government in indirect ways, the complexity and ambiguity of Hotline's actions did lead to breakthroughs in Taiwan's international space. However, Taiwanese activism was supported by the I(N)GOs, which reflects the two-way interaction that Tongzhi Diplomacy stands for. Unlike the West exporting LGBT rights to other countries, Taiwan not only inspires others but is also supported by the West.

The queer case of Tongzhi Diplomacy also challenges the fundamental assumption of the 'state' in the discipline of international politics. Taiwan's queer status does not fit neatly into the standard International Relations approaches. It is often positioned as a source of potential instability in Sino-US relations or in East Asia, and Taiwan's ambiguous status is sometimes seen as destabilising the international order. However, Taiwan's foreign relations strategies have evolved over time and due to the queerness of Taiwan's statehood, it has developed an unconventional diplomacy that is unlike that of other states. Tongzhi Diplomacy as explored in this chapter is one of these approaches for Taiwan to resist marginalisation in international politics.

The cases examined in this chapter reveal that since non-governmental actors play a huge part in this kind of diplomacy, trying to measure its success or failure is very challenging. Moreover, as Tongzhi Diplomacy is new and still evolving, there are no regular institutionalised grants from the government to support organisations such as Hotline to continue their international initiatives. Whether Hotline will continue its engagement in global LGBT rights really depends on its ability to raise enough funds and attention. Perhaps the fundamental issue for Tongzhi Diplomacy will be the future of Taiwan's LGBT rights movement and its ability to gain greater societal and political support. But it is clear that Tongzhi Diplomacy is not the transplanted version of the Western style of LGBT rights diplomacy. Due to Taiwan's queer status, Tongzhi Diplomacy has different approaches and goals. In other words, LGBT rights diplomacy is about 'making queer people in other countries normal,' but Tongzhi Diplomacy is about 'making Taiwan normal through its queer people.'

## Note

1 Gin Bookstore was the first gay bookstore in Taiwan. In 2003 the Criminal Investigation Bureau confiscated much of its stock. The owner of Gin was charged with a sex offenses crime and was fined. Several gender-related organisations then applied for a constitutional interpretation and Interpretation number 617 was made which further explained and narrowed down the definition of 'obscene' when applying the Criminal Law in 2006. Sister Radio, a radio station

focusing on women's issues, was fined by the Government Information Office of the Executive Yuan in 2004 due to an imitation of a women's sexual moaning on its lesbian programme. Sister Radio refused to pay the fine as the imitation was in the context of promoting safe sex. When the case went to the Supreme Administrative Court, Sister Radio was acquitted in 2005.

## Bibliography

Chen, N. 2018. 'Taiwan Through the Prism of Marriage Equality: A Study of Media Exposure in the English-Speaking World.' *Taiwan Sentinel*. Available at: https://sentinel.tw/taiwan-through-prism-marriage-equality/

Chen, Y. and Wang, P. 2010. 'Obstacles to LGBT Human Rights Development in Taiwan.' *Positions: East Asia Cultures Critique*, 18(2), pp. 399–407.

Chi, D. 2015. 'Translation/Public: AIDS, "Tongzhi," and "Ku'er."' *Bulletin of Taiwanese Literature*, 26, 75‑112.

Chou, W. 2000. *Tongzhi: Politics of Same-Sex Eroticism in Chinese Societies*. New York: Haworth Press.

Chu, W. 2003. 'Queer(ing) Taiwan: Sexual Citizenship, Nation-Building or Civil Society.' *Journal of Women's and Gender Studies*, 15, 115–51.

Cole, J. 2017. 'U.S. Hate Group Mass Resistance Behind Anti-LGBT Activities in Taiwan.' *Taiwan Sentinel*. Available at: https://sentinel.tw/us-hate-group-anti-lgbt/ [Accessed 9 September 2018].

Damm, J. 2011. 'Discrimination and Backlash against Homosexual Groups.' In: T. Ngo and H. Wang, eds., *Politics of Difference in Taiwan*. London: Routledge, 152–180.

Encarnación, O. 2016. 'The Troubled Rise of Gay Rights Diplomacy.' *Current History*, 115(777), 17–22.

European Economic and Trade Office. 2017. 'EU-Taiwan Factfile 2017.' [online] p. 26. Available at: https://eeas.europa.eu/sites/eeas/files/2017_eu_taiwan_factfile_1.pdf [Accessed 15 August 2018].

Fan, C. 25 May 2017. 'Facebook.' Available at: https://www.facebook.com/chifei.fan/posts/1313487745386431 [Accessed 9 June 2020].

Fan, Y. and Wu, W. 2016. 'The Long Feminist March in Taiwan.' In: G. Schubert, ed., *Routledge Handbook of Contemporary Taiwan*. London: Routledge, 313–25.

Fell, Dafydd. 2018. 'How Liberal is Taiwan? Adultery, the Death Penalty and Marriage Equality.' *Taiwan Sentinel*. Available at: https://sentinel.tw/how-liberal-is-taiwan-adultery-the-death-penalty-and-marriage-equality/

Geldenhuys, D. 2009. *Contested States in World Politics*. Basingstoke: Palgrave Macmillan, 208–33.

Gofyy. 2016a. 'Tai Wan Tong Yun Xian Chang: Shui Bao Guang Le Tong Xing Lian- AG Jian Shen Zhong Xin Shi Jian.' [online] Available at: http://ageofqueer.com/archives/10522 [Accessed 20 April 2018].

Gofyy. 2016b. 'Tai Wan Tong Yun Xian Chang: Zong Tong Fu De Di Yi Mian Cai Hong Qi.' [online] Available at: http://ageofqueer.com/archives/8893 [Accessed 20 April 2018].

Ho, J. 2010. 'Queer Existence under Global Governance: A Taiwan Exemplar.' *Positions*, 18(2), 537–54.

Ho, J. 2017. *Xing Bie Zhi Li Yu Taiwan Min Zhu*. Taoyuan City: The Center for The Study of Sexualities, i–x.

Hong, L. 2016. 'Fen Hong Xing Nue Yu Di Guo Fen Shi.' [online] Available at: https://www.facebook.com/notes/%E6%B4%AA%E6%B3%A0%E6%B3%A0 %E5%87%8C/20160305%E7%9A%%2084%E7%99%BC%E8%A8%80%E7%A8 %BF%E5%A4%A7%E6%94%BE%E9%80%81%E7%94%AD%E9%80%20%9F %E8%A8%98%E5%9B%89/10153387523125887
Human Rights Campaign. 2017. 'HRC Global Innovator Helps Bring Marriage Equality to Taiwan.' [online] Human Rights Campaign. Available at: http://www. hrc.org/blog/hrc-global-innovator-helps-bring-marriage-equality-to-taiwan [Accessed 14 September 2018].
ILGA Asia. 2017. '7th ILGA Asia Conference Agenda.' [online] Phnom Penh: ILGA Asia. Available at: https://ilgaasia2017.files.wordpress.com/2017/11/ ilga-asia-2017-conference-program-final.pdf [Accessed 24 August 2018].
Lim, S. 2008. 'How to Be Queer in Taiwan: Translation, Appropriation, and the Construction of a Queer Identity in Taiwan.' In: F. Martin, ed., *AsiaPacifiQueer: Rethinking Genders and Sexualities*. Urbana: University of Illinois Press, 235–50.
Lim, S. 2009. 'Queer Theory Goes to Taiwan.' In: N. Giffney and M. O'Rourke, eds., *The Ashgate Research Companion to Queer Theory*. Surrey: Ashgate Publishing, 257–76.
Lin, Irene. 2000. 'Rights Seen as the Path to Statehood.' [online] *Taipei Times*. Available at: http://www.taipeitimes.com/News/local/archives/2000/05/21/0000036946 [Accessed 19 July 2018].
Lin, J. 2017. 'OPINION: Is Taiwan Really a Beacon for LGBT Rights in Asia?' [online]. *The News Lens International Edition. The News Lens International Edition*. Available at: https://international.thenewslens.com/article/85204 [Accessed 26 August 2018].
Lin, S. 2013. 'Fu Yun Yu Tong Yun De You Zhi "Yi" "Tong": Yi Fu Nu Xin Zhi Ji Jin Hui De Chang Yi Li Shi Wei Li.' *Forum in Women's and Gender Studies*, 99, 32–41
Liu, L. 2018. 'Hu Wei-Zhen Xin Shu Fa Biao Ma Ying-Jiu Fen Xiang Tongzhi Wai Jiao Qu Shi.' [online] *The Central News Agency*. Available at: http://www.cna.com. tw/news/aipl/201805110276-1.aspx [Accessed 6 June 2018].
Liu, P. 2015. *Queer Marxism in Two Chinas*. Durham: Duke University Press.
Liu, W. 2016. 'Queer China and Homonational Taiwan? The Troubles of Queer Transnationalism. In: North American Taiwanese Studies Association.' [online] Toronto. Available at: https://www.researchgate.net/publication/309188562_Queer_China_ and_Homonational_Taiwan_The_Troubles_of_Queer_Transnationalism? enrichId=rgreq-0977ffb4dc9f01c7a6d895e49c65a9cf-XXX&enrichSource= Y292ZXJQYWdlOzMwOTE4ODU2MjtBUzo0MTc5MDI4MTg4MDc4MDh AMTQ3NjY0NzIwNDM5NA%3D%3D&el=1_x_3&_esc=publicationCoverPdf [Accessed 14 August 2018].
Lu, J. 2017. 'Facebook.' [online] Available at: https://www.facebook.com/Jennifer LuTw/posts/1873315716079345?__tn__=-R [Accessed 14 September 2018].
Lu, J. 2018. 'Jennifer Lu. Facebook.' [online] Available at: https://www.facebook.com/ JenniferLuTw/photos/a.1093153577428900/2011457895598459/?type=3&theater [Accessed 14 September 2018].
Lu, X. 2015. 'Tongzhi Wai Jiao —Shi Jie Ren Quan Ri De Guo Ji Chang Yi Gong Zuo Jing Yan. [Blog] Yan - Fu Nu Yi Ti Gou Tong Ping Tai Dian Zi Bao.' Available at: http://www.iwomenweb.org.tw/cp.aspx?n=076B9FAB784626CD [Accessed 24 August 2018].

Maxon A. 2018. 'Gay Games Team Renamed "Taipei."' [online] *Taipei Times*. Available at: http://www.taipeitimes.com/News/front/archives/2018/07/27/2003697448 [Accessed 9 September 2018].

Ministry of Foreign Affairs, Republic of China (Taiwan). 2006. 'Foreign Policy Report.' Ministry of Foreign Affairs, Republic of China (Taiwan).

Ministry of Foreign Affairs, Republic of China (Taiwan). 2015. 'Lian He Guo "Fu Nu Di Wei Yuan Hui" (CSW) Di 59 Jie Da Hui Ji Fei Zheng Fu Zu Zhi Zhou Bian Hui Yi - Chu Xi Guo Ji Hui Yi Qing Xing.' [online] Available at: https://www.mofa. gov.tw/igo/News_Content.aspx?n=106241E966C563C0&sms=9C13959F19F93 B2F&s=0281EFEC1F380271 [Accessed 14 September 2018].

Ministry of Foreign Affairs, Republic of China (Taiwan). 2016. 'Foreign Policy Guidelines.' [online] Available at: https://www.mofa.gov.tw/en/cp.aspx?n=B7411 BDCD003C9EC [Accessed 14 September 2018].

Ministry of Foreign Affairs, Republic of China (Taiwan). 2019. 'Taiwan, EU Stage LGBTI Human Rights Conference in Taipei.' Available at: https://nspp.mofa. gov.tw/nsppe/news.php?post=164786&unit=376&unitname=Policy-Framework& postname=Taiwan, -EU-stage-LGBTI-human-rights-conference-in-Taipei.

Ministry of Justice. 2001. *Draft Basic Law on the Guarantees of Human Rights*. Taipei: Ministry of Justice.

Office of The President Republic of China (Taiwan). 2007. *Zong Tong Fu Ren Quan Zi Xun Wei Yuan Hui She Zhi Yao Dian*. Taipei: Office of The President Republic of China (Taiwan).

Office of The President Republic of China (Taiwan). 2019. 'News Release: President Tsai Attends 40th Congress of International Federation for Human Rights.' Available at: https://english.president.gov.tw/News/5893

Open Society Foundations. 2017. 'On the Verge of Marriage Equality in Taiwan.' [online] Available at: https://www.opensocietyfoundations.org/voices/push-marriage-equality-taiwan [Accessed 14 September 2018].

OutRight - LGBTIQ Human Rights. 2017. 'UN New Yorker - The UNGA Edition.' [online] Available at: https://www.outrightinternational.org/content/un-new-yorker-unga-edition [Accessed 9 September 2018].

Rawnsley, Gary. 2017. 'Soft Power Rich, Public Diplomacy Poor: An Assessment of Taiwan's External Communications.' *China Quarterly*, (232), 982–1001.

Taiwan Association for Human Rights. 2000. '2000 Nian Taiwan Ren Quan Bao Gao.' [online] Taipei: Taiwan Association for Human Rights, p. 143. Available at: https://issuu.com/digitaltahr/docs/a012 [Accessed 13 September 2018].

Taiwan Tongzhi Hotline Association. 2017a. '2016 Annual Report.' [online] Taipei: Taiwan Tongzhi Hotline Association. Available at: https://hotline.org.tw/ sites/hotline.org.tw/files/field_upload/2016%E5%B7%A5%E4%BD%9C%E5%A0 %B1%E5%91%8A%E6%9B%B80428_%E7%B6%B2%E8%B7%AF.pdf [Accessed 14 September 2018].

Taiwan Tongzhi Hotline Association. 2017b. *International Exchange and Collaboration Program of Gender and Human Right. Report of the Taiwan Foundation for Democracy Grant*. Taipei City: Taiwan Foundation for Democracy.

The International Lesbian, Gay, Bisexual, Trans and Intersex Association (ILGA). 2017. 'Sexual Orientation Laws in the World. Criminalisation.' [online] ILGA. Available at: https://ilga.org/maps-sexual-orientation-laws [Accessed 9 September 2018].

United Nations Development Programme. 2015. 'Leave No One Behind. Advancing Social, Economic, Cultural and Political Inclusion of LGBTI People in Asia and the Pacific - Summary.' [online] p. 6. Available at: http://www.asia-pacific.undp.org/content/rbap/en/home/library/democratic_governance/hiv_aids/leave-no-one-behind--advancing-social--economic--cultural-and-po/ [Accessed 9 September 2018].

# Index

Note: **Bold** page numbers refer to tables, *italic* page numbers refer to figures and page numbers followed by "n" refer to end notes.

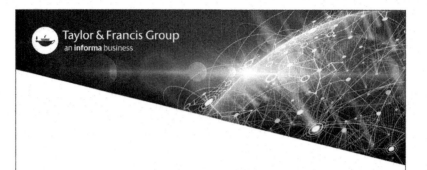